lotus
publishing

CW01271481

HIGH PERFORMANCE LIVING

The Complete Lifestyle Book with Healthy Recipes and Strength Training Program

Ru Anderson

First published in 2014 by Exceed Nutrition Limited, 67 Lanesborough Court, Newcastle Upon Tyne, NE3 3BZ, www.ExceedNutrition. com.

This edition published in 2015 by Lotus Publishing, Apple Tree Cottage, Inlands Road, Nutbourne, Chichester, PO18 8RJ.

The right of Ru Anderson to be identified as the author of this work has been asserted by him in accordance with the Copyright, Designs and Patents Act 1988.

Cover Design Tom Wallis
Text Design Mary-Anne Trant
Printed and Bound in the UK by Bell and Bain Limited
Recipe Photography Aleksandra Witkowska

British Library Cataloguing-in-Publication Data
A CIP record of this book is available from the British Library.
ISBN 978 1 905367 61 0

Disclaimer
This book is written as a source of information only. The information contained in this book should by no means be considered a substitute for the advice of a qualified medical professional, who should always be consulted before beginning any new diet, exercise, or other health program. All efforts have been made to ensure the accuracy of the information contained in this book as of the date published. The author and the publisher expressly disclaim responsibility for any adverse effects arising from the use or application of the information contained here.

DEDICATED TO BEING YOUR BEST.

Contents

Contents

INTRODUCTION

Build your strongest, most capable, most powerful body

Right now, no matter what shape you are in, your body is an amazing machine. But it has the potential to be even better. And knowing how to take care of that body is the most important information you can learn. Ever.

> ## "Training" and "nutrition" are not just words: they are tools.

It's important to develop the fittest, healthiest, strongest, and most powerful body you possibly can. You must learn how to listen and respond to its demands if you are to be your best. But you can't do that if you don't know how.

"Training" and "nutrition" are not just words: they are tools. By understanding how these tools can work for you, you can rapidly fine-tune your powerful body so it looks, performs, and feels the way you have always wanted it to.

Does this sound like you? You're training hard and eating good food yet are still frustrated at your lack of results. You're feeling tired and angry because, despite your best motivated efforts, you haven't achieved what you deserve.

It's not your fault. You simply haven't found the right tools for you—yet. And that's because the majority of training and nutrition advice and information we receive today is unqualified and unproven. It leads us to misguided decisions, resulting in substandard results. Time and time again. This inferior information leaves you overwhelmed and unsure, and wastes your precious time and energy, when you could be getting results. It doesn't have to be this way.

Once you learn to match the correct proven tools to your unique body, something amazing starts to happen: you discover that you can succeed at your goals and have a body that performs at its best. All the time. This isn't about diets, quick fixes, or transformation challenges. It's about finding the training and nutrition system that works for you, for life.

What Can You Look Forward To?

- You'll quickly improve your body, whether your goal is fat loss, muscle gain, or to generally look great naked. It's maintainable, not just a quick fix, and you'll enjoy balance in your life.
- You'll feel healthy and energized. Your body becomes boundless and you'll

see and experience the world in ways that you couldn't previously.

- No matter what sport, hobby, or general activities you get up to, you will be able to complete them to your maximum ability. All day, every day.

This is what I call High Performance Living (HPL). It's what you get to enjoy when you acquire these powerful tools and apply your new knowledge to experience the endless benefits. It's the most effective and proven system I've ever developed to help people like you look, feel, and perform at their best.

I strongly believe that educating yourself about your body is the most important thing you can do. So I'm going to show you how you can achieve HPL and apply it to your health, training, and nutrition. With my HPL System you're going to learn about nutrition and how to feed your unique body nutritiously and deliciously. I'll provide you with every bit of valuable knowledge and all the essential tools you need to finally be in complete control of your own nutrition. You'll have the power to transform your body, once and for all. You'll quickly improve your body using my proven, powerful, yet actually pretty simple, nutrition cornerstones.

You see, because you're reading this, I already know a few things about you:

- You're not willing to settle for average.
- You have more discipline, dedication, and drive than your friends or colleagues.
- You work on your fitness daily to be better than you were yesterday.
- You want to gain the edge so the work you put in gets results.

My HPL System is for you. It's for that small percentage of people willing to work with a system tailored to their specific needs and requirements. It's for those hungry for the best results, who are ready to apply the personal direction and knowledge they receive. And it's for those who want effective up-to-date information so they can be confident they're following a personalized approach created for them. That's what makes my system so special—it is unlike every other "nutrition" book out there.

We'll put the urban myths to bed (even those that somehow endure the test of time), and replace them with researched and field-tested methods that actually work. You'll get the hard facts—the stuff that gets results—with no "fluff" or gimmicks. I promise. The HPL System is for the motivated, proactive, and hard-working person who wants cutting-edge and proven nutrition strategies so they can finally achieve the results they deserve. In other words, it's for you.

By applying the power of my HPL System, you'll get all this (and more):

- Perform better
- Grow muscle
- Get stronger
- Lose more fat, consistently
- And feel better, every day.

Welcome to my world—because it's about to become yours, too. Welcome to High Performance Living.

ABOUT ME

Ru Anderson, BSc (Hons). Performance nutritionist, writer, speaker, competitive athlete, owner of Exceed Nutrition.

Ru is a performance-focused nutritionist. He helps motivated and driven people to be at their best, to look, feel, and perform better, all day every day.

Ru is the founder and owner of Exceed Nutrition, which has become the industry's "go-to" online nutrition coaching web site in just a few short years. Using this platform, Ru personally coaches his clients through the fundamentals of achieving the body and health they've always wanted, with nutrition being the cornerstone. He also created the Exceed Nutrition Certification for elite and ambitious personal trainers to excel in their coaching business and get better results with their clients using the power of nutrition.

Ru has also toured the UK to deliver his invaluable HPL nutrition seminar, and has been a guest speaker at some of the biggest fitness events. He's a former "fat guy" turned nutritionist, and has also competed at national level in drug-free bodybuilding.

In Ru's HPL podcast he interviews some of the industry's most successful and knowledgeable people. As of summer 2015, Ru's podcast is in the top one hundred fitness and nutrition podcasts in iTunes.

Oh—and he's also about to make you more awesome. Let's not forget that bit.

WELCOME TO HIGH PERFORMANCE LIVING

Here's my story. For years, I held an image in my head of how I wanted my ideal body to look. I was just a young lad, and the dreams and desires quickly began to consume me. My drive to accomplish my goals was unquestionable: it wasn't a matter of "if," it was a question of "when?"

My goal was to look freakin' awesome.

But in my mission to add large amounts of muscle, lean up, and build my strength, I forgot about two other major components: how I felt and how I performed. And I didn't realize how they would radically affect me. I was so focused on changing the outside of my body, that I neglected (and ignored) how I was performing and feeling on the inside. I was doing a lot of hard bodybuilding training and following the typical magazine nutrition advice. The result? I felt pretty horrendous and my performance in day-to-day life wasn't much better. I was constantly fatigued from the intense training, lacked concentration throughout the day, and had little energy left for any other activities. Aside from my dedicated "gym time," I was pretty damn useless.

To top it off, the mainstream nutrition advice I was being told to follow by magazines and forums was actually destroying my health, giving me irritable bowel syndrome symptoms and skin issues like acne. It was clear I had to find another way.

Finally, I'd had enough. I set myself a new goal; to look, feel, and perform my best—all day, every day. This is what I now call High Performance Living. The problem was, back then I didn't know where to start.

Achieving HPL is really pretty simple (I'll give you my ten-step formula soon), yet many people will never quite attain it. How come, if it's not difficult? It's down to the lack of information focusing on improving both the body *and* performance that is widely available to us. There is a lot of advice out there aimed at helping people lose body fat quickly, yet it fails to consider how someone will feel or perform during or after the process. Of course it might work, there are many ways to get to an end goal, but most people cannot sustain it long-term. In the end, they revert back to old habits and lose their results.

So, armed with my new goal, I decided to study and experiment with a huge number of nutrition and training protocols. The aim was simple: to discover whether I really could achieve HPL. After throwing out the rubbish (which was most of it), I was left with a surprisingly powerful yet pretty simple set of principles. I've since gone on to prove them time and time again. These principles, the HPL System, allow me and my clients to create and maintain healthy, lean, strong, and energetic bodies. What was the primary ingredient for success? Great nutrition. As a result, nutrition quickly became my key interest and passion, and I learnt that this is where the focus should be placed to achieve every health and fitness goal.

I developed a set of criteria to work from, in order to achieve HPL:

1. To Look Better—You need a system to help you quickly improve body composition. This must be maintainable, not a quick fix, and you must still be able to achieve balance within your new lifestyle.

2. To Feel Better—You need a system to instantly improve your overall health. It must give you more energy, better sleep, improved mood, increased confidence, and a clean bill of health.

3. To Perform Better—No matter what sport, hobby, or general activities you get up to, you should be able to complete them to your maximum ability, every single day. Get up, smash it, and repeat.

If you are not able to achieve this, something is missing. More often than not, it comes back to nutrition. Every nutrition plan or training program I design must adhere to these HPL criteria, otherwise it is incomplete.

From now on, your aim should be to set goals that include the HPL criteria. In my experience, this will always bring faster results and more long-term success. This new perspective makes it a lifestyle and ensures we are always freakin' awesome in all areas of our life. These are the new fundamentals to performance nutrition.

This book guarantees that you too can discover, develop, and maintain HPL to build your strongest, leanest, and healthiest body. It really is possible to look incredible, eat amazing food, and feel awesome in the process. I promise it's possible to get stronger and build muscle without adding body fat and feeling sluggish.

HPL is a lifestyle. It's not a "one-off" nutrition plan or diet book, nor is it a quick fix. This system is much more than just a nutrition book, it is an educational tool that should be constantly referred to as life gets busier and goals change. A change in plans or a disrupted routine no longer means missed meals or unhealthy choices. I will teach you the nutritional principles behind awesome nutrition, so you can always be in charge and reach your goals, whatever your situation.

This is a performance-focused nutrition system that combines the most researched and scientifically tested nutritional methods to provide you with a tailor-made eating plan. Adhere to my nutrition cornerstones and reap the reward of perfect body composition and optimal health. It really is that simple, and I will show you how.

Base nutrition on one key strategy: continually seeking more from your body. Daily maximum performance is a fundamental component to achieving your health and fitness goals. By keeping it at the front of your mind, you will learn how to be healthier, stronger, and leaner, while feeling awesome in the process.

Your body ultimately wants to remain the same. When most people try to change it, they only get a change in their metabolic rate (as it slows down on reduced calories), which leads to stagnated progress. We will avoid that with this system. How? By basing nutrition on seeking maximum performance. You need to be able to push your body, to force it to change. We must work with the body, not against it.

If your goal is to get leaner, then you must use a nutrition system that gives you the correct nutrients for performance. Your body will change because you can do more. It will be forced to build more muscle as a result of your strength improvements, and it will strip the body fat it sees as a burden.

Correct nutrition will ensure you perform at the highest possible level and then aid the recovery process, quickly repairing your body so it is faster, stronger, and leaner.

As I guide you to your own High Performance Living throughout the HPL book, keep this section in mind. We will work closely to build and develop your ultimate perfect nutrition system, and I'll answer all your questions. By the end, I will have passed all the relevant and important information on to you, so you can successfully control your own nutrition forever.

Ready? Let's do it!

PART I
THE TEN
ESSENTIAL HPL
CORNERSTONES

We are creatures of habit.

We like routine and do well by following guidelines and advice. On the flip side, most of us do not do well with strict rules. They usually mean restriction and limitation, right?

The same applies when it comes to nutrition. Give someone a set of guidelines to follow and they'll do it. But set strict rules and the chances are they will break the rules or just give up. After years of coaching people, I realized that people don't need rigid nutrition plans containing repetitive boring meals. They do much better with a simple set of guidelines and daily habits to follow.

I've summarized my core nutritional principles into ten essential HPL cornerstones: ten key guidelines I know will deliver the best results. Understand and follow these simple, highly effective cornerstones daily, and you will be the best that you can be.

It doesn't matter what level you are at. That's the beauty of these simple cornerstones. They can all be broken down, to provide you with tailored information to suit your knowledge level and experience.

Is this you: just starting your journey to improved nutrition and health? Perfect! The cornerstones will kick-start your good eating habits and provide a long-term strategy to reach your goals.

Or is this you: already eating good food and training hard? Great stuff. My cornerstones will show you how to fine-tune your nutrition to get way better results.

1. LISTEN TO YOUR BODY

You're here because you want to build the strongest, most capable, most powerful body possible. You want some HPL. And that's why I have written this book: so that together we can learn how to be the best versions of ourselves and enjoy the power that comes with being in complete control of our own bodies.

> **The connection with your body is the most precious thing you have.**

I'm not a scientist. I'm not a doctor. What I am is a man who has spent the last fifteen years learning about nutrition and what my body is capable of, whilst helping others do exactly the same. This has been the most rewarding experience of our lives. Everything I'm about to share is the combination of my study and experiences. It is the knowledge I have gained from working with my own body, and those of my clients.

I want to show you how to do this for yourself. I want you to know yourself, to unlock your power, and to become the best that you can be.

The connection you have with your body is the most precious thing you have. It is your past, present, and future. Understanding how your body can work for you, and processing the knowledge to make it perform optimally, is the most important information you can ever learn.

To begin, you must understand and accept your current situation. To do this, you must start listening to your body. It will always tell you what it wants and what it needs, but you have to learn to hear it. You know that feeling when you just have to go to the toilet, or when you just can't keep your eyes open while watching TV? That's your body communicating with you in urgent and powerful ways. Our bodies send similar messages throughout the day regarding nutrition and wellbeing. Right this second, your body is telling you what it wants and needs. It's your responsibility to hear, learn, and translate these signals.

Your body is a well-designed machine. And, just like any other machine, it needs fuel to run. When it doesn't get any, it grinds to a halt. And when poor-quality fuel is used (or when too much or little is put in), it doesn't function optimally. For our bodies, fuel is the nutrients in the foods we eat.

Nutrition is an evidence-based science. Nutritional scientists advance our knowledge of nutrition by building on prior research and examining new areas. Nutrition is a constantly evolving field of study, updated and supported by research, studies, and trials. It's this research that provides the foundations to most of our most well-known dieting practices and guidelines, such as the food pyramid, recommended daily allowances (RDAs), dietary reference intakes (DRIs), and tolerable upper limits (TULs).

One area of nutritional science that has yet to be explored in detail is how our daily nutritional choices impact the internal workings of the body. Many people believe it's a case of "eat less to lose weight" or "get stronger to build muscle," but never consider the metabolic or physiological changes that result from this. What we do know is that the fuel we give our bodies provides the energy to the internal workings known as cells.

A cell is considered the smallest and most basic unit of life. Cells are found in all life forms: bacteria, plants, animals, and, of course, humans. It is these cells that distinguish a living organism from a non-living object, as they conduct self-sustaining biological processes. The cell was discovered by scientists back in 1665, and then, after another 150 years of study, scientists began to formulate the "cell theory," which is applicable to all living organisms.

Right now, your body is made up of trillions of cells. But that has not always been the case. In the womb, we initially consisted of just one cell. It was this cell that carried

our genetic information (DNA) and began making new life. This cell divided into other cells with specific roles, which led to the formation of tissues, the numerous body organs and systems, blood, blood vessels, bone, and skin. Every cell within the body is compact and efficient, integrated into a complex system that functions as a whole. All cells have the ability to perform the essential processes of life, including energy capture, waste excretion, relocation, movement, respiration, growth, and reproduction.

We must eat food to survive, because our bodies demand energy to carry out biological processes. This energy comes from the nutrients in the digested food we eat. For the body to function optimally, our energy intake must match our output. When we manage to achieve this correct energy balance, we reach what's known as metabolic homeostasis. Maintaining this correct energy balance is important to ensure bodily functions don't suffer and overall health is maintained.

Every organ and system in the body requires energy from the nutrients we eat. Without this energy, there would be no output ... and with no output, the human body would fail. To put it simply: food keeps you alive, and nutrition is survival.

The body has successfully adapted so it is efficient at exporting nutrients for energy production to all eleven major organ systems. This process starts with the digestive system. When nutrients reach the small intestine, they are directly transported to the liver. The liver is the only organ in the body capable of exporting nutrients to other organ systems. Nutrient levels in the blood, and the hormones that respond to them, tell the liver how it should distribute nutrients throughout the other organ systems in the body.

But we want to do a *lot* more than just survive! We want to thrive. So we must listen to what our bodies are asking from us, so we can provide our cells with exactly what they need to function optimally.

I spent years ignoring what my body was trying to tell me. My knowledge of what was best for my body and health was based on someone else's advice. Ever since my teenage years I have suffered with bad acne on my face. I spent years trying out lotions and potions prescribed by doctors and dermatologists. My symptoms got worse, which later led to me being prescribed with Roaccutane (the last-resort treatment for acne) when I was fifteen years old. Throughout all those years of antibiotic treatment for my skin, I was never told that it could harm my digestive system. Sure enough, within a couple of years I was experiencing symptoms of irritable bowel syndrome (IBS) and fatigue. And my skin hadn't got a whole lot better. Something was triggering these flare-ups.

Around this time my passion for weight training had started to gather pace. I wanted to be strong and confident like the cover models on my fitness magazines. This led me to follow various training and nutrition "gurus," diets, and programs that only told me how someone else had achieved results. My goal was to add muscle to my scrawny ten and a half stone, so I followed the typical mainstream "bulking" advice.

At the same time, I noticed my skin and IBS getting worse. I carried on regardless, only to discover that I was gaining way more fat that muscle. In fact, I made myself overweight in my quest to look better. I was left frustrated and angry, with worsening health problems. And I was no closer to my goals.

Why am I telling you this story? I want you to see that our bodies will find ways to highlight the things we do wrong. I had failed to listen to my own body.

When I finally began to tailor training and nutritional information to myself, I was able to reach my goals. I want you to do exactly the same with the information from this book. Make it your own. Always ask yourself, is this right for me? There are no rules. Only good guidelines and classic cornerstones.

My favorite question to ask my clients is: "and how's that working for you?" This encourages them to listen to their body. I want you to start doing the same: start listening to the signals your body is sending. It wants to function optimally. Up to now, it's only your own mistakes that have held it back. But that's about to change!

The best way to go about this is to ask yourself daily: how did I look, feel, and perform today? Your nutrition should change in response to your answer, and this book will show you how to do that.

You'll know you've got it spot-on when your answer to that question is always "AWESOME!"

2. YOU ARE WHAT YOU EAT

I love food.

I love the entire adventure of planning, preparing, and cooking. I look forward to every single one of my meals each day, as each is filled with flavor and nourishment. I also love to share this passion for food with as many people as possible. You'll see this a lot on my social media pages, but the real magic happens when I get to cook for others. These days I've swapped nights out in town for house parties where I can show off my culinary skills.

Why? Because I get great joy from showing people what great-tasting, healthy, and nutritious food really looks and tastes like. A key factor in eating good food for the long term is ensuring it tastes great. You'll be glad to hear that the recipes at the back of this book will show you exactly how to do this.

It hasn't always been like this. In fact, I used to view food simply as a means to achieve my goals: calories, protein, fats, and carbs. Today, I know that the food we eat, meal by meal, day by day, is what dictates our health.

The word health gets used a lot these days, so let me tell you what being healthy really means to me. I'm talking about a body

that can do EVERYTHING we want it to do. A body that works at peak performance, all day every day, firing on all cylinders. A body that energizes, protects, and heals you, makes you happy and keeps you strong. Because you are what you eat. That's why the food you consume is so damn important, because nutrition is health and health is everything. I can't believe it took me so long to grasp this fundamental component to my nutrition. But that's the reason I wrote this book, so you don't make the same mistake, and to fast-track you to the knowledge you really need.

I've realized that if I eat rubbish, I'll also feel rubbish too. But if I eat the nutritious healthy foods that agree with me, my days are filled with energy, clarity, happiness, and productivity. Back when I was making poor food choices, I could not have written this book. I simply didn't perform well enough to get it done.

So a fundamental component to achieving HPL is good health. The type of food you eat will have a massive impact on your end results. For a performance-seeking person, a calorie is not just a calorie. Your nutrition is geared for maximum performance. Whatever your performance and physique goals, there are certain foods that are better choices. Every day I strive to maintain my HPL and will do whatever it takes to ensure my body works exactly as I want it to.

Now and again I will get a minor illness, like a common cold, and my body doesn't do what I ask. This frustrates me so much that it enforces my passion to keep my body healthy. After reading this book, you'll be thinking this way, too. No matter where you're starting from, one of the most important things you can do for yourself is eat the right nutrition that gives your body (and taste buds) exactly what it needs to help you be the best.

Stay Single

When I talk about eating for nutrition and good health, I mean good, real, whole food. I'm talking about single-ingredient foods that have grown in the earth and haven't been manufactured or processed in a factory. This means choosing foods that are as close as possible to their natural state.

Avoid fast food and processed items as much as possible. That's because most of these products are devoid of real nutrition. They are packed with sugars, artificial sweeteners, preservatives and other man-made chemicals. Who actually feels good eating this stuff anyway? Not me. I don't feel they offer me any health or HPL benefits. In fact, they lower my health and make me feel like the "old" me. Now that I understand that, I actually create the experience of my entire life by what I eat.

Knowing which foods to eat and which foods to limit should be something everyone knows about, right? But, shockingly, this isn't the case, and many people know very little about the nutrition of the food they are eating. Society on the whole is getting fatter, sicker, and unhappier, and poor nutrition is a key factor. Overeating, along with the consumption of over-processed foods, is ruining people's health. This is why eating single-ingredient foods is my nutrition cornerstone number two, and is often the first piece of advice I give clients. Making the correct food choices is a must if you want to support your goals.

One of the nutrition world's favorite arguments is that of "quality" vs. "quantity" of food intake. When it comes to changing body weight, quantity is an important factor. But high performance people want a lot more than just weight loss! For us, quality and quantity of our food is equally important. We want to understand why some foods give our bodies the energy to power through intense workouts, whilst others leave us lethargic. Throughout this book I'll show you how to make the best food choices, in both quality and quantity, for your time, money, and environment.

When I first learnt about the benefits of certain foods (and the lack of nutrition in processed foods), I took it to the extreme. I cut out all processed foods and drastically limited any man-made products. I essentially tried to live on meat and vegetables alone. This was a bad diet! And it threatened my relationship with food. Today, I have more respect for lifestyle balance. I realize that we create a better relationship with food by maintaining an inclusive diet, over an exclusive one. This approach is much more sustainable in the long term. By restricting my food choices, I created an ongoing mental battle. We are constantly surrounded by processed foods and food advertising, making it increasingly difficult to avoid temptation.

Understanding the role of food quantity in your diet is an important tool, helping you develop a diet that focuses on being inclusive, rather than good vs. bad food.

A great advantage of this style of eating is having the options to eat a wider variety of enjoyable foods. You'll never lack key nutrients, nor send yourself into a spiral of cravings that only a large pizza and chocolate dessert will satisfy. You will also find that even when you do fancy a change from the typical weekly menu, you choose healthy and nutrient-packed options.

The best bit? We can eat for both nutrition and enjoyment. Eating whole, single-ingredient foods doesn't mean you are confined to boring and bland chicken and salad meals. We want real food. Good food. Delicious food! Meals bursting with flavor and packed with the nutrients your body needs. I will show you how to combine food quality and quantity, and turn that into great-tasting meals that take you directly to High Performance Living.

Lastly, my advice to help you get this balance right is to follow the ninety percent rule. So for every ten meals, have one that doesn't match the rules. The same applies if you are only following your plan seventy percent of the time, so seven meals out of ten. If you want to see further progress, this needs to increase to eighty percent and then ninety percent. Only then will you see optimal progress and discover whether your current choices are truly working for you.

3. PROTEIN IS POWER

If you come over to my house (please drop me a line first, I'd hate you to turn up whilst I'm out at the gym!), you'll find the fridge and freezer stocked up with all kinds of meat. I admit that, in the past, I stuck to typical lean meats like chicken and turkey. Now though, I've gone exotic: kangaroo and buffalo feature regularly on the menu Chez Anderson.

That's because I love protein and I know the benefits it can bring to my body and daily performance. Of course, we can get protein from other sources, including plants, eggs, and dairy products. In fact, protein is present in most plant- and animal-based foods.

The word protein means "of prime importance"—and protein is certainly important to health. When I follow a high-protein diet, my body just feels powerful— my muscles get bigger, my strength goes up, and I recover from training much faster too. Its high thermic effect helps boost the metabolism, building lean muscle tissue and reducing body fat to make us look better. Despite it being the key macronutrient for optimal body composition, many people are drastically under-eating protein.

High-protein diets have occasionally grabbed the headlines for being unhealthy, but the research never holds up. So I'm going to show you the importance of a high-protein diet, and how much you actually need. Protein is incredibly important. Without it our body composition and health suffer.

Proteins are an essential nutrient and can be broken down into twenty building blocks known as "amino acids." Out of these twenty amino acids, nine are considered essential, as the body cannot synthesize its own, meaning we must obtain these from animal and plant sources. The other eleven are nonessential, as they can be synthesized by the body.

Within the nine essential amino acids, there are three branched-chain amino acids (BCAAs): leucine, isoleucine, and valine. They do not require metabolizing by the liver, and are therefore taken up directly by the body. These three amino acids are the most important for the manufacture, maintenance, and repair of muscle tissue. Of the three, leucine has shown to be the most effective at stimulating protein synthesis (the process of building muscle protein and therefore growth), yet the three work better together to provide a host of benefits and even boost energy during workouts. Studies show that BCAA supplementation alone can blunt the catabolic hormone cortisol (think stress) and decrease delayed-onset muscle soreness (DOMS). Essentially, these amino acids alone will add more muscle to your body and aid recovery from your intense training.

I often get asked what protein sources and food groups are best to eat. The table shows a breakdown of some typical foods and their protein content.

Animal Protein Foods	Edible Protein (g per 100 g)	Plant & Dairy Protein Foods	Edible Protein (g per 100 g)
Beef top round, lean	36.12	Pumpkin seeds	32.97
Pork bacon	35.73	Peanut butter	25.09
Beef brisket, lean	33.26	Cheddar cheese	24.90
Beef steak, lean	31.06	Monterey cheese	24.48
Beef top sirloin, lean	30.55	Colby cheese	23.76
Pork top loin	30.48	Peanuts	23.68
Bluefin tuna	29.92	Mozzarella cheese	22.17
Turkey bacon	29.60	Almonds	22.09
Chicken dark meat	28.99	Pistachio nuts	21.35
Oyster	28.81	Flaxseeds	19.50
Beef tenderloin, lean	28.51	Tofu	17.19
Turkey white meat	28.48	Egg yolk	16.89
Beef kidney	27.27	Cashew nuts	15.86
Halibut	26.69	Hazelnuts	15.31

Animal Protein Foods	Edible Protein (g per 100 g)	Plant & Dairy Protein Foods	Edible Protein (g per 100 g)
Trout, cooked	26.63	Walnuts	15.03
Veal, cooked	25.93	Fried egg	15.03
Salmon, cooked	25.56	Soybeans	13.63
Beef liver	25.51	Whey	13.10
Goose	25.16	Cottage cheese	12.93
Caviar	24.60	Ricotta cheese	12.49
Lamb, cooked	24.52	Pecans	11.26
Freshwater bass	24.18	Lentils	9.50
Flounder	24.16	Wheat bread	9.02
Beef T-bone	24.05	Acorn nuts	8.80
Hamburger, 80% lean	24.04	Lima beans	7.80
Duck	23.48	Macadamia nuts	7.79
Turkey	23.00	Mung beans	7.54
Pork chop	21.91	Cranberries	5.54
Turkey gizzard	21.72	Green peas	5.36
Turkey heart	21.47	Pinto beans	4.86
Shrimp, moist heat	20.92	Kidney beans	4.83
Lobster	20.50	Yogurt	3.47
Anchovy	20.35	Nonfat milk	3.37
Turkey liver	20.02	Whole milk	3.22
Alaska king crab	19.35	White rice	2.69
Chicken white meat	16.79	Brown rice	2.58

Complete Your Proteins

Not all protein is created equal. When considering what type of protein to eat, I encourage you to look at food quality by its "biological value" (BV).

The biological value of a protein is based on the quantities it contains of the essential amino acids. So a food with a high BV (also known as a complete protein) contains all nine essential aminos. This is commonly seen in animal and dairy products. A food with low to medium BV does not contain all of the essential amino acids. This is commonly seen in plant-based protein sources. We need to combine these low-BV foods to create a higher-quality BV in meals.

This explains why animal proteins (meat and dairy) are so important in our diets, and why they top that list for highest protein content. Buy the highest-quality protein sources you can afford. Not only will you get better-quality protein, but more protein as a result. As the saying goes, you get what you pay for…

It's Not All About the Muscles

So far I've told you that by eating high-quality protein regularly you'll turn into a high performance muscle-building machine. Awesome. But there are a ton of other reasons why protein is so important in our daily diets. Let me give you the whole picture.

I've mentioned that tissue growth and maintenance are primary functions of protein, as they provide the building materials (amino acids) for growth and repair. That makes them vital for forming skin, nails, hair, bones, organs, tendons, and, of course, our favorite… muscles!

But protein also plays a regulatory role in the body, managing enzymes, hormones, antibodies, fluid balance, and nutrient transportation. Lastly, if the body really needs to, it can use protein to provide the calories to meet the body's energy needs.

It's clear that protein has a ton of important functions outside of just making your muscles look good. But let's get back to those muscles, shall we?

How Much Is Enough?

Ah, the million dollar question, how much protein do you need? But before we look into specific numbers or guidelines for particular macronutrients (there's a separate chapter for that), you need to understand why you should be eating so much protein.

The debate continues on daily protein intake, but there is general agreement that active individuals need a higher intake than sedentary people. The DRI (dietary reference intake) suggests 0.36 grams of protein per pound of body weight, or 0.8 grams per kilogram.

This means an intake for a man weighing 177 lb (80 kg) is 64 g.

And an intake for a woman weighing 132 lb (60 kg) is 48 g.

As you can see, this isn't a lot of protein and we now know that for optimal body composition and health, we need a lot more. It's difficult to put an exact figure on how much protein everyone should really be consuming, as it all depends on your goals, activity levels, caloric intake, muscle mass, training schedule, and current health. We can turn to research to help us make the right decisions, yet it varies from source to source. So based on this, use the numbers given below as a starting point, and experiment with your daily protein intake (remember cornerstone number 1).

Your Options

If you're reading this book then you don't want to be average (and quite rightly so). Perhaps you want to lose that unwanted body fat, or build a ton of muscle. Here are the protein intake recommendations for each of those goals:

When Losing Body Fat

Protein has a high thermic effect, meaning it boosts our metabolic rate (we burn more calories) and reduces our appetite (we eat fewer calories). This increase in metabolic effect has been shown to be most effective when protein is set to 25–30% of daily caloric intake. For most, this works out to be around 1.0–1.5 grams per pound of body weight, daily. Having a high protein intake during a calorie deficit is also important, as it is very anabolic, meaning we are more likely to preserve lean body tissue.

When Building Muscle

The key to building muscle is protein synthesis. A higher protein diet will up-regulate protein synthesis (providing you have evenly spaced meals), which creates a net positive protein balance, resulting in that anabolic (building) environment. The studies that look at muscle mass and protein intake tend to vary from 0.8 to 1.0+ grams per pound body weight, so around 1 gram per pound body weight is seen to be highly effective.

Finally, if the numbers game is all too much for you, the easiest and simplest method is following the guideline of "eat protein at every meal." I have used this simple habit with many clients in the early stages and it works remarkably well. If you want to take this one step further, I recommend two palm-sized portions of protein (both width and thickness) per meal (halve this for females). This instantly boosts protein intake and monitors portion control without imposing a single number.

A typical serving of protein from a palm-sized lean meat will give approx. 15–20 g protein. Therefore two servings will give approx. 30–40 g protein—an ideal amount of protein to be consuming per meal.

Playing the Waiting Game

Now you know how much protein to eat, it's a matter of deciding how to split that up over the course of a day. Research has shown that to maximally stimulate muscle protein synthesis (the main goal of eating protein) we should consume our protein approximately every four hours.

Proteins that contain high levels of BCAAs, particularly leucine (approx. 3 g per meal is good), will produce greater protein synthesis, improve insulin signaling, and spare glucose in muscle cells.

So it makes sense that we should split our daily protein intake into evenly spaced meals, as opposed to one large protein hit once per day. In a later chapter, we'll look at exactly how many meals this should be based on your goals.

Dangers of a High-Protein Diet

I was going to write a good rant about the misguided information in mainstream publications, telling us that a high-protein diet is bad for us, linked to cardiovascular disease, dehydration, calcium loss, and impaired liver and kidney function. But I'm going to get straight to the point:

Show us the *accurate* research.

tumbleweed

You see, the small amount of research that may support these dangers appears to have been greatly exaggerated. There is no link to protein causing diseases or organ damage. It's all good. So let's get back to it!

The Protein Fix

I will continue to consume my high-protein diet, kangaroo steaks and all. Protein is the power behind my High Performance Lifestyle and it will be yours too. Every time I train hard in the gym, go sprinting, or even carry a heavy bag, the protein I eat throughout the day gives my body the resources it needs to perform optimally.

My priority is being as strong, energetic and healthy as possible. So I eat my protein from a variety of different sources, and in the correct quantities, every single day. It's protein that nourishes my body and allows it to build and repair.

4. FAT IS ESSENTIAL

Back in the day I believed the saying "fat makes you fat." I fell for it and cut fats out of my diet entirely. Luckily, my love for great-tasting, nutritious, and satisfying fats was just too much and I started to eat them again.

The drive to demonize fats started in the 1980s, when government guidelines and media messages told us that foods containing fat make us overweight and increase risk of cardiovascular diseases. This was wrong. What wasn't made clear was that food choices and overall intake were the key factors.

To understand fat, we need to know about the "right" kinds of fat, and how much to eat. Get this right, and you'll discover the incredible benefits that healthy fats have to offer, including better energy, increased nutrients, improved fat loss, and enhanced flavor to your meals. But before you go off and start smothering all your meals with extra cheese and a side of peanut butter, let me give you a word of warning. With fats, moderation is key, as a little goes a long way. So let's take a look at what fat really is and finally put the "should you eat fats" myth to bed...

Getting to Know Fat

Fat is also known as "lipids," a collective name for a wide variety of water-insoluble chemicals, including all fats and oils in our diets and bodies. Fat is the most concentrated source of energy, and one gram of fat provides around nine calories (compared to four calories per gram for protein and carbohydrates). That's why understanding portion size is so important, as calories from fats (even "healthy fats") can quickly add up!

There are three major types of fat: saturated, monounsaturated, and polyunsaturated. The difference lies in the structure of the fatty acids they are made of. Examples of foods containing a high proportion of saturated fat include animal products such as cream, cheese, butter, ghee, and fatty meats. Certain vegetable products have a high saturated fat content, such as coconut oil, palm oil, and even cocoa. Many prepared foods are high in saturated fat, such as pizza, processed dairy, bacon, and sausages. Yep—most of the tasty stuff!

Poor old saturated fat has been at the forefront of the attack on fat, with the World Health Organization and many governments all advising that we avoid this type of fat. However, if we actually look at recent research, we'll find nothing to support fears that saturated fat contributes to cardiovascular diseases or increases obesity risk. It appears it's not so bad after all.

Next, we have the family of unsaturated fats (polyunsaturated and monounsaturated), typically known as "less stable" than saturated fats, owing to their chemical structure. That doesn't mean they are more likely to harm you, but it does mean they shouldn't be used for cooking at high temperatures. Always use saturated fats for cooking. There are two important polyunsaturated fatty acids, linolenic acid (an omega-3 fatty acid) and linoleic acid (an omega-6 fatty acid) in foods. We call these the essential fatty acids, because they must be obtained from our diets. There's also a lot of research to support the health benefits of a balanced omega-3 to omega-6 fat ratio, and you'll often see people use omega supplements. Foods such as walnuts, sunflower seeds, sesame seeds, and natural oils like flaxseed and linseed are rich in omega fatty acids.

Last but by no means least is monounsaturated fat. This has a higher melting point than polyunsaturated fat and a lower melting point than saturated fat. It is liquid at room temperature and semisolid or solid when cold. Monounsaturated fats are found in natural foods such as red meat, whole milk products, nuts, and high-fat fruits such as olives and avocados. Olive oil is about seventy-five percent monounsaturated fat.

It's also important to mention that fat products should come from high-quality sources. Ideally, buy meats classified as "organic/grass-fed/wild," and oils labeled "extra virgin." Potentially harmful toxins can be stored in the body fat of animals fed a poor diet or kept in less than ideal environments.

Eat foods from this list and you will have no trouble building high-quality, balanced meals containing good fats:

- Essential fatty acids—omega 3/6 oil
- Extra-virgin olive oil—sprinkle this on food/salads—do not cook with it
- Organic virgin coconut oil—including coconut flour, butter, milk—cook with this oil
- Nuts and natural nut butters—not just peanut butter, but almond and other nut butters
- Milk and whole eggs—organic/free-range being best
- Fish—fresh wild Alaskan salmon
- Fresh avocado
- Butter—organic being best
- Dark chocolate—80%+ cocoa content
- Grass-fed/organic beef.

The True Bad Fat

So far I've been raving about the benefits of healthy fats. What I haven't spoken about is the fat that you should avoid: hydrogenated fats. Hydrogenated fats are chemically classified as unsaturated fats, yet behave more like saturated fats in the body. The term "hydrogenated" means manufacturers are blasting the chemical structure of the fat, making the fat solid at room temperature, and creating a man-made saturated fat. Here's the bad news: hydrogenated fats are poisonous to our bodies. When we eat them, they replace normal saturated fat in our cells, and sometimes the essential fatty acids as well. Hydrogenated fats have been linked to heart disease, diabetes, certain cancers, and obesity. By limiting the amount of heavily processed foods in your diet, you'll be avoiding these nasty fats.

The Role of Fat

So you don't think I'm some madman simply telling you to eat more fats, here are some interesting benefits we see from including fat in our diet:

Fat Is an Energy Source

Fat is the most energy-dense nutrient and is also easily stored and transported within the body. The body can store unlimited amounts of fat. Excess carbohydrates and protein can be converted to fat, but cannot be made from fat. Fat therefore serves as an excellent energy reserve.

Fat Can Keep You Fuller for Longer

Eating more fat greatly increases satiety levels, theoretically making it difficult to overeat (when compared to a refined carbohydrate diet). Therefore you can eat less, yet feel more satisfied in the process. Despite fats containing over twice as many calories (nine calories per gram) compared to protein and carbohydrates (four calories per gram), they will keep you much fuller for longer, and you will not need to each as much per sitting.

Fat Is a Key Player in Managing Inflammation

Fat that is typically found in fish contains the essential omega-3 fatty acids EPA and DHA, which are known to have highly anti-inflammatory properties. Reducing inflammation within the body is one of the best things you can do when seeking optimal body composition and health. From a health perspective, these fatty acids appear to reduce the risk of heart disease and stroke. From a performance aspect, they can help to prevent muscle breakdown, enhance joint healing, improve brain function, and promote greater fat loss.

Fat Can Improve Your Hormonal Profile

It has now been proven that dietary cholesterol, such as that from fat, has no effect on cholesterol levels in the blood. In fact, quite the opposite: dietary fats can actually improve our good cholesterol readings (HDL) by converting the bad (LDL). The benefits are clear and even the health authorities are accepting that monounsaturated fats can reduce the risk of cardiovascular disease, and that fatty acids (omega-3 and omega-6) are essential. Even the once-vilified saturated fat is now "not so bad after all," which is great as it's necessary for proper cell membrane function.

Fat Is High in Micronutrients

Many fats contain high levels of fat-soluble vitamins such as A, D, E, and K2. These vitamins are typically lacking in low-fat diets, yet are essential for maintaining good health and performance. Fat is also required to properly digest and assimilate these fat-soluble vitamins.

Fat Requirements

Just as with protein and carbs, there are a number of factors that determine the ideal amount of fats in your diet. When looking at the metabolic processes and their ability to supply energy, it is very clear that fat is an essential component of anyone's diet. There's no clear definition of ideal intake: it depends on age, gender, body composition, activity levels, personal preference, food culture, and current metabolic health. These factors will determine what percentage of dietary fat is required, but we can also look at the current research to help us in making our decisions.

Average Fat Intake

For a healthy individual seeking a balanced diet, 30% of daily caloric requirements should come from healthy fat. This can be broken down into the three different types:

1. 10% should be consumed from monounsaturated fat
2. 10% should come from polyunsaturated fat (omega-3 and omega-6)
3. 10% should be from saturated fat.

Hydrogenated fat should be avoided.

Intake for a typical 2,500 kcal diet would equal 83 g of dietary fat per day.

When Seeking Fat Loss

We have typically seen recommendations to reduce fat intake when seeking fat loss. However this appears to come down to personal preference, as those following a lower calorie diet see benefits from keeping protein and carbohydrates higher.

A daily intake of 20–40% of total daily calories is a good starting point for fats. I wouldn't recommend going lower than 15% (at this point, the negatives appear to outweigh the benefits). However, for some competitive athletes, fat levels may need to drop slightly lower than this (only for three to seven days) in order to successfully peak (usually via carbohydrate loading) for an event.

When Seeking Improved Health

A large proportion of the population stands to benefit from a balanced healthy-fat diet. In fact, reducing refined carbohydrates and increasing healthy fat has been rigorously proven as effective for those who are:

- Overweight or obese
- Type II diabetic
- Suffering metabolic syndrome.

From a health perspective, here's what we see from balancing healthy fats in our diets:

- Blood sugar levels are reduced
- Triglycerides tend to go down
- Small, dense LDL (bad) cholesterol goes down
- HDL (good) cholesterol goes up
- Blood pressure improves significantly.

Eat Your Fats

So there you have it: the truth about fat (and some myths obliterated). I know exactly what's getting added to your next shopping list—healthy fats to pour, whisk, and drizzle on your meals. Adding a small serving of healthy fats to each meal is a great habit to adopt, and you'll quickly start to feel the benefits. Enjoy.

5. THE FUEL OF LIFE

Carbohydrates! My favorite topic. Although I might be biased, as they are also some of my favorite foods. I love carbs!

Although, this wasn't always the case. In fact there was a time when I was actually afraid of carbs. And I know I'm not the first person to have experienced that. Whenever I wanted to lose some body fat, the first thing I reduced was carbs. That meant cutting out the foods I liked and wanted to eat. It made dieting difficult, limiting, and restrictive. But I felt that by cutting carbs out of my diet I would lose fat much faster. I thought that carbs made me fat. I was wrong.

I have since discovered how to eat hundreds of grams of carbs per day and maintain a lean physique. Nowadays, carbs are the last thing I reduce for fat loss in myself or my clients. BYE BYE low-carb diets, you're not welcome here.

I now believe that everyone can and should have carbs in their diet. That's because they can provide some awesome benefits: increased metabolism (better fat loss and health), full glycogen stores (more energy), increased leptin levels (controlled appetite and fewer cravings), improved libido (you know about this one), and increased anabolism (more muscle mass/strength). Without carbs, we are missing out on some great performance and health potential. As a high performance seeking person, it makes sense to include carbs in your diet.

Re-Friending Carbs

The term "carbohydrate" comes from the carbon, hydrogen, and oxygen that these molecules are based on. They are present in foods like fruit and grains. Unlike essential proteins and fats, there are no essential carbohydrates. This means we can obtain everything we need nutritionally from other food sources, so carbohydrates are not necessary to maintain life.

This has brought about much debate over the inclusion and requirement of carbohydrates in our daily diets. Some experts claim we do not need them, while others suggest they should never be excluded. As a result we now have a number of different diet protocols based on manipulating carbohydrates.

Dietary carbohydrate exists in three major classes: the monosaccharides, oligosaccharides, and polysaccharides. Monosaccharides are the simplest form of carbohydrate (mono: they only contain one subunit of sugar). The three most important monosaccharides are glucose, fructose, and galactose. These are known as "simple" carbohydrates and are recognized by their sweet taste.

Glucose is the body's preferred type of carbohydrate and is usually the end product after the body digests the more complex carbohydrates. Glucose is easily used by the body and typically undergoes one of the following three processes:

• Used for immediate energy
• Stored within muscle or liver cells
• Converted to triglycerides to be stored as body fat for later use.

Fructose is another monosaccharide, which has to be metabolized within the liver in order for it to be converted to glucose. It is found in many natural and artificial foods and is considered the sweetest of the carbohydrates, hence its popularity in food manufacturing. Over the years fructose has been the subject of debate, but there's nothing to worry about if you're eating it from natural food sources.

Fructose can be found in many fruits (and veggies), and it doesn't just taste good. It also contains a host of vitamins, minerals, antioxidants, fiber, and polyphenols. So eliminating these foods just because they contain fructose would be stupid—the benefits far outweigh the negatives. The body does just fine at handling modest amounts of fructose, and the typical guideline is around 15–25 grams per day. Many common fruits do not even surpass single-figure amounts of fructose, so you can eat a number of pieces of fruit per day and stay within the guidelines. Maintaining a diet low in processed foods and refined carbohydrates will help you stay well within

the recommended guidelines. It really comes down to one thing—balance.

The last important monosaccharide is galactose. Just like fructose, this carb molecule must be metabolized in the liver and will then be used in the same manner as glucose. Unlike the other two monosaccharides, galactose is not typically found alone in foods.

When monosaccharides join together they form disaccharides (two monosaccharides) and oligosaccharides (three to ten monosaccharides). There are three common disaccharides: sucrose, lactose, and maltose. Sucrose is also known as table sugar and is therefore the most popular disaccharide. This carbohydrate occurs naturally in many of our foods (fruits, vegetables, beet sugar, cane sugar) and is essentially a combination of glucose and fructose.

Lactose is another common disaccharide yet it only exists in milk from lactating animals, and is a combination of glucose and galactose. The body requires a special digestive enzyme called lactase to digest this type of carbohydrate. Those who have difficulty digesting dairy products are typically low in this lactase enzyme.

The final important disaccharide is maltose, a combination of two glucose molecules. In nature this occurs during the sprouting of seeds, but can also be artificially induced (known as malting) by the introduction of heat. This process is seen mostly in the production of alcohol, where this carbohydrate is used to provide the sweet taste in certain products.

The last of the saccharide categories is polysaccharides, a bonding of more than ten monosaccharides to form linear or complex chains. These types of saccharides are typically found in animal and plant sources, and the two main groups of polysaccharides are starch and fiber. The starch molecule is the storage form of carbohydrates in plants (e.g., grains, legumes, and potatoes). Starches that are not digested in the stomach (and remain intact) are known as resistant starches, and may then be broken down in the gut to benefit digestive health.

Fiber is considered a non-starch and is found in plants, and despite large benefits to our health, can only be broken down by the large intestine. There are essentially two kinds of fiber and each possesses unique and specific beneficial qualities.

Soluble Fiber

This fiber type is very resistant to breakdown by the digestive enzymes in our mouth, stomach, and small intestine. It is therefore partially digested in the large intestine, where good bacteria ferment it, producing butyric acid (found in butter) and acetic acid (found in vinegar). This helps the digestive system maintain its acidity and good health.

Insoluble Fiber

This is the most digestion-resistant fiber and therefore passes through the digestive system intact. Its main role is to aid transport of other foods and liquids. It does this by absorbing water and thus adding "bulk" to our stools, making our feces move faster through the intestines. The recommended average daily intake for fiber is eighteen grams for adults and proportionally less for children.

Despite all of these fancy names and various forms of carbohydrates, you will

actually eat all of them on a daily basis if consuming a variety of carbohydrate foods. Here are some of the most common carb sources I recommend:

- Rice (plain rice, rice cakes, rice milk)—jasmine rice tastes awesome!
- All types of potatoes
- Oats
- All type of beans, including lentils
- Fruits—limit to one to two servings per day
- Maltodextrin, dextrose, waxy maize starch, Vitargo (barley starch), Palatinose (isomaltulose)—workout window only
- Vegetables
- Manuka honey

The Carbohydrate Sweet Spot

Hopefully I've shown you the importance of having some carbs in your diet, and explained what they can do for you. Your next question might reasonably be: "How much should I eat then, Ru?" Sadly, there's no clear definition of exactly how much carbohydrate should make up someone's diet (but by now, you probably knew I'd say that). I've said it before and I'll say it again: an individual's optimal intake depends on age, gender, body composition, activity levels, personal preference, food culture, and current metabolic health.

When looking at the metabolic processes and their ability to supply energy for athletic performance, it is very clear that carbohydrates are an essential component of someone's diet. There are a number of indicators that I use to help me find the right level of carbohydrates for my clients.

Body type can play a factor in one's ability to handle carbohydrates, with typical ectomorphs being able to consume more carbs than their endomorph or mesomorph counterparts. Some people put a lot of emphasis on body typing and how that can influence someone's nutrition and training. I see it as one of the many factors that we can consider when creating nutrition plans, and use it as a rough guideline.

Ectomorph—typically tall and skinny with a small frame. This body type finds it difficult to gain muscle. This is because of a fast metabolism that results in reduced muscle mass and fat on the body. Higher caloric intakes are required to build more muscle and a greater level of carbohydrate sensitivity is typically seen.

Mesomorph—the guy or girl we all want to be, with a hard body and defined muscles. Mesomorphs are naturally strong and gain muscle easily, with an athletic body and broad shoulders to match. They can gain fat more easily than their ectomorph counterparts, but this can be easily controlled by watching calorie intake.

Endomorph—typically classified as "short and stocky," with soft features and a rounder-looking physique. Endomorphs gain muscle easily, along with body fat too. This is because of a slower metabolism, meaning carbohydrate tolerance is lower than the other body types and calorie intake should always be monitored.

Current body fat to muscle ratio shows how tolerant someone is likely to be to carbs. Typically, the more muscle mass you carry and/or the less body fat you have, the higher chance you will be able to consume greater quantities of carbohydrate on a daily basis.

Activity levels play a large role in how much energy you burn and therefore how much you require to "top-up." The more active a person is, the more carbs are required to replace the energy used to perform and recover. This is why I always recommend high-intensity weight training over most other exercise techniques, as it has been shown to burn much more energy during and after training. On top of this, you build some nice muscle too.

When you exercise more, you can eat more. And when you eat more, your body has a greater ability to change. This is basic energy turnover; the relationship between the amount of energy put in from your nutrition and the amount of energy out via exercise.

Our goal should be to create the highest energy turnover we can on a day-to-day basis, and intense exercise is essential for this. Central to this is improved nutrient partitioning—our body's ability to use the food we give it. In other words, more calories go to our muscles for growth and repair, while fewer are put to fat cells for storage. We are also eating more high-quality foods, meaning greater amounts of vitamins, minerals, and antioxidants are available to us, providing a much better recipe (pardon the pun) for long-term success.

Based on these factors, you can form a ballpark figure for how much carbohydrate you should consume to find your sweet spot as quickly as possible. Over the years I've tested out a lot of different carbohydrate levels for myself and clients, and here's my general outlook:

High-Carb Diet: >200 Grams per Day

Some people do very well on a higher-carb diet, and some of my clients can eat 300–400 g per day while still losing body fat. Jealous yet? Most are not so lucky, and those who are usually fall into the same category—young, lean, and metabolically efficient with an active lifestyle. If you do not tick all those boxes then the chances are you will not lose weight optimally eating this amount (while maintaining a balanced diet).

Moderate-Carb Diet: 100–200 Grams per Day

This is a very common daily carb range for the majority of active and healthy people looking to cut the body fat. This still allows for some starch in the diet, yet limits the amount quite significantly. You can still get all the benefits of having carbs in the diet (so you feel good and perform well), yet lower the intake and overall amount to therefore optimize fat burning (to look good).

Low-Carb Diet: <100 Grams per Day

This could be described as ketogenic diet—one in which no starchy carbs (or very few) are consumed daily. This is when the body is forced to use fat for energy. To do this, the person will go through a fat adaption phase, when the body releases ketones for muscle and brain fuel. This can be the most difficult part of such a diet as energy levels can significantly drop until this process is complete.

This energy slump is also common for those transitioning to a moderate-carb diet plan. Most people lose weight quickly on this type of plan, but it especially suits those who are inactive, diabetic, or seeking that last bit of fat loss. A low-carb diet also works better for women, as they carry much less body weight than men, and require less energy as a result.

Love Your Carbs

I rarely use low-carb diet plans with my clients, with the majority of females eating in the moderate-carb diet bracket and most guys in the high-carb diet. If you couldn't even dream of eating that many carbs while getting leaner, let me show you how to do this in Part II.

My guess is this has been your favorite chapter to date (right after the part I told you everyone should be eating more carbs... that line always wins everyone over!). As you can see, I'm not here to preach a low-carb or low-fat diet to you. In fact, I've shown you the benefits of having a balanced nutrient intake. To achieve HPL, you're going to need all the nutrients and energy you can get, and carbohydrates will be a focal point.

6. MAXING YOUR MICROS

If I think back to all of those years I wasted, eating foods I hated and avoiding the foods I liked, I could cry. All for the sacrifice of being "healthy" and lean.

Remember back when you were a kid, I bet your parents told you to finish everything on your plate. Yeah, I hated that too. And those leftovers were always your vegetables, right? There's just something about vegetables that makes us want to skip them, perhaps so we have more room on our plate for the really tasty stuff. Now, without trying to sound like your parents all over again, I'm here to tell you to eat more veg. OK, I did sound like them, but there's a good reason for that, so let me explain…

By eating a wide variety of fruit and vegetables, you'll get a ton of micronutrients, also known as vitamins and minerals. These are potent, indispensable compounds that make your body work properly. They boost our health and vitality while promoting growth, reproduction, and energy. Just as "macro" was the term given to suggest the majority, "micro" is given to this set of nutrients to suggest a much lower quantity.

The more handfuls of spinach, sides of carrots, or pieces of fruit I eat daily, the more effectively I am improving my body. By simply eating fresh fruit and vegetables, I get heaps of calcium for my bones, iron for my blood, and vitamin C for my immune system. I do this by adding nutrient-dense leafy greens, seasonal vegetables, fruit, and berries to my plate at every meal. It makes me feel sharper, stronger, and more capable than ever.

The three macronutrients are usually measured in grams. Micronutrients are typically measured in milligrams. However, it's important to note that this is only related to quantity, and micronutrients are vital to everyone in terms of optimal body composition, health, and performance. Most vitamins and minerals are classified as essential, as the body cannot synthesize them so they must be obtained from the diet. Whatever we choose to call them, micronutrients are vital for life. Although we get these nutrients from most of the foods we eat, some foods have more vitamins and minerals than others. Most of the time, micronutrients are found within the macros we eat, and they are important in the metabolism of those macronutrients.

There are two classifications of vitamins: water-soluble and fat-soluble.

Water-Soluble Vitamins

- Thiamin
- Riboflavin
- Niacin
- Pantothenic acid
- Vitamin B6
- Folic acid
- Vitamin B12
- Biotin
- Vitamin C

Fat-Soluble Vitamins

- Vitamin A
- Vitamin D
- Vitamin E
- Vitamin K

There are a number of key characteristics that separate the water-soluble and fat-soluble vitamins, but the clues are in the name. Water-soluble vitamins are broken down in water and excreted easily if required. The possibility of toxicity is low as a result. With the fat-soluble vitamins, excess tends to be stored in fat storage sites and there is therefore higher risk of toxicity. Deficiency symptoms are much slower to develop with fat-soluble vitamins than water-soluble ones.

Thankfully, the minerals aren't so complicated, and they are simply classified as inorganic substances:

- Calcium
- Magnesium
- Potassium
- Sodium
- Phosphorous
- Iron
- Zinc
- Copper
- Manganese
- Chromium
- Selenium

Let's summarize three important facts:

- Micronutrients are all natural compounds found in food.
- They are essential nutrients to the body for important functions such as growth, repair, protection, and reproduction.
- Deficiency can occur when micronutrient consumption is reduced or limited.

Scientists have investigated the possibility that large doses of certain vitamins and minerals will help stave off chronic diseases such as cancer and heart disease. This work is leading to exciting findings and future recommendations. Here's what we are currently sure of: with a deficiency of micronutrients, athletic performance and general health markers are reduced. So, mind your micros!

To Supplement, or Not to Supplement?

I know what question is currently on the tip of your tongue, so let me answer it. "Should you supplement with a multi?"

Micronutrients are essential components of our diet. The body cannot make any of the micronutrients (except vitamin D, from sunlight) so we need to take in an adequate amount from food, or supplement if required.

There isn't a lot of research to show that increasing daily dosages of micronutrients above the recommended daily allowance (RDA) levels significantly improves health or athletic ability. So supplementation isn't essential. But there is evidence to suggest that supplemental vitamins C and E, acting as strong antioxidants, may enhance recovery after exercise by reducing oxidative stress. And those with low iron levels, particularly menstruating females, could benefit from an iron supplement.

Ideally, by eating a well-balanced and complete diet, we should receive all the micronutrients in sufficient amounts, but this is not always the case. If you do find your diet lacking in fruit and vegetables, you may suffer from deficiencies. Those who follow a low-calorie intake for significant time periods may not get sufficient micronutrients from their diet. In these cases, supplementation can ensure no deficiencies are present.

Overall, a multivitamin and mineral supplement can be important for those who are not meeting recommended daily intakes. More recently, greens powders have been popularized, to help us get more micronutrients into the diet. Either is a good option.

The Secret Nutrients

Perhaps you knew all this. After all, you've always been told to eat your vegetables! Hopefully I've got my point across: if you really want some HPL, you're going to need to eat some more veggies and fruits.

Before we move on, I'm going to get my geek on and introduce you to a collection of nutrients that you might not have heard of before: phytonutrients, also known as phytochemicals. The phytonutrients are a class of substances found in plant foods. They're not essential nutrients, yet appear to help promote health and reduce risk of cancer, heart disease, and other conditions. Phytonutrients are responsible for providing plants their colors (the red of tomatoes, for example) and distinctive aromas (such as garlic). They occur naturally and protect plants from environmental factors such as sunlight and insects.

Humans, too, can benefit from eating the phytochemicals in fruits, vegetables, legumes, whole grains, herbs, and seeds. As they do not provide energy or building blocks to the body, they are not classified as essential nutrients, but they still play a key role by serving as powerful antioxidants that can help reduce blood pressure and cholesterol, prevent cataracts, minimize menopause symptoms, and reduce osteoporosis.

There are thousands of known phytochemicals, yet most foods only contain a small number of these and few contain them in high doses. Have I got you excited for these yet? Awesome, then you'll be pleased to hear that getting some more of these into your diet isn't going to be difficult…

A well-balanced diet based on whole foods, with ample amounts of fruit, vegetables, legumes, whole grains, herbs, and seeds should provide the body with plenty of phytochemicals. Below are just a few of my favorite foods high in micronutrients and phytochemicals:

- Cruciferous vegetables (e.g., cauliflower, cabbage, broccoli)
- Seaweed
- Fresh berries
- Garlic
- Kale
- Avocado
- Spinach
- Beets (beetroot)
- Most fruit

The whole-food approach is likely to be more effective than supplementation, as we know the absorption, metabolism, and distribution of some nutrients is dependent upon the presence of other nutrients. The same goes for phytochemicals. Simply taking individual amounts (from supplements) may not provide the same functions and protection as combining various sources.

Foods high in micronutrients should be present at every meal, and the recipe section of this book will help you do this successfully.

7. WATER IS LIFE

The topic of water doesn't sound too exciting, even I'll admit that, so let me spice it up for you. It's actually the most important nutrient in your diet. Nothing else comes close. Got your attention?

Let me explain. Imagine you crash-landed in the Sahara Desert. You're all alone and nothing else exists as far as the eye can see. You'd be panicking, but your body will be asking for something pretty quickly: water. As the baking hot heat hits you from every angle, you begin to wilt like a plant and your mouth gets drier by the second. Before you seek shelter or food, you'll be looking desperately for some water. That's because we can only survive three or four days without water, yet can survive weeks without food. (Did you know: Mahatma Gandhi survived 21 days of complete starvation?)

Water is a truly vital resource for the human body. We know it is indispensable for life itself, and provides essential functions for good health. In fact, it is the most widely used nutrient involved in the processes and makeup of the body.

Since you aren't lost in the desert, you need to understand how water can maximize your performance and make you better at what you do. So let's look at it in more detail. A typical male is made up of around sixty percent water, a woman around fifty percent, and our brains (regardless of gender) around seventy-five percent.

Daily water intake is extremely important in helping to replenish water lost through bodily processes including urination, sweating, and breathing. When the water is not replaced, we become dehydrated. Check out these scary stats:

- 1% dehydration—we become thirsty, with reduced concentration
- 5% dehydration—we become hot and tired, with decreased performance
- 10% dehydration—delirium and blurred vision
- 20% dehydration—may result in death.

It's clear that even a small amount of dehydration can hold us back from being our best. As a performance-seeking person, being dehydrated is never a wise option.

Water does plenty aside from simply quenching our thirst:

Transports Nutrients Through the Body

Once a substance is dissolved, water becomes vital for transporting it throughout the body. Blood—83% water—transports oxygen, CO_2, nutrients, waste products, and more from cell to cell. Urine—another important transporter—is also mostly water and removes waste products from the body.

Moistens Eyes, Mouth, and Nose

Water is needed for protection, keeping your mouth moist and washing away dirt and grime from your eyes. Water even lubricates our joints, keeping them from getting stiff and making sure motion is smooth.

Can Help Maintain pH and Electrolyte Balance

Our bodies must maintain a very specific pH level of 7.4. Values of pH less than 6.9 or greater than 7.6 are life threatening, so it is essential that we have ways to keep pH from deviating too far from normal. Water is a reactant within a very important process that maintains pH at 7.4.

Water is essential to maintaining electrolyte balance within our bodies. Electrolytes are charged ions (such as Na^+ or Cl^-), which must be kept at certain levels to maintain the proper amount of water in our cells.

Participates in Many Chemical Reactions

As a chemical reactant, water is involved in many processes and pathways of the body. We use it to digest food in the gastrointestinal tract, to access stored energy for muscles and organs, and for countless other reactions. Water:

- Helps maintain normal body temperature
- Reduces chances of kidney stones
- May reduce constipation
- Hydrates our skin
- Ensures adequate blood volume
- Forms main components of body fluids.

As you can see, it's pretty important stuff.

How It Works

Water is the fundamental solvent for all biochemical processes in the body. A solvent is the dissolving medium to which a solute (the substance to be dissolved, like a solid, liquid, or gas) is added. When a solvent dissolves a solute, it is known as solvation. Solutes that solvate into ions are known as electrolytes. These play important roles in our bodies including in nerve transmission and muscle contraction.

Electrolytes are single electrically charged particles, key to maintaining water balance and the balance of acids and bases in the body. Sodium, potassium, phosphorous, and chloride are examples of electrolytes—substances dissolved in blood and body fluids that carry electric charges. The key role of electrolytes is to balance the fluids inside and outside of cells, so they can function properly, transporting nutrients while removing waste products. Electrolytes also help create the environment in which the cells' work (for example nerve–nerve communication, heartbeats, and contraction of muscles) takes place.

For all of that, there is another reason why remaining hydrated is so important. When we lose fluid from the body, we also lose electrolytes. Maintaining healthy concentrations of electrolytes is critical to support the important activities of the vital organs.

Which Type of Water?

One of the top questions I'm asked about water is "which type of water should I be drinking?"

The first thing to say is that, when I say water intake, I really do mean pure water. The best source of water is water. Not energy drinks, not coffee, not juice, and definitely not alcohol. If you need a drink, get some fresh water.

In the UK, most drinking water comes from the tap, but this is also used for toilet flushing, washing, and landscape gardening (if you're into that sort of thing). It's one hundred percent safe enough to drink, as it has been "treated" before use. So drink up.

But you might find bottled, filtered, or mineral water tastes better and gives you a higher level of minerals for improved hydration levels. Bottled water is big business and many people buy it because of perceived health and safety benefits, for its improved purity, or for "taste free" factors. These reasons might not hold water (excuse another pun). There are no existing guidelines requiring bottled water to meet higher standards for quality (such as a maximum level of contaminants), than standards imposed on public drinking water supplies. As a matter of fact, it is suggested that anywhere between twenty-five and forty percent of bottled water comes from the same municipal supplies as tap water, and has only been filtered to remove chlorine to improve taste.

It's important to understand how the source of your bottled water may affect its overall quality. My personal choice is to look for a natural mineral water that is drawn from an underground source as it should contain higher levels of minerals than the others.

How Much Water Do You Need?

Yes, you guessed it: "how much water do I need to drink?" is the second question I'm asked by friends and clients. The answer to this is highly individual, as the amount of water you need will depend on your age, health, activity level, environment, and diet.

Water leaves the body through several routes—the evaporation of sweat, in the moisture of exhaled breath, in the urine, and in the feces. It is also used to facilitate all the previously mentioned functions in the body. This amount equals between 1.4 and 2.8 liters (between 3 and 6 pints) per day.

Adults are advised to consume 1.0–1.5 ml of water for each calorie expended daily.

For example: if your daily energy expenditure (basal metabolic rate × activity level) is 2,000 kcal per day, then you would require 2–3 liters (approx. 4–6 pints) of water per day. I've personally found that many people do better at the higher end of this spectrum. In fact, studies conducted on strength and power athletes noted optimal hydration levels for these athletes in the range of 3.8 liters (8 pints) per day for men and 2.6 liters (5.5 pints) for women.

Water consumption throughout training should be a given, and it is suggested for every pound in body weight lost between the start and finish of training, 500 ml (1 pint) of water should be replaced.

When recommending daily water intake to clients, these general guidelines work very well:

- Get hydrated ASAP in the morning
- Continue to sip throughout the day
- During high heat and exercise, drink enough to compensate for lost fluids.

Listen to your body—it will tell you when it needs more water. Don't wait for thirst cues, that's your body's way of saying it's been too long. If you are feeling thirsty, that doesn't mean you'll need water soon, it means you've needed it for a while. You can also check your pee: a pale yellow color means you're optimally hydrated, and a darker yellow color means you need some more water.

8. THE POWER OF SLEEP

I've told you a lot about my own journey through nutrition and lifestyle. I believe our experiences are what make us truly individual.

Without my previous experiences, this book would just be full of my reading and studies and would have no personality (like a lot of nutrition education books). So far, I've shared my difficulties with getting this nutrition lark right for myself. It's all different now.

You see, this chapter's topic—sleep—is something I have always got right. As my Mom will often remind me, from a very young age I complained of not getting to bed early enough. So it's safe to say I have always loved my sleep. In fact, I'm not the same without it. One bad night's sleep can knock me off my usual high performance self for days. It's a fine line and one that I try never to compromise.

Sleep always makes for an interesting topic as everyone has plenty of experience of it (good or bad) and can relate to it. It is accepted that every being within the animal kingdom must sleep, yet the exact purposes and mechanisms of sleep are only partly understood.

Understanding the power of sleep and how to get as much high-quality sleep as possible is one of the healthiest things you can do. We can all relate to how loss of sleep can take its toll on our energy, mood, decision making, and ability to handle stress. Sleep should therefore be your top priority. Many people try to sleep as little as possible, but just as exercise and nutrition are essential for HPL, so is sleep. No other activity delivers so many benefits with so little effort. Sleep has a direct correlation to the quality of your waking life.

The Role of Sleep

The study of sleep looks at the neuro-scientific and physiological basis of sleep and its functions. It is assumed that the benefits we get from enough sleep have evolved over time, creating greater dependence on getting sufficient and good quality sleep. Sleep is a naturally occurring state characterized by reduced or absent consciousness, and the inactivity of nearly all voluntary muscles.

In humans, sleep timing is controlled by the circadian clock and (to some extent) by willed behavior. The circadian clock (also known as circadian oscillator) allows us to coordinate our biology and behavior with daily and seasonal changes in the day/

night cycle. This inbuilt biological clock receives daily corrective signals from the environment, primarily daylight and darkness. Circadian clocks are the central mechanisms that drive circadian rhythms.

The term circadian comes from the Latin "circa," meaning "around or approximately," and "diem," meaning "day." It works over a 24-hour period.

The Circadian Clock

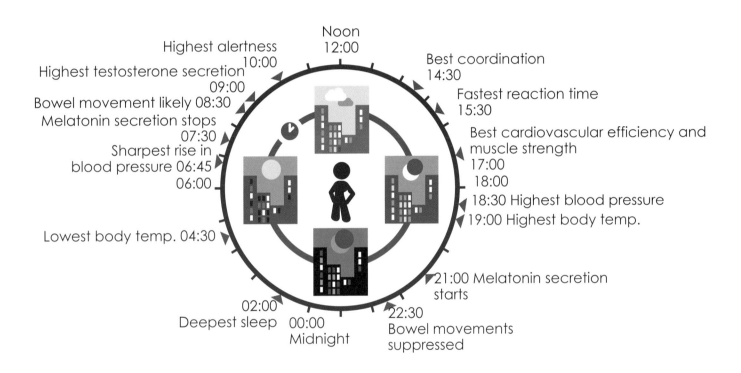

This clock is reset through our ability to sense external cues. The primary one of these environmental changes is light. The circadian clock is considered to be intertwined with most cellular processes. When you sleep, the body doesn't just shut down and switch off. In fact, while you rest, the brain oversees a wide variety of biological maintenance that improves your health markers and aids recovery. Here are some quick facts on how quality sleep helps you be more awesome:

Restoration

Sleep is restorative, and without it you are not able to work, learn, create, or communicate at your highest level. Over time, lack of sleep can even lead to mental and physical breakdown.

Sleep has been linked to the immune system. Sleep loss can impair our immune function, so by sleeping longer we can invest in strengthening our immune system.

When we sleep, our metabolic rates reduce and free radical production is decreased, allowing restorative processes to take over. The metabolic phase during sleep is anabolic, as we see a greater release of anabolic hormones such as growth hormone. This further adds to the restorative processes of sleep.

Memory Processing

Numerous studies have been conducted into the correlation between sleep and memory. Sleep deprivation is linked to a reduction of "working memory," which keeps information active for further processing and supports higher-level cognition functions such as decision making, reasoning, and memory.

So, the next time you forget to buy your protein powder, you know why!

Preservation

It's been suggested that sleep can serve as a "preservation and protection" system to reserve energy and to keep us out of harm's way.

The Stages of Sleep

A number of stages of sleep occur every time we get some rest. These stages represent what's happening beneath the surface, and all play an important part in the benefits of rest. There are two main types of sleep:

Non-REM (NREM) Sleep

This is essentially a three-stage sleep cycle, with each being a deeper level than the previous one.

- Stage N1 (transition to sleep)—The stage between sleep and wakefulness. The muscles are active, the eyes roll slowly under the eyelids, muscle activity slows down, and we are easily awakened.

- Stage N2 (light sleep)—Considered the first stage of true sleep, characterized by an increase in "theta" activity within the brain. We become harder to awaken, eye movement stops, heart rate slows, and body temperature decreases.

- Stage N3 (deep sleep)—Known as "slow-wave sleep," characterized by an increase in "delta" activity within the brain. Blood flow to the brain is decreased and passed to the body to enhance its restorative benefits. We are difficult to awaken at this stage.

REM (Rapid Eye Movement) Sleep

REM sleep has been given this name as our eyes can be seen moving back and forth in this stage. It can also be known as "dream sleep" and usually occurs about sixty to ninety minutes after falling asleep. Eye movement, heart rate, and blood pressure increase, yet arm and leg muscles are paralyzed.

Every time we sleep we are likely to go through all stages of this cycle. Our bodies move back and forth between REM and N3 sleep to form a complete sleep cycle. Each cycle typically lasts about ninety minutes and repeats four to six times over the course of the night. Typically, the majority of deep sleep occurs in the first half of the night, with REM stages becoming longer with more light N2 sleep later into the night.

This is why many people report waking up after a number of hours' sleep, as their sleep is getting lighter. Each sleep within this sleep cycle has potential benefits to you.

A normal adult spends around fifty percent of total sleep time in stage N2 sleep, twenty percent in REM sleep, and thirty percent in stages N1 and N3.

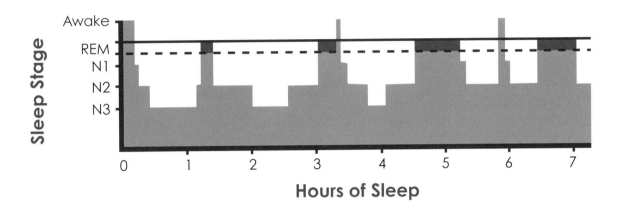

Stage N3, deep sleep, is considered one of the most important for making us feel energized and refreshed from rest. It is heavily involved in maintaining your health, providing growth and development, repairing muscles and tissues, and boosting the immune system. It essentially renews the body.

REM sleep renews the mind, and is important for a healthy memory and learning ability. During REM sleep, the brain consolidates and processes the information we have learnt that day, while forming neural connections to strengthen the memory. It also replenishes its supply of neurotransmitters, including feel-good chemicals like serotonin and dopamine.

It's evident that we need a mixture of all sleep stages for optimal health and restoration.

How Much Sleep?

With modern lifestyles, people are sleeping less than ever, with the average person getting fewer than seven hours per night. Whilst sleep requirements vary from person to person, this average is not enough for most, and is leading some people into chronic sleep disorder. Most people sleep as much as they need, but not as much as they should for optimal health and performance. In reality, most healthy adults need between seven and a half and nine hours of sleep per night for best results. Young adults and children require even more.

There is no system to show exactly how many hours you should sleep, and the best way to evaluate it is how you feel throughout the day. If energy is low, memory is poor, and you don't feel alert, the chances are you need more sleep. A common sign that you require more sleep is that you always want to sleep in if you don't set your alarm clock. This is your body telling you that it requires more sleep. You are essentially playing catch-up. If you wake in the morning and feel like you could sleep a lot more, then you likely should.

Sleep Deprivation

Everyone experiences trouble sleeping from time to time, and this can be the result of a number of factors. A problem may occur when regular disturbances happen frequently and these affect daily life. This problem alone can lead to a number of health problems. Remember, even a minimal loss of sleep can affect health and performance.

In case I haven't got my point across on the importance of sleep yet, here's a quick rundown of the common side effects from lack of sleep:

1. Fatigue, lethargy, and lack of motivation
2. Moodiness and irritability
3. Reduced creativity and problem-solving skills
4. Inability to cope with stress
5. Reduced immunity, frequent colds and infection
6. Concentration and memory problems
7. Weight gain
8. Impaired motor skills and increased risk of accidents
9. Difficulty making decisions
10. Increased risk of diabetes, heart disease, and other health problems.

How To Sleep Better

Every night, I fall asleep within minutes of my head hitting the pillow. I don't wake up again until my alarm. This isn't the case for everyone, and I know some people can struggle for a good night's sleep. So here are a number of sleep-promoting techniques and considerations that can be easily integrated into your evening routine.

Get a Routine

Syncing with the body's natural clock, the circadian rhythm, is one of the most effective methods we have for getting a good night's sleep. Getting into a strict and consistent routine of going to bed and getting up in the morning can have huge benefits.

It's also important to experiment with different sleep and wake times, as various setups will benefit people differently. Aim to not only find the ideal length of sleep, but also the times your sleep should start and finish.

Control the Surroundings

On top of finding the best sleeping routine, we can naturally encourage the body to feel more alert or relaxed. A hormone known as melatonin is released when we are in dark surroundings, as it helps the body regulate the sleep–wake cycle. If we are exposed to little or no sunlight during the day, we release melatonin, making us sleepy during the day. In a bright environment, melatonin production is stopped. The same can occur at night. If we are exposed to bright light or electrical equipment just before bed, it can slow down the release—just when we do want a release of melatonin in order to induce sleep.

The goal should be to spend more time in daylight during the day, with less exposure to light (including artificial light) at night.

Keep the Bedroom for Sleep

It's essential to ensure the bedroom is optimized for relaxing, unwinding, and sleep. The bedroom should therefore become a place associated with sleep, which will send a powerful signal to help us nod off.

Other important factors here are:

- Eliminating any noises that may disturb your sleep
- Keeping the bedroom at the right temperature
- Removing any electronic equipment
- Ensuring the room is dark enough
- Ensuring the bed is comfortable enough.

Improve Nutrition and Exercise Habits

Good nutrition habits—particularly in the last hours before bed—can drastically improve sleep quality. Some important considerations are:

- Avoid eating large meals before bed
- Avoid drinking too much liquid
- Avoid caffeine in the latter part of the day (2–4 pm is good cutoff)
- Avoid alcohol before bed.

A small bedtime snack containing a balance of protein, fat, and carbohydrates can be ideal to help you fall asleep, as that feeling of being satisfied can help the body rest. Daily exercise can also lead to improved sleep, while exercising too late may disturb the body's natural wake–sleep cycle as it can act as a heavy stimulus on the body.

Reduce Stress and Relax

Stress related to family, money, work, or other day-to-day difficulties can be a common sleep disruptor. Managing these stressors and using pre-bed relaxation techniques can be effective in aiding a better night's sleep. Some common techniques are:

- Write down any problems or issues
- Conduct some deep-breathing techniques
- Use progressive muscle-relaxation techniques
- Avoid any stressful tasks or thoughts before bed
- Keep the bedroom clean and tidy
- Have a hot shower or bath
- Do something you enjoy before bed.

Start applying some of these techniques and you'll be sleeping like a baby very soon. Sweet dreams!

9. THE SILENT PHYSIQUE KILLER

I get stressed just thinking about the topic of stress. Maybe that's why it makes the penultimate nutrition cornerstone. I've decided to rename stress the "silent physique killer" when explaining it to my clients. Let me clarify.

A common theme I see amongst those with high stress levels is a lack of results when trying to change their body. Stress holds them back from being the best that they can be, and they never quite achieve HPL. In a very similar way to poor sleep, it can put the brakes on progress, even if training and nutrition are spot-on.

Of course, we all suffer stress at some point in our lives. We are involved in regular stressful life situations, including exhausting training schedules. Stress is a burden on the body, and if it becomes chronically elevated and prolonged, we can end up massively fatigued and run down. That's when it can put a halt to any body composition changes. What we don't always realize is the potential damage stress is doing to the inside of our bodies and how it affects our health.

Stress 101

To show exactly what happens internally during a typical "stressful" situation, let's look at an example:

Imagine you are walking on the sidewalk and start to cross the road after checking it's clear in both directions. Suddenly a car appears out of nowhere and is forced to swerve out of the way to avoid a collision with you. What happens to you? Your heart is racing, you are breathing heavily, sweating, and shaking. You are in a state of shock. Here's what happened internally:

- Above the kidneys you will find a pair of triangular-shaped glands known as the adrenals. Their main role is to help your body cope and survive during stressful situations.
- At the time of noticing the car hurtling towards you, the brain sent a nerve impulse directly to your adrenals, causing them to secrete adrenaline.
- Adrenaline is the reason for the heightened state you felt after the event, as its role is to ensure you have the focus and energy you need to survive a life-threatening situation. This results in high blood pressure, respiration, and heart rate.

- The brain requires more glucose during this stressful time, so that the body and brain have more energy to survive. This causes the release of a number of hormones, which tell the adrenals to produce cortisol.
- The increased blood glucose levels we see associated with stressful events are due to the increased cortisol levels. Our bodies have actually adapted well to these sudden stressful events and can therefore effectively manage our near-death experience. That's good news for you... in the short term.

We also see cortisol being released during other stressful situations such as intense training sessions. Under normal conditions, cortisol rises rhythmically throughout the night, and peaks first thing in the morning.

These natural "one-off" releases of cortisol can actually be a good thing for the body, as they help regulate immune function, repair tendons/ligaments, and may even accelerate fat loss. The problems we see with cortisol are when the hormone is elevated for long periods of time. This chronic, low-level stress that never quite goes away leads to physical problems. So let's look at this process again, but in a little more detail.

What is Stress?

One of the most common medical issues seen by the health-care industry is stress-related illness. Whether we recognize them or not, there are a number of stresses that we will come into contact with daily. It is the intensity, frequency, and duration of each stress that combine to form our total stress load.

There are four major categories of stress:

1. Physical stress—such as overworking, poor nutrition, lack of sleep, or athletic over training
2. Chemical stress—from environmental pollutants, food intolerances or IBS, poor diet, and endocrine gland intolerances
3. Thermal stress—from overheating or over-chilling of the body
4. Emotional and mental stress—from family, friends, money, work, etc.

It's the combination of these stresses on the body over time that can cause stress-related illnesses.

You'll likely never experience full-blown adrenal fatigue, but you could experience a number of other negative symptoms during high-stress times:

- Increased blood sugar levels (store more body fat)
- Suppressed pituitary function (low testosterone)
- Suppression of the immune function
- Insomnia
- Reduced liver detoxification
- Increased inflammation
- Learning and memory issues.

This is what occurs on the inside, but spotting the issues on the outside can be difficult. Common symptoms are:

- Difficulty falling asleep
- Feeling lethargic most of the day
- Suffering from allergies or falling ill frequently
- Suffering from mood swings or feeling emotional
- Excessive perspiration, dizziness, or blurred vision.

See why getting on top of our stress levels is a must?

The Adrenal Glands

Our two adrenal glands, situated just above the kidneys, are the "command centers" for certain hormonal operations. They have a significant effect on the functioning and operation of every tissue, organ, and gland in the body. We cannot live without them, and how well they function has a drastic impact on how we think and feel. The adrenal glands largely determine the energy of our responses to every change in our internal and external environment.

From a nutritional stance, the adrenal glands closely affect the utilization of carbohydrates and fats, the conversion of fats and protein into energy, the distribution of stored fat, normal blood sugar regulation, and proper cardiovascular and gastrointestinal function. The protective activity of anti-inflammatory and antioxidant hormones secreted by the adrenals helps to minimize negative and allergic reactions to alcohol, drugs, foods, and environmental allergens.

As we age, the adrenal glands become the major source of sex hormones in both men and women. These are strong and powerful hormones, responsible for a range of emotional and psychological effects, including sex drive and the tendency to gain weight. The adrenals are also linked to our disposition to develop certain diseases and our ability to overcome them. Essentially, the stronger the illness, the more critical the adrenal response becomes. This is why those with hyper- and hypoadrenia will likely experience more frequent illness and longer-lasting symptoms.

The Stress Hormone

Many consider cortisol to be a "bad" hormone that should be always suppressed—but this isn't correct. Cortisol is responsible for many life-sustaining functions attributed to the adrenal glands. Many of the symptoms associated with adrenal fatigue actually occur from decreased levels of cortisol in the blood or inadequate levels during times of high stress.

Cortisol is known as the stress hormone because the body releases cortisol in order to help cope with stressful situations. Are you starting to see why we do actually need it? The immediate effects of increased cortisol are increased levels of fatty acids, proteins, and glucose in the blood. It is a catabolic hormone, that's true. It takes protein from muscles and fatty acids from fatty tissues, increases gluconeogenesis (the process of making glucose), and decreases the body's uses of glucose.

We see peaks and troughs in cortisol levels naturally throughout the day, with highest levels typically seen at 8 am and the lowest between midnight and 4 am.

Don't underestimate the power of cortisol in your body, it has a number of important functions to play:

Blood Sugar

Cortisol is necessary for maintaining blood sugar levels; when levels are low, the adrenals produce more cortisol. Cortisol up-regulates gluconeogenesis, which converts fats and protein into energy for the body.

Inflammation

Cortisol is anti-inflammatory and works effectively at reducing and preventing responses to allergies in nearly all tissues.

Immune System

In reaction to an autoimmune or inflammatory response in the body, blood cells are sent to defend the body and attack the invaders. Cortisol plays an important role here, as it reduces irritation such as swelling or redness caused by the attacking white blood cells.

Cardiovascular System

Cortisol can help regulate blood pressure through the contraction of the walls of the arteries. The higher the levels of cortisol in the body, the more contracted the mid-sized arteries become. This increase in blood pressure directly affects the heart, and can increase the strength of contractions.

Central Nervous System

Cortisol influences behavior, mood, and excitability—behavioral changes that are a result of excessive or deficient cortisol levels.

Stress

We find ourselves back at the topic of stress and how to manage it. The body signals the adrenals to produce cortisol in times of stress. During stress, cortisol must simultaneously provide more blood glucose, mobilizing fats and proteins for reserved energy, and modify immune reactions, heartbeat, blood pressure, brain alertness, and nervous system responsiveness. Without cortisol, these processes will not occur quickly enough to help us deal with the stress.

When we exhaust our system with too much chronic stress, the body responds by dampening down its response, resulting in low cortisol levels. This is also known as adrenal fatigue, or hypoadrenia.

Living Stress-Free

It's fair to assume you currently have some stress in your life. It's important to know what we can do nutritionally to support our health and reduce negative impacts from stress. I'll outline some of the key points I use with my HPL clients. The more stressed they are, the more these factors are applied in greater detail.

Eat Little and Often

You've learnt that in times of stress your body is burning through more carbohydrates for energy. It's therefore common for those under stress to experience low blood sugar levels, as demand for glucose is higher. This can result in hypoglycemia or, at the very least, increased cravings for sugar. Those with high stress levels are typically on a constant blood sugar roller coaster and always looking for their next sugar fix. On top of this, they rely on stimulants such as coffee and sodas to see them through the day.

These uncontrollable food urges are likely to cause overeating, as the body constantly strives for homeostasis to balance blood sugar levels. And that overeating generally leads to weight gain. It is important for those with a sweet tooth to eat regularly throughout the day, with consistent meal timings. The goal should be never to go hypoglycemic. Meals should be nutritionally balanced with adequate protein, fats, and carbs from high-quality food sources. Sugary food, caffeine, and alcohol should be limited as these have a negative effect on blood sugar levels.

Don't Fast

Intermittent fasting (IF) has become one of the most debated modern nutrition protocols, and rightfully so because it breaks a lot of rules. For decades we have been told to eat every two to three hours, and to eat breakfast upon waking to "kick-start" our metabolism for optimal body composition and health. IF goes against this by reducing meal frequency and delaying breakfast. Many fasting protocols suggest eating less during the day and feasting at night.

Fasting isn't a tool I'd recommend for those with high stress levels as it puts even more pressure on the adrenals to maintain the level of blood glucose.

When recommending IF protocols it's important for the user to be in a good state of health, already eating whole unprocessed foods, getting sufficient sleep, managing stress, and exercising well. It should therefore be used as an addition to an already effective and consistent training and nutrition strategy.

Eat Your Carbs

Carbohydrates are the body's preferred source of energy, and this becomes more apparent during times of stress. To provide the energy to support recovery from stress, follow a higher-carbohydrate diet.

Don't Starve

A low calorie intake during stressful times or recovery from high stress will only heighten the depletion of glycogen and breakdown of muscle tissue, and put more demand on the adrenals. Therefore you should look to eat at calorie maintenance level or a slight surplus during stressful times. We will be working out these levels for you in Part II.

Chill Out

Family, friends, career, and money can all be stressful issues at times, and it's important to manage these as much as possible. Find the root cause(s) of stress and then put procedures into place to reduce, manage, or eliminate them. Remember to relax, laugh, sleep, and have sex as much as possible, as these reduce stress levels in the body. Reduce the main stressors in your lifestyle and remember not to take life too seriously all the time.

One of the best things I ever did to reduce my own stress levels was taking more time out for myself. Each day I start with an activity that I really enjoy doing. That's currently going for a brisk walk around the park while listening to a podcast on my phone. It means I start the day with exercise and learning, before I do anything else. So if I have to work late or if a change of plans happens, I'm cool with that because I've already had some "me" time. But I always try to do something similar on the evening too, as it's the perfect way to unwind from a busy day. Give it a go and see for yourself.

10. ALL ABOUT DIGESTION

Forget "you are what you eat." A more accurate way of looking at it is to say, "you are what you eat, absorb, and don't excrete."

In today's busy society, it's our lifestyles, nutrition, and environment that hold us back and put negative strain on most of our body's systems. The digestive system is one of these systems.

My eyes were first opened to this when I started taking antibiotics for my skin. Just as your body is made up of trillions of cells, it is also host to trillions of bacteria. The role of antibiotics is to kill off bad bacteria to make us feel better again, yet they also destroy the good bacteria. When antibiotics destroy some of the good bacteria in our guts, we can experience poor digestion. As a result of my antibiotic use, I experienced symptoms of irritable bowel syndrome (IBS) for years. At the time I wasn't knowledgeable enough to join the dots, so I just lived with it. As I learnt more about the digestive system, I quickly realized that I did actually have full control over it. I want you to have this power too.

How It Works

Close your eyes. Now imagine your favorite meal sat before you. The smell of it fills the air and you can already feel that first bite on your tongue. Ok, stop now. My guess is that has just made you hungry, and your mouth is watering too. The brain kick-started your digestive system before you even got your first bite.

If you were to eat that meal, you would take a bite and start chewing. This chewing, or mastication, will increase the surface area of the food, while the salivary glands start releasing an enzyme called amylase to breakdown carbohydrates.

From here, with the help of a process called peristalsis, food is passed down the esophagus and enters the stomach. The stomach mixes the food some more, with protein being the main nutrient digested here. This occurs via the activation of the proenzyme pepsinogen, which is converted to active enzyme—pepsin. For this process to occur, the body must release adequate amounts of HCl (hydrochloric acid), which signals the rest of the digestive system to "get ready."

After being in the stomach for one to three hours, the stomach contents are passed along to the small intestine. Most digestion and absorption takes place as food reaches the first section of the small intestine, the duodenum. In order for fats to be fully broken down, bile is required from the liver and the gallbladder to emulsify the fats, before the pancreas adds its pancreatic enzymes so all of the macronutrients can be broken down further. These enzymes are made of protein. Micronutrients, vitamins and minerals, are already small enough that they don't have to be broken down, and the small intestine can just absorb them. The final digestive role for the pancreas is to release bicarbonate to neutralize stomach contents. The process of peristalsis continues, further moving the digested food through the small intestine. At this point, the villi (tiny little fingers that stick out of the small intestine's inner surface) secrete more enzymes that help with the final stages of digestion. The results of this process are:

1. The carbohydrates you ate have been turned from larger sugars to single sugar units, like glucose, fructose, and galactose. These will act as the primary energy source for the body, or be stored as fat.
2. The proteins you ate have been broken down into small units—amino acids and small peptides. These serve as the building blocks for the body.

3. The fats you ate have been broken down to fatty acid chains, which will be used for energy and absorption of vitamins and minerals.

All this is the fundamental reason for the digestive process: so the body can obtain simple sugars, amino acids, and fatty acids from the food you eat. These are absorbed into the intestinal cells, eventually reaching the liver. The liver is responsible for the processing and storing of the nutrients, as well as breaking down toxic substances.

To conclude this energy cycle, your blood delivers these nutrients along with oxygen to your cells. Here, the mitochondria within the cell get to work. These structures are considered "cellular power plants" because they generate most of the cells' supply of adenosine triphosphate (ATP). ATP is also known as the "energy currency of life," and its creation is the main goal of the entire food/digestion/energy cycle. Your body is fueled by ATP, and this is why the digestive system is so important.

The remains of the digestive process pass into the large intestine (colon) in a semifluid form. Minimal absorption of nutrients occurs here, with the main function of the large intestine being to create a more solid stool. You know what happens next.

What Can Go Wrong?

In the real world, things don't always work like they should. In my case, the introduction of antibiotics was enough to disturb this system and cause a host of negative impacts. For some, it may just be one or two smaller factors affecting the functioning of this system.

Basic issues could start at the mouth, such as a lack of saliva to digest carbohydrates, or not chewing your food enough, letting large chunks of food go into the stomach. But the most common issue is low stomach acid, which reduces the stomach's ability to break down proteins. The small intestine can also experience problems if insufficient bile is produced by the liver to break down fats, or if a dysfunction of the pancreas results in reduced pancreatic enzymes. In the small intestine there could be damage to villi and microvilli, which can lead to less breakdown of food and less absorption of nutrients. Lastly, if transit time in the small intestine is decreased, we are at risk of not digesting our food properly, and potentially missing out on vital nutrients. With the large intestine, we commonly see a different disruption in transit time: if transit time is increased, this can lead to potential reabsorption of toxins or hormones that were to be excreted.

Food Allergies and Intolerances

My guess is you want to know how to get your digestive system working at its best. If you are having consistent difficulties, there's a lot of further information you need to learn and apply that is beyond the scope of this chapter. But if you want to maximize the performance of your gut and make it "bulletproof," focusing on food allergies and sensitivities is a great place to start.

Food allergies and intolerances are considered a "sensitive" topic, and many conventional medical practitioners deny that food sensitivity is a real condition. On the other hand, there is a strong argument from alternative medical practitioners that the food we eat is a frequently overlooked origin of disease. It's important to consider research and findings from both groups to ensure the most accurate and balanced approach to understanding gut health.

With a food allergy or sensitivity, the problematic food can set up a cascade of immune and chemical reactions in the body, usually within days (if not minutes) of ingestion. If this food is continually consumed over time, it can cause an ongoing inflammatory reaction in the lining of the intestines, which can result in the lining becoming unhealthy.

Our gut prevents dangerous toxins and compounds getting in whilst allowing the foods and water we consume to enter the body. When our gut is not working optimally, or is in a state of distress, these dangerous compounds can enter our system, yet the body will not fully absorb key nutrients from food.

It's important to highlight the fact that not everyone has an allergy or intolerance to foods or food groups. Those who have never experienced an allergic reaction can find it difficult to understand how even a food that is usually good for us can cause some people such problems.

It's becoming a popular dieting trend to restrict the diet to avoid any chance of reactions or responses to certain foods. This shouldn't be a general starting point for a diet. Food sensitivities do exist and are very real, but probably do not even need to be considered for most people. The take-home point here is that you don't need a "gluten-free diet" or "dairy-free diet" unless you experience negative symptoms from eating those foods or food groups. Read that line again. You with me?

Food Allergies

We understand the strength and importance of our immune system, a complex and connected network designed to protect the body. If the immune system's cells brand a food as an "invader," it will be dealt with by the same process as any other immune response. It's a smart system, and will remember the problematic food and respond in the same fashion with each subsequent exposure.

This response calls forth the body's energies, using up macro- and micronutrients to keep the body safe. This is why those with food sensitivities often experience increased levels of tiredness.

Histamines are the trigger to common allergic symptoms and this process is also known as "degranulation." These are typical instant responses caused by common allergies: a sneeze from dust, watering eyes from pollen, or a skin reaction to nuts. The severity of reactions is varied but they follow the same response pattern, are easy to identify, and the culprit food can usually be easily found.

Food Intolerances

Sensitivities and food intolerances are different to food allergies. The onset of symptoms may take several hours to a couple of days to occur, owing to a delayed immune response. As a result, they can be much harder to diagnose.

The pathways or mechanisms underlying food intolerances appear different to those of the allergies previously mentioned. Most probably they are the immune system cells reacting to a chemical that either naturally occurs in a food or is added to it at some stage. There are many elements within a food and any one of them may be responsible for activating the immune system.

Why It Happens

There are three main factors that contribute to people experiencing an immune response to certain foods or food groups:

A Hyperpermeable Gut (Leaky Gut Syndrome)

Leaky gut can be triggered by a number of things, including an inflamed gut lining, unbalanced bacteria levels, nutritional deficiencies, and underlying allergic conditions within the gut. The source can typically be linked back to a number of lifestyle factors. A diet containing foods you're intolerant of is the most common, but any food that has been shown to inflame the gastrointestinal tract can cause issues. Stress can also be a trigger as it can greatly reduce blood flow to your important digestive organs. A diet low in fiber can play a significant role too, as fiber keeps you regular, excreting dangerous compounds in the process. Lastly, antibiotics and anti-inflammatory drugs will cause havoc in your gut and kill off good bacteria.

A Slow or Deficient Detoxification Pathway

The detoxification system is the primary way that toxins are removed from the body. If this is not operating efficiently, problems can arise. A slow detox may exist if the body's detox system is already under strain—it finds it difficult to keep up with demand. As a result, toxins remain in the body and cause an immune response (such as a food intolerance) to occur.

This can also happen when a certain detoxification enzyme is deficient. Detoxification enzyme deficiency makes it difficult or impossible for the body to break down a dietary toxin. This can be linked to a poor diet, as an optimal detox system requires adequate levels of the nutrients necessary for proper liver detoxification.

The liver is said to be the most hard-working organ in the body, and conducts a number of important functions that are vital to life. It plays an important role in digestion (breaking down nutrients) and assimilation (building up body tissue) and can be considered one of the most important organs for detoxification. It has further responsibilities, such as acting as a storage site for essential vitamins and minerals (iron, B12, vitamins A, D, E, and K). Kupffer cells, which destroy micro-organisms in the blood to help fight off infections, are located in the liver. Red blood cells—responsible for carrying oxygen around the body—are broken down in the liver.

The liver detoxifies harmful substances through a complex series of chemical reactions. The role of the enzymes activated in the liver is to convert fat-soluble toxins into water-soluble substances that can be excreted in the urine or the bile. The liver neutralizes a wide range of toxic chemicals, including those produced internally and externally of the body. When the liver is not functioning optimally, or our metabolic processes are disrupted, this neutralizing effect is greatly reduced, leaving the body open to attack from toxins. This is becoming increasingly more common owing to the rise of genetically modified foods and poor diets.

Genetic Predisposition

Some people are more likely to react to a particular food substance than others. This can be related to place of origin, ancestry, previous exposures, migration, and food modification. It has also been suggested that blood types may have some predictive value in whether there will be an adverse reaction to certain foods.

When we continually expose the body to a food it is intolerant of, it can lead to a chronic activation of the immune system. This constant response leads to increased free radicals in the body, taxing the detoxification pathways and increasing inflammation. This inflammation can cause potential physical damage and premature aging, and is now believed to be linked to diabetes, cardiovascular diseases, and obesity. This sets in motion another cascade of events in the body that may result in symptoms of "malnutrition" or nutrient deficiencies.

It's clear that those who have a food intolerance should act on it and remove the food from their diet. There are a number of tests and procedures we can use to source the problematic food(s), but first let's look at some of the common symptoms and responses.

Symptoms and Responses

There are a number of common reactions within the body when it is exposed to a food that causes an allergy or intolerance. It is important to understand these so we can spot potential issues.

Fatigue

Can be linked to an overactive immune system constantly being taxed by the consumption of foods to which the body is intolerant. Fatigue can also be the first alert to a food intolerance.

Headaches

Can become a recurring problem in those experiencing allergic reactions to food. These may range from mild headaches right up to full-blown migraines that require medical treatment.

Skin Reactions

Common skin problems such as eczema, acne, or irritation may be reduced or prevented through elimination of foods to which the body is intolerant.

Weight Gain

Food sensitivities can result in malnutrition, as the body no longer absorbs the nutrients correctly and expends more of them to keep up the immune response. The body will naturally crave more food to replace the lost and expended nutrients, and with the over-consumption of calories, we see subsequent weight gain.

Irritable Bowel Syndrome

Irritable bowel syndrome (IBS) is a common condition of the digestive system. It can cause bouts of stomach cramps, bloating, diarrhea, and constipation. The exact cause of IBS is unknown, but most experts agree it's related to an increased sensitivity of the entire gut, which can be linked to a prior food-related illness. This may be caused by a change in your body's ability to move food through your digestive system, or may be due to you becoming more sensitive to pain from your gut.

Inflammatory Bowel Disease

Inflammatory bowel disease (IBD) is a term mainly used to describe two diseases: ulcerative colitis and Crohn's disease. Both are long-term (chronic) diseases that involve inflammation of the gastrointestinal tract (gut).

Respiratory Disease

There is medical research to suggest that food we eat can have an impact on airway conditions. Allergic airway disease may be due to food intolerance, molds, and chemicals such as preservatives and food dyes, as well as airborne allergens. Typical problems are asthma, hay fever, and sinusitis. These intolerances represent more load on the body, with the air passages a target for a system weakened by the elements.

Hopefully this has highlighted just how important the digestive system is, and how it can be linked to many common illnesses and symptoms.

Finding the Problem

The good news is that, in most cases, it's perfectly possible to treat food allergies and intolerances. This is can be done much more easily and at less expense than for other chronic medical conditions. This normal, predictable sequence of events can be stopped at any time by removing any foods or chemicals to which the body is intolerant. The results can be instant, and my clients usually see significant improvements in symptoms within the first two to four weeks.

It can be difficult to find trigger foods, but as you become more in tune with your body, you'll begin to notice which foods work best and which slow you down. Listen and experiment with this feedback. If this doesn't work for you, food sensitivity testing can be a great addition, helping reinforce findings and confirming some of the more uncommon food intolerances. It can also help save time, as you can instantly remove the troublesome foods and test again when symptoms are resolved.

Blood tests can be the most accurate form of testing, particularly those that test for changes in white blood cell size and number. These tests mimic (as closely as possible) what actually happens when a food is consumed or chemical exposure occurs, and can detect the effects of a wide range of biological mechanisms.

Standard allergy testing (skin, urine, hair) may not prove as accurate as blood tests, as they only measure a single mechanism. They can, however, serve as a quick, easy, and affordable starting point. Not everyone needs to start cutting out all common allergens and foods that commonly cause intolerance from their diet. Yes, the side effects of food problems are pretty harsh and unwanted, but by following a healthy diet of whole, single-ingredient foods, your gut health will likely take care of itself.

If you are experiencing difficulties, then this chapter might just change your life. I wish I had been given this information when I first experienced negative digestive symptoms as a teenager. It would have changed a lot of things for me. You now have more knowledge, and that knowledge is power.

PART II
YOUR
NUTRITION
PLAN

In Part I of the book, we explored the ten essential cornerstones to High Performance Living. This has laid the foundations for your knowledge so you understand the "whys and hows" of great nutrition. The basics need to be in place because they dictate every step afterwards. Skip them (or don't give them the respect they deserve) and it'll result in a constant struggle. When I work with clients using the online HPL coaching system, these ten cornerstones continually provide the biggest improvements to people's bodies and health.

I learned an important lesson a few years ago:

Learning = study + application

Say what? For all of this new information to be of real use to you, you must APPLY it. So Part II of this book is dedicated to showing you how to apply the previous cornerstones and be successful with them.

I'm also going to show you how to make it personal, so you are finally applying information that is right for YOU. You'll be armed with the right tools for your goals and have all the information you need to kick-start instant results.

You're not going to find any nutrition plans or templates in here (sorry!)—that's just not how I coach people. That's because my goal as a coach is to show people how to be in complete control of their own nutrition. A traditional rigid nutrition plan tells you to eat X food, at X time, in X amount. But what happens when you need to make your own decisions? That's not teaching anyone anything, it's just telling them what to do.

What you will need to do as we move through Part II is calculate and crunch a few numbers based on your own personal information. So get a pen and paper ready.

Let's get learning!

11. HOW DIETS REALLY WORK

"Ru, are you a paleo guy, into intermittent fasting, or a 'insert a popular diet' coach?" Whenever I'm asked this, my response is: "That's all wrong."

I am focused on personalization, the fundamental component to achieving great results from nutrition. This section will show you how to do that too. That's right, it's time to throw away the "cookie-cutter" approaches on how you eat, as there is no "one size fits all" when it comes to nutrition. This book is not just something you try for a while and move onto the next thing. It's your final solution to eating right for the long term.

A question I asked myself many years ago was, "is there really one 'right way' to eat, considering our diverse goals, lifestyles, and dietary history?" Surely not. Yet I think this is why people are still struggling with body composition and poor health markers. They have yet to make nutrition personal—they are not listening to their own bodies.

This section of the book is not a set diet or protocol that will force you to do something to the letter. The High Performance Living System is an educational tool that you can develop to find the right nutritional strategies for you. It will make your nutrition "personal," which we now know is the only "secret" to

achieving great results. Personal nutrition is not just about following the current trend, or a particular diet protocol you have read about. It needs to be built around:

- Past and present dietary history
- Goals (short- and long-term)
- Hobbies/sports
- Lifestyle
- Environment
- Likes/dislikes
- Sustainability

And much more...

Current Philosophy

Here's an interesting test I use when hosting a seminar or guest-speaking at an event. I ask the attendees to identify themselves as an "eating type." The typical answers I get are: paleo, vegan, vegetarian, intermittent faster, omnivore, or even the "eat everything" type.

Eating is tribal, and humans are always seeking to belong somewhere. When we belong to a group, we become defensive of it and feel that it is the best system, often failing to see the bigger picture. And because people want to hold onto their beliefs and belongings, they make common nutritional mistakes.

With regards to nutrition, that bigger picture is personalization. This is the problem I have with many of the current "popular diets"—they do not account for the individual needs of the user. If your goals include long-lasting results, health, and maximum performance, you'd better forget about regular and popular diet regimes and start listening to your body.

What To Do Instead

Another common question I get is, "What makes these popular dieting protocols so ineffective long term?" That's a great question, and once we learn how diets should really work, you'll begin to see the flaws in many of the common diets out there. Below, I'll outline how diets actually work while highlighting the fundamental component we must consider to have success. By understanding this, you will be able to create your own bespoke nutrition plan.

1. Food Quantity (Calorie Surplus/ Calorie Deficit)

Most diets only work on the basis of manipulating overall calorie intake (sometimes on a drastic scale). If you under-eat for a period of time, you will lose weight. If you overeat, then you will gain weight. It all comes down to the "calories in vs. calories out" equation, which we will look at later, as this is generally regarded as the main principle behind weight gain or loss.

In fact, it's impossible to override this fundamental fact, so we always have

to consider it. When we want to gain weight, we must eat more than we need to supply the body with sufficient energy and nutrients in order for it to be able to lay down new muscle tissue. The same can be applied for fat loss. We must eat less than we need to ensure the right signals are being sent to break down body fat and use it for energy.

2. Food Quality (Macronutrient Balance)

A good diet should focus on improving daily food choices, replacing typical high-calorie, low-nutrient foods with low-calorie, high-nutrient foods. This ensures you are eating a high-nutrient diet, which in turn brings visual changes and improved health markers, and increased performance. This usually means you have more energy and will exercise more often. In addition, this also:

- Helps naturally control calorie intake
- Provides longer periods of satiation (fullness) between meals
- Reduces overeating
- Provides higher total essential nutrients in the diet
- Highlights the importance of adequate vitamins and minerals (micronutrients), including water and fiber. Placing emphasis on whole, single-ingredient foods ensures sufficient amounts of fruit and vegetables in the diet, which are the cornerstones to keeping ample amounts of micronutrients in the diet.

3. Food Timing and Frequency

A good diet should also educate you on the importance of nutrient timing (when certain nutrients can be consumed to enhance nutrient partitioning and sensitivity). For example, I'm sure you've heard of the "anabolic window." It's that important time post training when your body becomes more sensitive to nutrients, increasing its ability to better partition them. Your diet should take full advantage of this time period.

A good diet should also have specific meal frequencies. How often you eat can have a significant impact on the two factors we just discussed: how much you eat and from what food types. We can manipulate this variable for further progress and enhanced dietary compliance.

4. Supplementation

What would the world of nutrition do without the supplement industry? It's no surprise that many diets introduce some supplementation in the process of changing someone's nutritional habits and routine. There are a number of supplements that have been field-tested and research proven, but we must always consider the following before taking any supplement:

- Quality and quantity—does the quality of the supplement meet recommended manufacturing standards and compliances? Have the key ingredients been significantly researched to prove results, and at the dosages prescribed in the supplement? If any of these factors are not met, you should avoid the supplement and find a better alternative, if available.
- Is it safe—are all the ingredients in the supplement approved by the World Anti-Doping Association (WADA)? If not, it's not worth the risk, and you should look for an alternative that is WADA-approved.

These are the fundamental components of any dietary plan. When we read success stories and testimonials from people who have followed a set and rigid diet protocol, we must understand that these are a result of manipulation of one or more of these factors. Many popular diets manipulate level one (food quantity), and that's how they alter the user's body composition. Others will incorporate factors two to four. Adhering to all four always brings the best results.

Many of the popular diet protocols use a variety of guidelines, restrictions, or techniques to achieve success. As a result, although they are all doing the same thing (or have a very similar objective) they will feel very different. This can make them difficult to follow, as they haven't been matched to your lifestyle or routine. In time, you find that you can't stick to these diets at all and resort back to your old ways.

But, by now, you understand how a good diet actually works. You've seen the fundamental components that should be involved, and in what priority. And you can tailor this information to your needs and wants. You are no longer following someone else's ideas or diet, but your own. This will bring you the fastest and greatest results, and—best of all—you can sustain your progress forever.

Redefining Nutrition

By now, you should feel a nice sense of freedom, as you've just learnt the exact steps to creating your own effective nutritional strategy for life. You no longer need to follow another "diet" that restricts you with rules and excessive guidelines. You now know the key nutritional factors that are important to change your body.

However, knowing what to do isn't the same as doing it. Being able to actually take action on this new knowledge is essential. When you turn this new knowledge into action, results will never be too far behind. Over the coming chapters I'm going to show you how to make these key steps and considerations personal to you, based on your own goals and lifestyle.

It's time for some work—and some results!

12. BUILDING A NUTRITION PLAN

All of those years I wasted, eating foods I hated and avoiding foods I loved. Just because I wanted to be healthy and lean, and didn't know that there was a better way.

I can't get those years back, but I can ensure that you don't make the same mistakes. Mistakes like living on chicken, rice, and peas while avoiding your favorite snacks like chocolate rice cakes and popcorn.

I know what you're thinking. "Ru, that's what I'm doing!" If you're still in that situation—refraining from the foods you like and feeling mega guilty when you give into your cravings—please keep reading.

Let me guess... it's protein powder with oats for breakfast, salad for lunch, and some meat with veg for dinner? It's working, but only on the days you stick to the "plan," avoid social outings, and prepare your food in advance?

That's no life.

I bet you're surprised to hear me say that, given my High Performance attitude, always wanting to be the best I can. You thought my advice would be, "suck it up and get on with it," didn't you? But you should know me better than that by now, since we've just debunked a ton of

nutritional myths together, and I've shown you how diets really work.

It's time to put your new knowledge into practice to create your own, personal High Performance nutrition plan. This time it's going to be different. There will be no fads, no gimmicks, and no restrictions or limitations. We will get straight to the details that matter. By calculating and applying numbers to your daily nutritional approach, you'll get the most effective tools to help you achieve your goals, while still letting you eat things you enjoy (like the tasty recipes in Part III of this book).

For this nutritional protocol to work, we need to do some groundwork, and you will need to learn how to keep a food diary to track progress. This protocol also requires counting and tracking calories and, more specifically, protein, fat, and carbohydrate intake. Creating a detailed nutrition plan that includes exact macronutrient numbers can be a difficult task if you don't know what you are doing. We have a host of calculators designed to help with this, yet these seem to over-complicate the simple procedure of finding someone's daily macronutrient numbers based on their goals.

Being able to do this yourself is a great skill. This chapter will let you stand on your own two feet by knowing how to calculate your own macronutrient needs. We are going to break down how to create a macronutrient number diet, by focusing on some very simple guidelines.

Firstly, there are no magic ratios, techniques, or programs that will create the "Holy Grail" macronutrient split. So stop looking. The key is getting a good starting point. Get started on a macronutrient number plan, assess the progress, and tweak it to achieve the results required.

Let's get started.

All I See Are Numbers

Most nutrition plans are set out with a daily breakdown of the number of meals, when to eat them, and the suggested food choices—e.g., Monday, breakfast (meal 1), three whole eggs and two rashers of bacon, with two fried tomatoes and a handful of almonds. This is perfect—you know exactly what to eat and how much—all you have to do is follow it. But behind this meal is a set of macronutrient numbers (see table), showing the amount of protein, fat, and carbohydrates in each of the foods, which then provides a total for the entire meal.

As we can see, each food contains a certain amount of each macronutrient, measured in grams. This is the same information shown on the back of the food packets. From this, we can work out the exact numbers of calories in this meal:

Food	Protein (g)	Carbohydrates (g)	Fat (g)
Egg (3 whole)	23	3	16
Bacon (2 rashers)	5	0	4
Tomatoes (2)	2	10	0
Almonds (10)	3	2	6
Total	33	15	26

- **Protein = 4 calories per gram:** 33 g × 4 kcal = 132 kcal
- **Carbs = 4 calories per gram:** 15 g × 4 kcal = 60 kcal
- **Fat = 9 calories per gram:** 26 g × 9 kcal = 234 kcal
- This gives a total overall calorie intake for this meal of 426 kcal.

Each food contains its own amounts of macronutrients, depending on size, quantity, and what it is. More on this topic later. For now, we know that macronutrients are the protein, carbs, and fats that make up our food. When it comes to creating nutrition plans, it is not purely the calories that we should focus on, but also the macronutrient breakdown.

Do You Even Macro?

There are a number of simple calculations you have to complete to work out your best starting daily macronutrient breakdown.

The first thing to consider is overall energy balance—the total number of calories you need in order to meet your primary goal. This is a two-step process and I'll use myself as an example (body weight of 180 lb):

Step 1. Calculate Your Basal Metabolic Rate

Your basal metabolic rate (BMR) is your daily energy expenditure in calories without any contribution from exercise or digestion. Think of BMR as the amount of calories you would need to consume daily to maintain your body's functions if you were comatose.

The quickest method for determining your BMR is to multiply your total body weight by a simple multiplier. Common values used are 10, 11, or 12 (I like to use a conservative 10). This is my favorite method, and it brings very similar results to the more advanced versions:

Body weight (in pounds) × 10 (multiplier) = 180 lbs × 10 = 1,800 kcal

The Mifflin–St. Jeor BMR formula is considered more accurate than the one above, and is generally the most reliable of the BMR formulas when body fat percentage is unknown.

The formulas used are:

- Male: (10 × weight in kg) + (6.25 × height in cm) − (5 × age) + 5
- e.g., (10 × 81.6) + (6.25 × 175) − (5 × 26) + 5 = 1,785 kcal

- Female: (10 × weight in kg) + (6.25 × height in cm) − (5 × age) − 161
- e.g., (10 × 81.6) + (6.25 × 175) − (5 × 26) − 161 = 1,619 kcal

As you can see, there isn't a huge difference between results from the two approaches, hence why I recommend using the quick multiplier to save the calculations for the number geeks. If you want the most accurate starting point, then use the Mifflin–St. Jeor formula.

Step 2. Calculate Your Total Daily Energy Expenditure

Your total daily energy expenditure (TDEE) is the total calories you require on a daily basis, including:

- Basal metabolic rate (BMR)—calculated above
- Non-exercise-associated thermogenesis (NEAT)—calorie requirements from normal daily activity (NOT from exercise) like walking, working, chores, etc.
- Exercise-associated thermogenesis (EAT)—calorie requirements from planned exercise and sports

- Thermic effect of food (TEF)—calories associated with eating and digestion. TEF varies according to macronutrient and fiber content of your diet, with protein having a TEF of up to 30% of the consumed calories, while carbs are around 6%, and fat a mere 3%.

Luckily, we can account for all of this in one very easy calculation. To account for TDEE, we simply multiply our BMR by an activity level:

- Sedentary: little or no exercise = BMR × 1.2
- Lightly active: light exercise/sports 1–3 days/week = BMR × 1.375
- Moderately active: moderate exercise/ sports 3–5 days/week = BMR × 1.55
- Very active: hard exercise/sports 6–7 days a week = BMR × 1.725
- Extra active: very hard exercise/sports and physical job = BMR × 1.9.

For my own example, I train three days per week, so I am moderately active:

TDEE = BMR × activity level
     = 1,800 kcal × 1.55 = 2,790 kcal

Therefore it requires 2,790 kcal for my body to maintain this body weight based on my total daily energy expenditure.

The problem is that you likely do not want to remain the same. Most people want to lose body fat or gain some muscle, while staying healthy in the process.

To lose one pound of fat:
We know that one pound of fat contains around 3,500 kcal, therefore if I reduce my diet by 500 kcal per day (3,500 kcal/week ÷ 7 days = 500 kcal/day), I will theoretically create a calorie deficit (essential for fat loss) with around one pound fat loss per week (the ideal).

An important point that must be understood is that the smallest possible calorie deficit should be used in order to retain as much lean body mass (LBM) as possible. We know that the rate of weight loss is directly related to the size of the calorie deficit used. Research also shows that the lower the caloric intake, the increased chances of losing LBM.

For example, weight loss = 2,790 kcal – 500 kcal = 2,290 kcal per day

To add muscle, we need the opposite—a calorie surplus—in order to grow new muscle tissue and cells. Depending on weight training experience, a 100–300 kcal per day excess is ideal for aiming at a weight gain of 1–2 lb per month (halve this for females).

For example, lean weight gain = 2,790 + 200 kcal = 2,990 kcal per day

Remember these calculations are merely good starting points to get going with a personalized macronutrient plan. You will likely need to adjust them based on results. Of course, your caloric intake will need to be adjusted with time too, owing to changes in body weight and any metabolic adaptations that occur. Gain weight faster than this, and you'll quickly realize within a month or two that you've gained more body fat than LBM. It's not worth it.

Let's Do the Splits

Up to this point, we have only worked out how many calories are needed by the body to maintain your current body weight, and then adjusted this to match your goal of weight gain or weight loss. The next step we should look at is how the macronutrients can be broken down into their respective protein, carb, and fat profiles. Again, to do this, I like to suggest slightly different setups for fat loss and lean weight gain.

Fat Loss

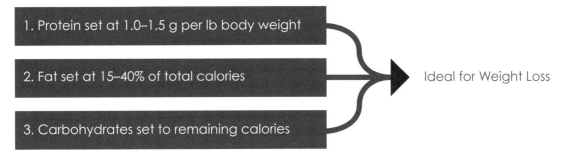

1. Protein set at 1.0–1.5 g per lb body weight
2. Fat set at 15–40% of total calories
3. Carbohydrates set to remaining calories

Ideal for Weight Loss

Lean Weight Gain

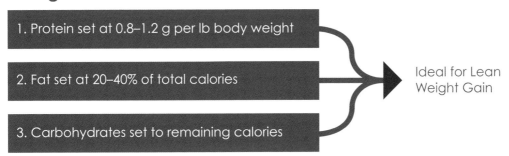

1. Protein set at 0.8–1.2 g per lb body weight
2. Fat set at 20–40% of total calories
3. Carbohydrates set to remaining calories

Ideal for Lean Weight Gain

As you can see, there are no precise figures on how to exactly break down each macronutrient for each goal. This calculation is highly individual.

So if you're not sure what exact figures to pick, you'll need to go back to the previous chapters where I outline my thoughts for each of the macronutrients. And if you end up getting really stuck, try starting with an equal split, so 33% for each of the macros. This works surprisingly well.

The above macronutrient ranges are those I typically use for the majority of clients, and these ranges will get results for 95% of people. Only if I were to complete a full consultation with you, like I do for my online HPL coaching members, could I dial this in any further for you. Again, the goal is to start somewhere and be open to making adjustments as required. There's no reason not to try several different ratios to find the one that works best. No ratio is intrinsically better than any other; the most important criteria are how you feel and perform.

From my own example, I know I carry ample amounts of muscle mass (I do, promise!), so protein can be high. I also train using high-intensity techniques, so carbohydrates are important in my daily diet, and therefore fats can be lower as a result.

- For example, goal for fat loss is 2,290 kcal (worked out from earlier example)
- Protein (1.2 g per lb body weight): 1.2 g × 180 lb = 216 g (= 864 kcal)
- Fat set at 20% of total calories: 20% × 2,290 = 458 kcal = 50 g
- Carbohydrates set at remaining: 2,290 kcal − (864 kcal (protein) + 458 kcal (fat)) = 968 kcal = 242 g

So the ideal starting point for me to lose weight is a diet adding up to 2,290 kcal a day, with a macronutrient split of 216 g protein, 50 g fats, and 242 g carbs.

If I were to eat four meals per day, I can simply divide each macro number by four to find how much of which nutrient I should be eating at each meal; e.g., 54 g protein, 12.5 g fat, 60 g carbs × four meals per day. (Note—this is neglecting any sort of nutrient timing or personal preferences.)

The Flexible Approach

As per the examples above, macronutrient number plans can be used for anyone with any goal. This numbers-based approach is an advanced template, and I get the best results by using it. But that's why you are here, reading this book—you want to be the best—so get calculating.

You do not need a macronutrient nutrition plan if you are not already following a "good" diet to start with. You just need a simple plan based on good foods and consistency. Just follow the ten nutrition cornerstones to help you do this. When you are ready and want more progress, get stuck into calculating your numbers.

If you are already eating what seems to be a great diet but are not seeing the progress you expect, macronutrient numbers can be a great addition to get things moving. Set overall calories to match your goals, and adjust each macronutrient to help you feel and perform better. It shows you how much of the good stuff you should be eating. Or more commonly, that you really require something less!

When you combine good food choices with ideal calorie intake, along with a balanced macronutrient breakdown, HPL will not be far behind. It's a solid nutrition system that is now used by most. It also gives you greater nutritional freedom, and this partly explains its recent popularity in the fitness industry. As long as you match good food choices (that you enjoy eating) to your daily macronutrient numbers, progress will happen. This flexible dieting plan even allows some people to add "treat" foods into their diets while still getting results. So as well as being an accurate and advanced method for dietary success, it gives great nutritional freedom and choice.

Take our original example for the breakfast: Monday, breakfast (meal 1), three whole eggs, two rashers of bacon, two fried tomatoes, and a handful of almonds. Instead of having to eat this exact meal every day in order to achieve results (as in a traditional nutrition plan), we can replace this meal with another one that meets the same macronutrient numbers—Monday, breakfast (meal 1), 33 g protein, 26 g fat, 15 g carbs.

After working out your calorie and macronutrient targets for your goals and lifestyle, it is a matter of matching the foods and meals that you enjoy to your numbers. It's not an excuse to fill your daily nutritional requirements with junk food, but simply lets you keep some balance in your diet while achieving your goals in the process. Keeping balance is something I have lacked in the past, particularly when dieting for fat loss, and this approach has eliminated that problem. It feels great, let me tell you.

If you have a good relationship with food, and are healthy and active, this nutritional approach will probably work very well for you. It can take some time to get used to, and I have found there is a significant learning curve at the start. To be the most accurate with it, you need to weigh your foods in order to know the exact amounts (people tend to overestimate their intake). Over time, you will be able to eyeball your food and know roughly what weight it is and what macronutrients it contains. I certainly don't advocate weighing your foods forever, it really doesn't need to be that accurate. In fact, being within ten percent of your numbers is considered accurate, so please see this as a tool to aid you and not something to become obsessed with.

Measuring Progress

Once you are nailing your ideal starting daily caloric intake and macronutrient breakdown, you'll likely need to adjust it for ongoing progress. It typically takes between two and four weeks to determine whether a nutrition or exercise routine is working. Consistency during this time is critical.

If changes need to be made, the first point of call is to adjust your daily calories. I'm a fan of only adjusting these by small amounts at a time—reaping the most from the least. If you require further or faster fat loss, I'd typically recommend reducing overall calories by no more than 200 kcals at a time, and assessing this every seven to fourteen days. For fat loss, you want see no more than one to two pounds weight loss every week.

The same goes for gaining weight or muscle mass. I'd typically recommend increasing overall calories by 100 kcals at time, and assessing every seven to fourteen days before further changes. For muscle gain, the ideal weight increase is one to two pounds per month. Your protein intake will likely stay the same throughout these adjustments, so make adjustments to your daily fat or carbohydrate intake.

When I talk about making adjustments to your macronutrient numbers, I'm talking about your daily totals. It's these that will deliver the results. Of course you can look into the exact breakdown of these for each meal too. You might find you do better with more carbohydrates in the morning, or perhaps less fat in certain meals. This is all about listening to your body and developing a nutrition setup that suits you.

This nutritional approach has made traditional and rigid nutrition plans outdated, and that's why I have included my awesome recipes at the back of this book. Get into the kitchen and cook up some of those great-tasting nutritious meals and match them to your daily numbers. It really is as simple as that. All the recipes have their respective macronutrient breakdown per serving. My team have even added every single HPL recipe to MyFitnessPal so you can quickly add them to your log. It doesn't get any easier than this! I want you to succeed.

What's MyFitnessPal? Right, Let's Talk Food Logs

If you've been thinking that this information is way too much hassle to keep track of, let me introduce you to a mobile app that will make the whole thing a breeze.

To get the necessary level of accuracy and individualization with your nutrition plan, you're going to need a food log. I use MyFitnessPal (www.myfitnesspal.com) to track my own daily food intake and to help my clients. It's a free food diary that lets you log every single food item, giving you the breakdown of calories and macronutrients.

Before starting your new plan, create a free account with MyFitnessPal and track your daily food intake for at least three days. Take the average of the three days to see how close you are to your calculated numbers (from the previous section). If you aren't far off these starting numbers, within 100–300 kcals, then you could easily transition over to your new plan. However, if you find that you are under-eating or overeating by more than 300 kcals per day, a slow and steady approach to transition to your new numbers will be a good idea. I would suggest following the previous suggestions for making changes to your diet at this point.

It's important to have an idea of what your energy intake looks like, but many people find the actual act of tracking food intake hugely beneficial. It's a behavior that takes just minutes a day, but every time you pull out your app or diary, you are reinforcing your healthy living desires and strategies. New habits are formed through regular and conscious efforts, and any behavior that helps keep your goals and intentions at the forefront of your busy mind is a good one.

Food diaries aren't there to tell you what you are or aren't allowed. A food diary is simply a source of information to help inform your decisions, as well as an incredibly powerful habit-building tool.

High Performance Living isn't about sacrifice and restriction, it's about finding the most effective nutritional tools to bring you to your goals in the quickest time possible, while creating a long-term system that is maintainable. For the majority of my clients, this nutritional approach has been the best way to achieving HPL. I've got a feeling you're going to love it. For my online HPL coaching clients, I do this exact process for them, to ensure they have the most accurate and personalized information they can get.

Summary

Let's wrap up what we have just looked at, and what you should now do before moving on. It's important to remember that all of the recommendations in this chapter are just that—starting points to creating your own personalized eating system. They're not set in stone and are not the final destination.

- Step 1—Calculate your BMR and multiply this by your chosen activity level. Adjust this number based on your goals.
- Step 2—Break this number down into your starting macronutrient split: how much protein, fat, and carbohydrates you need daily to match your set caloric intake.

- Step 3—Start food logging for at least three days, then assess how far away you are from your new calculated starting point. Test-drive your new nutrition plan and keep logging your numbers daily to assess compliance and accuracy.
- Step 4—If you get the results you want, then great, it's working for you. If not, make some of the prementioned adjustments to see results. This can be the most difficult part for some people, and that's why my HPL coaching system is so effective at getting results for members. This is when I am able to make the necessary tweaks and changes for ongoing progress, based on my years of experience and the best available research.

13. NUTRIENT TIMING AND FREQUENCY

The debate over "optimal" meal frequency rages on, and general advice ranges from one large evening feast to the tradition of six or more meals per day.

Which Approach is Correct?

Well, it depends. Nutrition must be matched to your physiology and current goals. And, of course, for long-term success it must also fit your lifestyle to be manageable on a day-to-day basis.

We can find "success" stories for almost every nutrition protocol/strategy, whether eating two meals per day or eight. This indicates that overall daily food intake is the key factor in someone's results, not how many meals they have had. The results usually come down to the fact that the person has found a nutrition system to suit them, one they can stick to consistently, that helps them adopt a set of healthy lifestyle habits.

What this shows us is that some of the time-honored myths can now be firmly put to bed. So let's do that.

Greater Meal Frequency Increases Metabolism

When we consume food we get what is known as the "thermic effect of food" (TEF).

This is the amount of energy expended by the body during digestion. When we eat food we get a slight rise in our metabolism; however, eating more meals per day does not provide any significant increase to metabolism. Eating a greater number of meals per day doesn't raise the metabolism enough to impact fat loss. It is actually the total amount of daily food consumed that equates to our daily energy expenditure on digestion.

Look at the numbers. If you consume three meals per day at 1,000 kcals each, you get exactly the same daily energy turnover as if you ate six meals per day at 500 kcals each.

You Must Eat Breakfast Upon Waking

It's often suggested that eating immediately upon waking helps improve fat loss. This is not the case, as it does not kick-start the metabolism for the day. In fact, it has been shown that going periods without food (usually skipping breakfast) can actually increase metabolism. We can get additional health benefits from short fasts, such as improved insulin sensitivity, nutrient partitioning, greater fat loss, and induced autophagy (the cellular cleanup process).

When To Eat More Frequently

When Building More Muscle Mass and Strength

To gain muscle we need to provide the building blocks—based on a high quality and quantity of food. This is when it would be best to eat more frequently—to ensure maximum muscle protein synthesis (MPS). Studies show approximately 3 g of leucine per meal is required for maximum MPS; hence, quantity and quality of protein per meal is the most important factor. There is a reason why physique athletes and bodybuilders eat a lot of lean meat, as it makes for a complete amino acid profile (with >3 g leucine) and typically offers the ideal 30–40 g protein per serving.

MPS has been shown to peak two hours following elevated amino acid levels (to allow for digestion); therefore, placing meal timings too close together is unnecessary, as you will see diminishing returns. An optimal eating strategy is around three to six meals per day, spaced every three to four hours, with a high-quality protein source of at least 20 g per serving per meal. So a typical eating schedule could be 8 am, 12 pm, 4 pm, 8 pm.

When Suffering from Metabolic Damage or Food Issues

If you are suffering from weight gain after "yo-yo" dieting, or have been using a low-calorie diet approach for some time, it would be best to return to a more regular eating pattern with increased food quantities. The aim is to restore homeostasis within the body and to balance hormones.

This is also true for those with previous or current physiological or psychological issues with food, such as cravings or binge-eating cycles. A regular eating schedule will ensure blood sugar levels are constantly steady and you never reach a point of hypoglycemia.

A typical approach of four meals per day, spaced every three to four hours, would be ideal, with healthy snacks between meals if required.

When To Eat Less Frequently

When Focusing on Fat Loss

If you have a good relationship with food and follow a healthy lifestyle and food choices, skipping meals could help you in your quest for lower body fat. It provides the opportunity to feast on larger meals to provide that feeling of fullness despite a lower overall daily intake of calories. A typical approach of three meals per day could be applied (such as 8 am, 12 pm, 5 pm), or you could utilize intermittent fasting (and eat at 12 pm, 4 pm, 8 pm).

Remember that the goal of your diet in this case is to lose body fat and retain as much lean body mass (LBM) as possible. Just as with building muscle, the key concern for the dieter is to remain in an anabolic state by maximizing MPS.

When Your Lifestyle Says So

Some people have extremely active and busy lifestyles, and eating every few hours may not be an option. Such people often don't particularly want to, either. Lifestyle doesn't have to hold you back from your goals. The body is well adapted to under-eating at periods of intense activity/workload and feasting afterwards. If you want only two meals per day, and enjoy this way of eating, then there is no problem with doing so, providing your overall nutrient requirements are met.

Match your nutrition to your lifestyle, and not the other way around. Good healthy food should enhance our lives, not hold us back.

The most simple method to decide how many meals you should eat is:

1. Eat when you are hungry
2. Stop when you are satisfied
3. Repeat.

Nutrient Timing

So far, you've worked out an ideal starting point for your daily calories and macronutrients based on your primary goal. You should now also decide how many meals you'll need in order to get this nutrition in, and form a nutrition plan that suits your lifestyle.

The next consideration is nutrient timing: how may calories you'll eat at each meal and what macronutrients they will contain. Over the years we've seen a large number of articles and books created around maximizing the benefits of nutrient timing. One of the most popular approaches to date has been "carb-cycling."

A cyclic ketogenic diet, or "carb-cycling," is a low-carbohydrate diet with planned periods of moderate or high carbohydrate consumption. Tradition tells us that we can only build muscle or lose fat, never both at the same time. This is because we must maintain a calorie deficit to lose fat and a calorie surplus to build muscle. Then carb-

cycling came along and was sold to us as an ultimate method for rapid fat loss while building muscle. Carb-cycling therefore goes against the typical advice of fitness professionals and has gained a lot of attention.

There is a lot of anecdotal evidence to show that this type of nutrient-timing protocol can get people lean very quickly, but we must look at the research to understand how this occurs and if it is any better than other approaches. It appears that the micromanaged details of carb-cycling protocols will not bring significantly better benefits than traditional calorie-controlled diets. My own experience backs this up. I have been able to get myself and clients equally lean without the need to use advanced carb-cycling protocols. On paper it makes sense, but there is little research to support it and I feel it makes the whole process more complicated than it needs to be. Remember, the best diet is one that you can stick to.

The research that exists to support nutrient timing for active people is typically for endurance athletes, and I'm going to assume that readers of this book are not regularly doing two or more hours of endurance training. Nutrient timing doesn't seem to be as important for gym goers and weight trainers, with studies showing that adequate recovery from training and glycogen replenishment can occur from simply meeting recommended intake of carbohydrates. Studies suggest that total macronutrient intake each day is more important than specific timings.

With this being said, there are two main nutrient-timing considerations that I want you to bear in mind:

Re-feed Days

If your main goal is to lose body fat, you know this will require a reduced-calorie diet for optimal fat burning. With time, a low-carb or low-calorie diet can lead to a reduction in metabolic rate, thyroid hormone output, sympathetic nervous system activity, reproductive hormones (testosterone and estrogen), and much more. This is when the inclusion of a planned and structured "re-feed" (classically known as a "cheat meal") can be of benefit.

A re-feed meal or day should be put in place if you are consistently under-eating on a daily basis. It will provide the body a break from reduced-calorie intake and reduce any fat-loss plateaus. It can also provide you with a short mental break and offer increased variety to the diet. Here are some pointers when setting up a re-feed during fat loss:

- A re-feed meal should be a day on which you eat above maintenance level in calories. I recommend keeping your calorie intake on these days to roughly one and a half to two times what you're eating on your fat-loss plan. For example, if you're eating 2,000 kcals per day for fat loss, don't go above 4,000 kcals for a re-feed.
- The re-feed should be kept to one twenty-four-hour period and then normal dieting continues. A re-feed can occur as often as every three days or only every fourteen days. My guidelines for this are:
  o 20%+ body-fat levels—no re-feeds required
  o 10–20% body-fat levels—once every seven to fourteen days
  o <10% body-fat levels—every three to seven days.
- This isn't an excuse to eat extra calories from junk food—it should be a continuation of your normal diet, but just more of that type of food.
- It can be a good idea to weight train on this day too, as all that extra energy can help go towards muscle building and recovery.

The Workout Window

Want to reap the most from your nutrition to aid performance and recovery, while maximizing muscle protein synthesis? Some studies show that some nutrient-timing recommendations around the workout window can be of benefit.

The workout window (before, during, and after exercise) is considered an important time for someone seeking maximum performance and recovery. Throughout this time, we have the ability to fully maximize protein synthesis. For the performance-minded individual, this should be an important component to seeing better results.

Protein synthesis is the body's ability to create new proteins for muscle repair and growth. In order to do this effectively, we must activate "mammalian target of rapamycin" or "mTOR" (a protein), the component that controls protein synthesis while also signaling growth within the body.

So, protein synthesis = mTOR activation

To successfully activate mTOR, we must adhere to the scheme shown in the diagram.

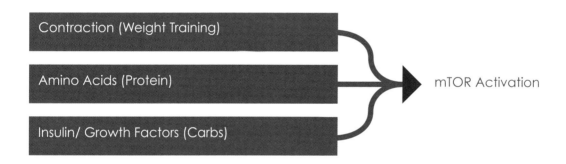

As we can see, in order to maximally activate mTOR, we need a combination of weight training and nutrition at the same time. We need to find the correct workout nutrition.

Contraction

Intense weight training takes care of the "contraction" part of the equation, along with providing growth factors such as growth hormone and insulin like growth factor (IGF). By including weight training, we increase insulin sensitivity but not fat sensitivity, and the body can make better use of the nutrients we give it around

the workout window. This occurs by the relocation of our GLUT (pronounced "gloot") glucose transporters.

GLUT comprises a family of proteins that acts as a solvent and carries things around the body. GLUTs can carry a number of nutrients, but their main role is to transport glucose. They are located in the jelly-like outer coatings of cells and are normally exposed on the cell surface. The anomalies are GLUTs 4 and 12, which are normally located below the surface of the cell membrane, preventing them from transporting glucose. These GLUTs also appear to be the main pathways through which high volumes of glucose enter the cell (both muscular and fat).

The more insulin sensitivity someone can develop, the more they can recruit GLUTs 4 and 12 and bring them to the surface of the cell to transport glucose. Resistance training does just this, but only for muscle cells, not fat cells. Therefore, by weight training, we can improve insulin sensitivity of the muscle cell to glucose. That's good news for you! It is also suggested that resistance training not only causes GLUT to relocate without insulin, but also increases the amount and concentration of GLUTs 4 and 12 in muscle cells.

So, resistance training encourages muscle cells to absorb glucose at a faster rate, either for storage or energy production. What remains is the amino acids (protein) and insulin (carbohydrates). To ensure we cover these bases, we can use a number of foods/supplements. These ensure we provide the body with exactly the right nutrients at the required times.

Amino Acids (Protein)

Protein intake prior to exercise can help maintain energy levels, increase levels of satiation, and provide ample levels of amino acids. Research suggests that, for the most benefit, the intake of protein should be alongside carbohydrates, just before or during resistance training. Research has also shown that the body will excrete certain amino acids from muscle and oxidize and metabolize them during training. Branched-chain amino acids have the greatest benefits for athletes at this time.

The consumption of branched-chain amino acids (BCAAs—leucine, valine, and isoleucine) may therefore promote improved athletic performance. It's not fully known why, with some studies suggesting BCAAs can be used for energy, insulin stimulation for heightened glycogen synthesis, and/or suppression of central fatigue. Protein at this time should be easily digested, and supplementation with BCAAs is a popular choice.

During the workout session, you could use BCAAs (10–20 g) or fast-acting casein hydrolysates (10–20 g). These types of protein powders provide us with sufficient and high-quality amino acids in order to activate mTOR throughout training. These amino acids are delivered to working muscles instantly to fuel performance and induce anabolism.

Protein will aid the recovery process from your training, too. Research suggests that consuming carbohydrates with protein after exercise gives greater glycogen replenishment than consuming carbohydrates or protein alone. A further benefit is that the increased levels of amino acids will aid recovery and muscle repair.

Protein should be consumed with fast-acting carbohydrates, thirty to sixty minutes post exercise. Choose easily digested "fast" proteins—e.g., whey protein powder. Approximately 30–40 g of protein post exercise is ideal (halve this for females). It should then be sufficient to eat high-protein whole foods in subsequent meals to continue the recovery process and meet daily requirements.

Insulin (Carbohydrates)

Insulin is a growth and storage hormone. So when you are trying to create maximum protein synthesis, it is important to have a spike in insulin (and even keep it elevated) by using fast-acting carbohydrate sources.

This helps shuttle the important amino acids to the muscle cells to improve nutrient uptake and further increase performance and recovery.

Research shows that carbohydrate intake in the hours and minutes leading up to resistance training can have positive results on increased performance. This works by increasing blood sugar levels, sparing muscle and liver glycogen stores more effectively. This is an important factor that people often miss, particularly those who exercise early in the morning. Studies have shown that carbohydrate can be eaten anywhere between one and four hours prior to training: the greater the amount consumed, the more time should be left. You can choose whole-food starchy carbohydrates before training to ensure ample amounts of insulin are being released.

As previously mentioned, carbohydrate intake throughout training may prove beneficial in order to maintain blood energy production and mTOR activation. Many trainers do well with 1 g carbohydrates per minute of activity, while some use 2 g per minute.

My favorite carbohydrates for achieving this during workouts are Vitargo and highly branched cyclic dextrins (HBCD). These are the perfect workout nutrition carbs for me, as they are high molecular yet low osmolality, providing a quick release from the stomach into the small intestine, to provide a rapid yet sustained form of glucose into the bloodstream.

Carbohydrates are critical to optimize recovery from resistance training and to replenish muscle glycogen stores. Trainers should aim to consume 30–40 g of carbohydrates (halve this for females) within thirty to sixty minutes following exercise. These could be consumed using carbohydrate powders. Consumption of high-carbohydrate whole foods in subsequent meals should be sufficient to continue the recovery process and to meet daily requirements.

To summarize: research suggests that a 1:1 ratio of carbohydrates to protein (approximately 30–40 g) from fast-acting sources, taken before and after training, can improve muscular size and strength.

Supercharging Your Workout Drink

All of the above information has focused on ensuring we are optimally activating mTOR, providing us with maximum protein synthesis with increased recovery and performance. Essentially, we are delivering key nutrients to the working cells in order to create new ones, trying to maximize performance and recovery using training and nutrition at the same time.

There are a number of other ingredients to consider during the workout window that will help promote delivery of key nutrients to boost your performance.

Leucine

Leucine is a BCAA, and research has shown that mTOR is activated the most from this amino acid. When taken in the right dosages (minimum 3 g), it acts as a trigger switch for amino acid transport and uptake via the mTOR pathway. Leucine also potentiates insulin release (even more so in the presence of carbs), which is another important factor when aiming for maximum protein synthesis.

Citrulline Malate

Citrulline Malate is a unique combination of the amino acid citrulline and the organic salt malate. It offers a potential method of improving performance, delaying fatigue, and accelerating recovery. It is particularly useful for people involved in high-intensity exercise such as weight lifting and sprinting. Citrulline aids in the removal of toxins such as lactic acid and ammonia, which are by-products of intense physical activity, protein metabolism, and catabolic states.

Glutamine

There are a number of benefits that glutamine is marketed under, but what we should really be using it for is to further enhance cell volume and protein synthesis around the workout window. Glutamine supplementation pulls water into cells and activates leucine uptake, both of which are needed to maximally turn on protein synthesis.

A cell has to load up on glutamine before leucine is imported. When the body produces its own, there is a significant lag time involved. You can probably guess that we do not want any delay of nutrients during the workout window.

The Protocol Summary

We want to achieve maximum protein synthesis during the workout window. We do this by activating mTOR by intense weight training, amino acids, and insulin. As a result, we can achieve optimal recovery and performance. To do this, we need:

1. Intense weight training
2. Amino acids via fast-acting whey isolates, BCAAs, or high-protein foods
3. Elevated insulin levels via fast-acting carb powders or high-carb foods
4. Enhanced performance and recovery via free-form amino acids:
- L-leucine, 5 g
- L-glutamine, 5 g
- Citrulline malate, 5–10 g

Suggested Dosages and Timings

Here's my typical "go-to" workout nutrition setup. It summarizes all of the previous information and gives you something you can instantly start using. Just like with the macronutrient calculations and splits, this is a starting point. Remember, this book isn't a set system, it's information you should personalize. Try the below protocol and play around with timings and quantities of the various nutrients to get them perfect for you.

- Pre-training (3–5 hours): balanced macronutrient meal from whole foods
- Pre-training (0–1 hours): 30–40 g protein with 30–40 g carbohydrates from fast-acting sources—e.g., whey protein isolate powder and a large ripe banana. Halve this for females.

- During training (optional): 10–20 g BCAA powder with 10–20 g fast-acting carbohydrate powder (Vitargo or HBCD powder).

- Post-training (0–1 hours): 30–40 g protein with 30–40 g carbohydrates from fast-acting sources—e.g., whey protein isolate powder and a large ripe banana. Halve this for females
- Post-training (2–3 hours): balanced macronutrient meal from whole foods.

This protocol doesn't need to change much to match your own goals. During fat-loss phases, you may have less carbohydrate to play with, so a 1:1 ratio of carbohydrate to protein may be ideal. During times of increased calories for muscle/strength gain, you could increase the amount of carbs at certain points, or go for a 2:1 ratio of carbs to protein. It's important to use this as a starting point to finding out what works best for your own goals, performance, and recovery.

14.
SUPPLEMENTATION

When I think back over how much money I have spent on supplements, it's quite frightening. It's difficult not to get drawn in to the hype that companies create around their products.

As humans, we naturally want to take the easy path to success. I used to fall for it, and it's safe to say I've tried most of them! I'm about to save you a lot of cash, and show you the supplements that really could help you. This isn't just based on my experiences, as there's plenty of research on supplements that helps us be confident in what we are taking.

It can be difficult to know what exactly we should be taking and if it will even work. If a supplement claims to do something that sounds too good to be true, then this is usually the case. So when are you better off saving your hard-earned cash?

There are a small number of supplements that have been scientifically researched and field-tested—and work. And guess what, the ones that work do not have fancy names or shiny packaging and are usually consumed already via our diets. The supplements recommended below are vitamins, minerals, or oils that are totally safe and can actually be sourced from foods.

So Why Should We Supplement When Following a Healthy Eating Plan?

Research shows that we should increase levels of certain vitamins and minerals to get the most benefit from them. Usually these levels are much higher than we can get from food sources alone, even when eating high-quality foods. We should also consider the overall quality of our foods: pollution is higher, crops are sprayed more, and items are often heavily processed. Food is lacking some key nutrients. You're also probably training hard, and this can deplete the body, adding further stress while demanding extra energy and nutrients for recovery.

So boosting some natural vitamins and minerals via supplementation is important for optimal performance and health. If your nutrition is dialed in and you are eating correctly with high-quality foods, research suggests supplements can be of benefit. Let's take a look at which ones can be of use to you:

Vitamin D

Vitamin D increases health and strength, and aids muscle building and fat loss. Many of us in the northern hemisphere are deficient in this vitamin owing to lack of sunlight. Vitamin D has been shown to improve mood, aid immune function, fight off cancers, burn body fat, and improve bone health. It also helps boost muscle strength and growth, mainly because of its potential to increase testosterone levels.

How to Take
You should be supplementing with vitamin D3 (cholecalciferol) form rather than D2 (ergocalciferol) owing to better utilization in the body. Take it with meals.

The majority of people will see benefits and prevent deficiency with a dose of 1,000–2,000 IU vitamin D3 daily. The dosage can be higher, but it's suggested to say within 20–80 IU/kg daily. I recommend that higher dosages be consumed in times of reduced sunlight, such as winter.

Omega-3 Fish Oil

This increases health and strength, and aids fat loss and muscle building. Fish oil contains the essential omega-3 fatty acids EPA and DHA, which provide a number of health and performance benefits owing to high anti-inflammatory properties. From a health perspective, these fatty acids appear to reduce the risk of heart disease and stroke, while from a performance aspect they can help prevent muscle breakdown, enhance joint healing, improve brain function, and achieve greater fat loss.

How to Take
We do get omega-3s from our diet, but combining this with supplementation may bring enhanced benefits. The important factor to consider here is not the total omega-3 consumed, but the total EPA and DHA it offers. This is where the real magic happens. Effective dosages of combined EPA and DHA are from 250 to 1,000 mg per day. For more dramatic and enhanced effects, dosages can be used up to 6 g, split over the course of a day. Liquid fish oil is usually more effective at providing these dosages than capsules.

Green Tea

Green tea promotes fat loss and energy production, and increases health. Green tea contains compounds called catechins, including EGCG, the primary active ingredient for its thermogenic properties. EGCG has the ability to inhibit an enzyme that breaks down norepinephrine, the neurotransmitter involved in regulating metabolic rate and fat burning. Green tea also contains caffeine, which boosts energy levels and provides further fat-burning actions.

How to Take
Research shows that for maximum fat-burning and metabolic capacity, a high dosage of 400–500 mg EGCG will be required daily. A green tea extract is therefore recommended, as one cup of green tea will only provide approximately 50 mg of EGCG equivalence. I suggest taking this alongside food, as some people can feel nausea after taking it on an empty stomach.

ZMA

This is a combination of zinc, magnesium, and vitamin B6. It increases health and strength, and aids muscle building and fat loss. Research has shown that hard-training individuals (people who sweat a lot) may be deficient in these important minerals. You will see improved hormone levels, aiding better recovery, sleep, and strength.

How to Take
- Zinc: for the hard-training individual, a high dosage of 25–45 mg daily is the ideal. If no training is taking place, 5–10 mg is likely sufficient.
- Magnesium: for magnesium, the type is of importance. Citrate or other bioavailable forms such a glycinate or gluconate are your best options to provide the best absorption rates. With these, a daily dosage of 200–450 mg magnesium is the ideal.
- Vitamin B6: around 10 mg per day is the ideal.

Vitamin K

Vitamin K increases health and strength and builds mass. Research is uncovering many roles for this vitamin in the body. There are two main types of vitamin K—K1 (phylloquinone) and K2 (menaquinone). What is currently known is that vitamin K plays a critical role in enabling certain enzymes in the body to function. Some of these enzymes help form blood-clotting factors and some are important for fixing calcium in bones. These roles appear to be performed by K1. A certain type of K2, known as MK4, has recently been shown to increase testosterone production.

How to Take
Look for vitamin K supplements that provide both K1 and K2. While most supplements use a form of K2 known as MK7, your best bet is to use a form that includes MK4 to maximize testosterone production. Take 100–1,000 micrograms of vitamin K1 and vitamin K2.

Whey Protein

Whey protein builds mass, increases strength and health, and aids energy production and fat loss. Whey is an effective protein for increasing muscle protein synthesis, the process in muscle cells that results in muscle growth. There are numerous reasons why whey is so effective, such as its high content of branched-chain amino acids (BCAAs) and its ability to boost blood flow to muscles. However, the most important characteristic of whey is its rapid rate of digestion. Whey protein is one of the fastest-digesting protein sources that you can get. It also makes achieving a high-protein diet super easy.

How to Take
Typical recommendations are 20–40 g first thing in the morning, thirty to sixty minutes before workouts, within thirty to sixty minutes after workouts, and between meals as needed.

Creatine

Creatine builds mass, increases strength, and helps with energy production. With regards to athletic performance, creatine has continually proved itself to be one of the most effective and safe nutritional supplements to increase strength, muscle mass, and performance.

To date, there have been hundreds of studies conducted on creatine, and they have included such areas as the ways to maximize creatine storage in muscle, which types of exercise may obtain the greatest benefit from supplementation, the potential medical uses of creatine, and the long-term safety and efficiency of creatine supplementation. Approximately seventy percent of these studies have shown positive results from creatine supplementation in the chosen areas. Safety reviews show that creatine is safe and well tolerated by most individuals.

Enhanced benefits:

- Increased muscle mass and strength
- Increased single and repetitive athletic performance
- Enhanced glycogen synthesis
- Increased work capacity
- Enhanced recovery

We typically store around 120 g of creatine, yet are capable of storing up to 150–160 g. If you want to enhance the effects, top up the total creatine pool and keep it full.

How to Take
Most of the studies on creatine supplementation were conducted using pharmaceutical creatine monohydrate in powder form, so this is what I'd suggest to use. The recommended dosage is 3–5 g per day, and you shouldn't need to cycle it using this amount. You should consume this alongside a meal, or at least some carbohydrates, to maximize uptake to the muscle cells.

What About a Multi?

Lastly, I often get the question, "Can I just take a multivitamin instead?" The answer to that is no. Multivitamins do not have high enough individual quantities to provide the benefits of a higher-dose protocol. The quality of our supplements matters. Always buy the highest quality product that fits your budget.

If a supplement falls well short on the typical dosages recommended, it is more than likely poor quality and a waste of money. And you would have to take more in order to reach the ideal dosages, so in the long run you would be spending just as much. Many of the cheaper products contain fillers and further ingredients to bulk up the product. Always buy the higher-quality option so you know exactly what you are taking.

Advanced Fat Burning

The previous supplements are those that I classify as "base" supplements: staples in your supplement regime that can and should be taken long term. But there are also a number of researched supplements that can be used to really enhance your fat-burning efforts. Let's look at those now.

When combining these supplements together in a "stack," remember that this can have a synergistic effect. Supplementing with stimulants should be done with caution. When done correctly, we can create a potent fat-burning supplement stack that is ideal to use during fat-loss plateaus or within the final phases of a strict fat-loss diet. I therefore suggest only using these ingredients for short periods of time (four to six weeks). If you do not tolerate stimulants well, or have little stimulant experience, I'd suggest starting with half the recommended dosages.

Caffeine

Caffeine not only acts as a stimulant but is effective at fat burning owing to its ability to increase the release of fat from fat cells. These fat-burning properties can be attributed to its thermogenic effect, increasing heat production.

How to Take
For fat loss and weight management, take 100–400 mg daily. For strength and power, take 200–400 mg one hour before workouts.

Synephrine

This is an increasingly popular ingredient in fat-loss supplements (usually called "bitter orange") as it appears to have a similar effect to its stronger counterpart, ephedrine. Synephrine is a natural compound found in citrus fruits and has a stimulatory and fat-burning effect.

How to Take
Take two doses of 20 mg per day.

White Willow Bark

This is the plant source of salicin, which is closely related to aspirin. It appears to produce a strong synergistic effect in promoting fat loss when combined with caffeine and synephrine.

How to Take
Take two doses of 90 mg of salicin per day.

Yohimbine

This is another stimulant, derived from the bark of the Pausinystalia yohimbe tree. It has been shown to increase fat burning, particularly when combined with other stimulants such has caffeine. It's important to note that excessive yohimbine dosages can cause elevated heart rate and anxiety.

How to Take
When using as part of the above stack, use 2.5 mg twice per day.

That wraps up the supplement section, with lots of supplements covered. Should you go out tomorrow and buy them all? No way. Find two or three supplements from the list above that best match your goals, and use them for a period of four to six weeks. Assess the results, and see if they are truly benefiting you and your goals. If not, then there may not be a need for them in your current diet. You might be better off saving your cash for good food instead.

15. THE DIET AFTER THE DIET

This might sound like an unusual title for a chapter. When I first learnt about this practice, I thought it sounded odd, too!

But it's actually pretty smart. It means exactly what it says—your diet after the diet. I know what you are thinking: "What on earth is that?" Let me explain.

I'm no stranger to a good dieting phase. The typical dieter's mentality is to quickly resort to old habits once our "diet" is over. I've done it myself. What happens? We usually end up back at square one, and need to diet again to achieve those same results. This happens over and over again. Now you can understand why some people are on a permanent diet.

This was what happened with my first ever "diet." I started eating less (calorie deficit) and training more to achieve my fat-loss goals. And there's nothing wrong with this either, it's the good old-fashioned "calories in vs. calories out" approach to ditching body fat. But the problem arises when we stop eating less and exercising more.

For most of us it is an overnight 24-hour transition from fitness buff to food addict. This is the result of completing the "dieting" phase with a specific time frame. It all has to stop sooner or later. In the past I would celebrate my success and good dieting behavior by breaking all the good habits and protocols I had set myself during the diet. That meant swapping the chicken for cake, the protein shakes for pizza, and exercise for an extra sleep-in. Because I felt I had earned it, that I now deserved to eat those foods.

The result was never pretty, and I would suffer from an almighty rebound. Bloating, tiredness, weakness, water retention, and, of course, the dreaded fat gain. Everything I'd worked so hard to combat for months basically came back at me with full force. And then some more. This situation occurred because I never stopped to consider the "diet after the diet." You need to apply just as much thought, effort, and planning to your new eating plan as you did to your diet. Fail to do this, and you will probably end up as a bloated, angry, and fat-gaining machine—like I was.

In this chapter, we'll look at what is actually causing this, while showing you a proven yet simple approach to ensure it doesn't happen to you. The result will be a way for you to maintain the results achieved from all your hard work!

Let's Chat Metabolism

The term "metabolism" is being used more frequently as people are becoming increasingly aware that their training and nutrition efforts influence what is happening on the inside too. But the debate is split on just how important the metabolism really is when managing how we look. One side believes it is key to achieving a better body and health, while the other side believes it has little importance. Before making your own decision, let's look at what metabolism really is.

Our metabolisms are the sum of the physical and chemical processes that occur in our cells to produce energy and assimilate new material. Essentially, everything happening in our body makes up our metabolism. However, when it comes to metabolism in regard to body composition and health, we focus on certain functions and processes, usually caused by the action of hormones related to thyroid hormones (T3, T4), or leptin, insulin, and cortisol.

I'm not here to argue how much of a factor these hormones might be. My main point is that what we do in terms of exercise and food intake is likely to be having a hormonal impact on the inside. It is the level of this impact that dictates the state of our individual metabolism and our health.

"Metabolic Damage"

In the health and fitness world, metabolic imbalance is typically seen in the "eat less, exercise more" people. That's you and me. If you eat less and exercise more, you'll create a caloric deficit that, over time, can create an unbalanced metabolism (it essentially slows down). This is known as "adaptive thermogenesis," and it's highly variable from one person to the next. For the average dieter, the metabolic downturn is about 300 calories per day, but up to 800 in some cases. This means after a period of dieting, the average person will burn 300 fewer calories per day than they previously did, without the inclusion of exercise.

This is the result of the body downregulating its "basal metabolic rate" (BMR) in response to a decrease in available energy on a calorie-restricted eating plan. The lack of available energy going in has forced the body to become more efficient over time. Due to this, many people can suffer from a "rebound" effect after a lower-calorie diet. What tends to occur is upon finishing the diet, body mass reverts towards pre-diet values. The mass gained also tends to be fat mass. The higher the initial caloric intake after the calorie-controlled diet, the higher rate of fat mass storage.

The Solution

You should now understand why suddenly resorting back to old habits after a diet phase can have a much stronger negative impact on the body than before. By quitting our diet after a period of consistent calorie restriction and intense exercise, the weight can quickly go back on. This is because of the decreased energy expenditure, even if you revert to what is considered the average food intake.

The solution? You need a structured and consistent plan in place following your original diet, so that in four days, four weeks, or even four months, you will still have the results to show for your efforts. The good news is that is doesn't need to be rocket science, but it is science. It's a simple case of giving the body time to play "catch-up" and get with your new program.

The key is calorie control. It's important to increase calories slowly with time and build up to the level you require for your new goals. For clients, and for myself, it's a simple case of adding an additional 100 calories each week while keeping an eye on the measurements. Using myself as an example, I finished my last fat-loss diet at 2,000 calories and increased them each week by 100. These extra calories were added to my carbohydrate or fat intake, depending on what I wanted to eat more of that week. After ten weeks I was eating 3,000 calories daily with no extra weight gain, bloating, or fatigue. The table shows how my own nutrition plan looked for those ten weeks.

The first goal was to increase carbohydrates, as I wanted to see how many I could consume while staying lean. In the past I was afraid of carbohydrates and believed I was "carb intolerant." This clearly isn't true and I actually lost more body fat (an extra 4 lb) in these first four to six weeks while eating more carbs. It is, however, common that your weight will increase slightly, as water and muscle mass increase at this point too. Once I was happy with the level of carbs in my diet, it was a simple case of adding the extra calories each week via my fat intake.

You shouldn't be gaining more than one to two pounds in weight per month (half of that for females) and you should adjust your intake based on your own results. Always keep a record of your weekly measurements. This might initially look like a complicated approach to your nutrition. But if you really want to keep the results from your hard work, I urge you to give this simple, but highly effective, approach a go after your next dieting phase. Reap all the benefits it has to offer.

Date	Total Calories	Protein (g)	Fat (g)	Carbs (g)	Body Weight (lb)
End of diet	2,000	200	50	190	174
Week 1	2,100	200	50	215	174
Week 2	2,200	200	50	240	173
Week 3	2,300	200	50	265	172
Week 4	2,400	200	50	290	171
Week 5	2,500	200	50	315	170
Week 6	2,600	200	50	340	170
Week 7	2,700	200	66	340	171
Week 8	2,800	200	77	340	171
Week 9	2,900	200	88	340	172
Week 10	3,000	200	99	340	173

PART III
RECIPES

My motto is "real food, real results." And the real food we eat must be great tasting, easy to make, and have plenty of variety.

In Part III of the HPL book, I'll show you exactly how to do this. We're going to look at the practical side to my HPL system, the stuff you will have to do, such as prepare your kitchen, go food shopping, and actually cook the meals. You now have the knowledge behind good nutrition so you can understand why these recipes have been created from these particular ingredients.

Within this part of the book you will find a wide variety of dishes that have been created to suit people of all tastes and cooking abilities—there is something for everyone. It is a collection of my favorite breakfasts, lunches, dinners, sides, snacks, and of course desserts.

That's right, desserts!

Eating great-tasting food is essential if you want long-term benefits and results through improved nutrition. Tradition has it that we must eat plain, tasteless, and repetitive meals in order to improve body composition and health. I put this book together to show you different—it really doesn't have to be that way.

Here's one of the common messages I get after introducing members to the HPL recipes:

"For the first time in a very long time I'm actually making progress. I can't believe that I'm eating better food and dropping body fat."—Ross, HPL Member

That is exactly what these recipes will help you achieve—how to eat great-tasting food while still achieving your goals. But we all know that great-tasting food doesn't make itself (much as we wish it did!). This means the responsibility is on you to make that happen. Just as improving your nutrition isn't just a simple case of saying "I'm going to eat better," you need to take action and cook yourself great-tasting food.

This means some preparation needs to be undertaken, along with plenty of consistency. Thankfully, the first part of the recipe section helps you do just that: prepare for the changes you need to make in order to cook up these awesome recipes.

There is an unlimited amount of nutrition information out there to help you get better results and improve your nutrition, yet people are still failing. Why? I believe it's because:

- This information is not tailored to the individual.
- This information may tell them what to do but doesn't prepare them for actually doing it.

What makes this recipe book different is that it shows you the nutritional breakdown of each meal (per serving) so you can match it to your own goals. The information that precedes the recipes ensures you will be prepared to successfully apply the information contained here.

16. EQUIPMENT

Before we talk about ingredients, it's important to look at the kitchen equipment you'll need to help you turn those foods into meals.

I've made every recipe in this book at home (several times!), so I've created the following list of equipment you will need. I've even included what you will use the different items for (just in case you don't you already know).

Kitchen Appliances

1. Refrigerator and freezer—a big freezer plays a big role in my kitchen; you need some room if you plan to buy the meats in bulk.
2. Oven and broiler (grill).
3. Kettle.
4. Food processor—not everyone's got one, but it's a great piece of kit: chops, mixes, mashes, and prepares ingredients for you.
5. Blender—reliable piece of equipment that blends everything you want, perfect for preparing shakes and smoothies.
6. Hand mixer/blender—essentially does what the two above do, but it comes with wide range of features to help make food preparation easier.
7. Slow cooker (Crock-Pot™)—great for cooking meats, you can set it up in the morning and it will all be ready in time for dinner.
8. Rice cooker—if you want your rice perfect every time without having to check on it, stir it, and so on, this is what you need.
9. Water filter—if you hate tap water, this is for you. I cannot imagine life without it. Provides you with great-tasting mineral water whenever you want. Saves you some coin on bottled water too.
10. Coffee maker—if you are a coffee lover you need this: perfect coffee every time. I recommend a simple cafetière (French press) or a stove-top espresso maker.
11. Tea pot—a ceramic or glass one is great if you drink loose tea; you will also need an infuser.

Cookware

1. Nonstick pots and pans—you probably already have these.
2. Sharp knives—if you have good quality knives it makes the job so much easier.
3. Ovenproof dishes and ramekins—a variety of these will ensure you can make any recipe.
4. Nonstick muffin tray—you will need it for the tasty frittatas.
5. Mixing bowls—you should have few different sizes, they can be plastic, stainless steel, or glass.
6. Storage containers—get your Tupperware ready, as meal preparation will be a key element to your success (any large supermarket will have a range of sizes).

Utensils and Accessories

1. Garlic press
2. Peeler
3. Grater—the best ones have an attached container
4. Can opener
5. Wine and bottle opener
6. Chopping boards—wooden is best for meats, plastic for veg
7. Kitchen scales, measuring bowls, and spoons—essential if you want to get the correct measurements to track your food
8. Strainer
9. Utensils: turner, spoon (wooden or plastic), ladle, whisk, spatula
10. Wooden or metal skewers
11. Aluminium foil—stock up on it, as it's such a pain when you need it and it's not there!
12. Plastic wrap
13. Waxed paper
14. Food and freezer bags

17. THE FOODS

It's now time to discover all the great-tasting foods you are going to need for the recipes. Don't worry, we will get to the meals soon, promise. Let's get stuck in.

Warning: this will make you hungry—don't say I didn't warn you!

Meat and Eggs

The quality of your meat matters and my motto is "quality over quantity." One of the best ways to source quality meat is from a local butcher; after all, these businesses are dependent on serving good meat. They are also usually happy to explain how the meat has been sourced. It is likely to come from locally reared animals, reducing travel time to your plate, meaning better quality and sustainability. Not everyone has time to go to the butcher every week, and there has been a rise in popularity of online butchers. Again, quality appears to be higher then supermarkets and the meat is cheaper too.

Budget depending, always buy the most expensive cuts you can afford, there really can be significant benefits. As the saying goes, we are not just what we eat, but what the food we eat has eaten, too. Aim for grass-fed and organic/free-range meat and poultry (rather than corn fed), as these will be of high quality.

Fish and Seafood

Having some fish and seafood in the diet can provide a nice break from the typical meats and can provide a number of health benefits. Aim to eat at least two to three portions of fresh fish per week.

Just as with our meat and eggs, the quality of our fish should be considered. Farm-raised fish has been fed pellets and antibiotics and forced to live in cages, but it is not always clear that this is what we are buying. The equivalent of grass-fed or organic meat in fish and seafood is "wild," so that's what you should aim to buy if budget permits. Again, a good local fish dealer is your best bet, if there is one.

Fruit and Veg

You can probably guess what I'm about to say here—source fresh, local, high-quality fruit and veg. Supermarket produce is usually imported and quality and freshness is therefore lower. It's not necessary to buy organic fruit and veg, but if you do then concentrate on the following twelve fruit and vegetables (known to have a higher pesticide content when non-organic):

- Apples
- Blueberries
- Grapes
- Nectarines
- Peaches
- Strawberries
- Bell peppers
- Celery
- Cucumbers
- Lettuce
- Potatoes
- Spinach and kale

You will notice that not a lot of fruit makes it into the recipes. That's because it's easy to overdo it. One to two pieces per day is more than enough to support a healthy and balanced nutrition plan.

Seeds and Nuts

Seeds and nuts not only taste good but pack a high nutrient punch too. That's why they will be included in a number of the recipes.

Something that may be new to you is "nut butter" in its various forms. This is simply a spreadable paste made from raw nuts. You can buy peanut, almond, cashew, and many more varieties. Most large supermarkets now sell these. Buy the most natural forms, with no added salt, sugar, or any "extra" stuff—we just want the raw nuts.

Dairy (Milk) Alternatives

Some people find they do not do very well with dairy in their diet. The most common complaint is digestive issues, and that person would likely be lactose intolerant, meaning they cannot break down lactose in dairy. Some report skin issues, and others find they just don't feel good. Luckily there are a number of alternatives to use. Here's a list of my favorites:

Coconut Milk

This is not the canned version but the carton alternative to milk. Most supermarkets should stock this. You can usually find it in the refrigerated section or on the "free-from" aisle. Note that the coconut milk is the one with the lowest carbohydrate content.

Almond/Hazelnut Milk

Another great alternative to cow's milk, with most supermarkets now stocking their own range of both. Go for the unsweetened variety.

Goat's Milk

This is considered to be the closest alternative to cow's milk that you can get. This is lactose free and therefore offers the same benefits as the other nondairy milks. Again, this can be found in most supermarkets.

Soya Milk

This is usually the first alternative people go to, but if you want my advice—don't. Small amounts of soy products are fine, but I wouldn't suggest drinking lots of it as soy has been shown to have negative effects on our hormonal health.

Herbs and Spices

A selection of herbs and spices is essential to boost flavors in your meals and enhance variety. Stock up with as many as you can, with the fresh options always being best. There are also a number of health benefits (including anti-inflammatory and antiviral) from eating them, so make sure to include them in your dishes. You should find a good range of herbs and spices in the large supermarkets.

Cooking Oils

The best cooking oils are those from saturated fat. That's because they don't oxidize and become highly inflammatory due to high omega-6 content when heated.

Believe it or not, this makes extra virgin olive oil a poor choice for cooking. Instead, when cooking, use extra virgin coconut oil, coconut butter, organic ghee, grass-fed butter, or goose/duck fat. Save the polyunsaturated fats (the ones damaged at high heat) as healthy oils to add cold after cooking, on salads, or in vegetable dressings. Examples of dressing oils would be extra virgin olive oil, avocado oil, and macadamia oil. You should buy these in dark-colored glass bottles to protect the oils from sunlight, and store them in a cool dry place to protect them from heat.

Tea and Coffee

Coffee is awesome. It is, however, one of the crops most sprayed with pesticides, so always buy organic.

Herbal teas serve as a tasty alternative to the traditional English tea and should be an addition to your daily selection. They are caffeine free and have a number of health benefits that can boost energy, improve recovery, and enhance sleep. Most supermarkets have a large selection of different flavors. I highly recommend buying them as loose herbs and using a tea strainer to reap the most flavor and benefits.

Salt

Salt gets used in a number of recipes here but it's important to highlight that this is individual and you can use as little or as much (within reason) as you like. I recommend salt that is unprocessed and as natural as possible, as this will have a higher mineral content and reduced additives. So avoid table salt and go for Celtic Sea Salt®, or Himalayan pink salt. You will find these in most supermarkets.

18. INGREDIENTS TO ALWAYS HAVE AROUND

Want to peek inside my kitchen cupboards? Here a list of the typical ingredients you'd find. Stock up on these and you will be able to prepare any dish from this book.

- Herbs and spices
- Cayenne pepper
- Salt
- Black pepper
- Smoked paprika
- Basil
- Tarragon
- Thyme
- Garam masala
- Curry powder
- Cumin
- Coriander
- Parsley
- Cinnamon

- Nuts and seeds
- Sesame seeds
- Peanuts
- Grated almonds
- Whole almonds
- Flax seeds
- Oils
- Coconut oil and olive oil
- Chicken stock gel pots
- Balsamic vinegar
- Light soy sauce
- Oyster sauce
- Stevia
- Honey
- Vanilla and almond extract
- Cashew and peanut butter
- Coconut flour
- 85% cocoa dark chocolate
- Frozen peas

Note: fresh herbs will always give you better-tasting dishes, so if that's what you are planning to use stock up on them weekly. I always have the above as dried versions in my cupboard and buy additional fresh herbs weekly, depending what is on the menu.

19. WEEKLY SHOPPING LIST

Here is my personal weekly shopping list. Use it to make the most of the recipes in this book—it will give you a huge variety of foods to choose from every day.

Fruit and Veg

1. Red onions
2. Mixed bell peppers
3. Sweet potatoes
4. Zucchini (courgette)
5. Organic baby spinach
6. Kale
7. Cucumber
8. Tomatoes
9. Avocado
10. Garlic
11. Scallions (spring onions)
12. Lemons
13. Blueberries
14. Strawberries
15. Raspberries
16. Bananas

Meats and Fish

17. Chicken breasts/drumsticks/thighs
18. Ground (minced) turkey and beef
19. Wild salmon fillets
20. Cod fillets

21. Smoked Canadian bacon (back bacon)
22. Parma ham

Dairy and Nondairy

23. Fat-free natural/Greek yogurt
24. Fat-free cottage cheese
25. Low-fat feta cheese
26. Coconut milk
27. Eggs

Cupboard Food and Other

28. Canned tuna
29. Canned chopped tomatoes
30. Tomato paste
31. Pickled onions and beets (beetroot) (for salads)
32. Rice
33. Rice noodles
34. Sun-dried tomatoes
35. Red pesto
36. Rice cakes
37. Popcorn

20. SETTING UP YOUR KITCHEN

You now know the equipment and ingredients you need to start creating these great-tasting meals.

But before you head off to the shops there is one more thing you to consider—where you are going to store it all. My guess is the kitchen, but is your kitchen ready for all of this? Perhaps not. So here's a short guide to preparing your kitchen for the new chef in you—out with the old, in with the new, and all that.

Get Rid of the Junk

By junk I mean anything that isn't on our previous food list. Now, I'm not saying you can't eat anything that's not in this book, of course you can, but I'm trying to create the most successful environment for you. So, if that means initially throwing out the cookie jar and bread box, so be it.

With time, you will find which foods work and can be included in your flexible diet approach, but to start with let's reduce them. Start with a blank slate and add things in from there. If they are not under your nose, the chances are you will not miss them.

And before you ask, no, don't try to eat them all this weekend before starting your plan next Monday. Bin it, donate it, or gift it. Don't worry, there are plenty of snacks, desserts, and treats you can make to replace them. Just wait until you see what we can do!

Give It A Scrub

Nobody wants to eat from a dirty kitchen. Plus, you are going to start spending more time in there now, so get it clean and tidy. Start from the tops and work your way down, and don't forget the inside of the refrigerator. A soap and cloth may come in handy here too—you know the drill.

Re-stock

It's now time to add in all the equipment and foods we just discussed. Keep the fresh stuff in the refrigerator and freezer and everything else can go in cool, dry cupboards. Simple.

Preparing Your First Meal

It's time to cook your first meal from the HPL recipe book (thank goodness, I hear you cry!). Here are a couple of things to consider before you start—they may just save you some time and effort.

Bulk Cooking

One of the best tips I can pass on is to never cook just for one meal. When you do hit the kitchen to make some great-tasting food, aim to get at least two meals from it. Some people like to cook for three or four days in advance. This will mean cooking a number of meals at the same time and storing them in Tupperware. This means they can grab a meal whenever they like and don't need to cook it, as it's already done. This could be ideal if you are really busy during the week and know time is against you.

Personally, I like to cook something fresh every evening (or every second evening), but I ensure there are leftovers for a lunch the following day. So it is worth spending some time on making something nice.

Think about what preparation style will suit you best and give it a go.

Plan Ahead

This recipe section will show you everything you need to make great-tasting meals, but won't tell you which days and times to eat them. This is where your nutrition plan comes in handy, as it will suggest certain meals on different days. The benefit is that it will take the "planning" process out of the equation. So, providing you always have the ingredients, you can make the suggested meals. It also serves as a great tool to help you plan, getting the correct meats out for days ahead, and taking time to gather any last-minute ingredients.

Let's do it.

You're now ready for some cooking.

Enjoy the recipes. I hope you like them as much as I do (I'm confident they'll help bring you closer to your goals).

21. SOUPS, SIDES, AND LIGHT BITES

When you want something more to eat, turn to nutritious, tasty, and homemade food. This section will show you how prepare light meals and sides from single-ingredient foods. It will help you avoid the trap of high-calorie and low-nutrient nibbles, ensuring you get even more of the good stuff.

Chicken, Leek, and Cabbage Soup

This soup is packed with protein, which makes it a perfect warming meal for any time of the day.

Prep: 15 mins
Cooking: 20 mins
Serves 2
Nutrition per serving: 273 kcals, 31 g protein, 26 g carbs, 4 g fat

What you need:
- 11 oz (300 g) chicken breast, skinless and boneless, diced
- 1 leek, chopped
- 2½ cups (175 g) savoy cabbage, shredded
- 1 carrot, thinly sliced
- 6 prunes, cut into quarters
- 2¾ cups (650 ml) vegetable stock, hot
- ½ tsp coconut oil

What you need to do:
1. Heat the coconut oil in a pan, and fry the chicken for a few minutes. Then add the leek, stirring from time to time.
2. Place the sliced carrot in a pot and cover with the vegetable stock. Bring to the boil and then simmer for 5–6 mins.
3. Add the cabbage and simmer for another 10 mins.
4. Place the chicken and leeks in the pot and add the prunes. Simmer for 1–2 mins and then season to taste with salt and pepper.
5. Once vegetables are soft, serve the soup in bowls.

Chicken Noodle Soup

Who says soups can't be high in protein? This protein-packed soup not only tastes great, but will also add muscle to your body faster than you can eat it!

Prep: 5 mins
Cooking: 20 mins
Serves 2
Nutrition per serving: 284 kcals, 32 g protein, 29 g carbs, 3 g fat

What you need:
- 2 cups (500 ml) chicken stock
- 11 oz (300 g) chicken breast, diced
- 1 tsp ginger, grated
- 1 garlic clove, crushed
- ¼ cup (50 g) corn (sweet corn), drained
- 1½ oz (45 g) rice noodles
- 4 shiitake mushrooms, sliced
- 2 scallions (spring onions), chopped
- 2 tbsp soy sauce
- Fresh chili, chopped
- Ground pepper, to taste

What you need to do:
1. Heat the chicken stock in a large pot. Add chicken, ginger, and garlic, and simmer for 15 mins, until chicken is cooked.
2. Now add noodles, mushrooms, corn, half of the scallions, soy sauce, and chili, and simmer for another 5 mins.
3. Serve in bowls with sprinkled scallions.

HPL Food Fact—Ginger
Ginger has been used in India and China since 5000 BC both in cooking and as a therapeutic spice. It contains an active constituent (gingerol) that may have anticancer properties.
It's also great when you are feeling sluggish as it stimulates and promotes detoxification by increasing perspiration and circulation.

Pea and Spinach Soup

This unbelievably light and fresh soup is quick and easy to make. Perfect for a quick bite.

Prep: 10 mins
Cooking: 18 mins
Serves 2
Nutrition per serving: 233 kcals, 14 g protein, 39 g carbs, 7 g fat

What you need:
- 1 onion, chopped
- 1 small potato (6 oz/170 g), diced
- 1 garlic clove, crushed
- 1¼ cups (300 ml) chicken stock, hot
- 1⅓ cups (180 g) frozen peas
- 3 cups (100 g) baby spinach
- ½ tsp coconut oil
- 1 scallion (spring onion), chopped
- 1 tbsp fresh mint, chopped
- 100g 0% fat Greek yogurt (or a dairy-free alternative)

What you need to do:
1. In a small bowl, mix the yogurt, mint, and scallions, and set aside.
2. Heat the coconut oil in a pot and add the onion, garlic, and potato. Cook for 2 mins, stirring often.
3. Pour in the stock, bring to boil, and simmer for 10 mins.
4. Add the frozen peas and bring back to boil. Simmer for 2 mins.
5. Add the spinach, and again bring to boil and simmer for another 3 mins.
6. Blend the soup using a hand blender or food processor. Serve with mint yogurt.

HPL Bonus
You can store this soup in the freezer for up to three months.

Indonesian Veg Stir Fry

This is a very simple recipe for an excellent and authentic-tasting Thai dish.

Prep: 10 mins
Cooking: 10 mins
Serves 2
Nutrition per serving: 334 kcals, 13 g protein, 51 g carbs, 10 g fat

What you need:
- 1 onion, chopped
- ⅔ cup (50 g) brown (chestnut) mushrooms, sliced
- 1 red bell pepper, chopped
- 1½ cups (100 g) pak choi, chopped
- ½ cup (60 g) bean sprouts
- 1 garlic clove, crushed
- ¼ cup (30 g) cashews
- ½ cup (50 g) edamame beans
- 1 tbsp Thai green curry paste
- ½ heaping cup (100 g) egg noodles, cooked according to instructions

What you need to do:
1. Heat the coconut oil in a pan and add the onion, bell pepper, mushrooms, and garlic. Cook for about 2 mins.
2. Add the cashews and cook for further 3 mins.
3. Now add the curry paste, noodles, and pak choi. Mix and cook for 2–3 mins.
4. Lastly, add the bean sprouts and cook for another minute, then serve.

HPL Bonus
- If the dish is too dry, add a few tbsp of water.
- If you are very short on time, buy an oriental vegetable mix instead of using individual vegetables.
- If you'd like to add some meat to this dish, do so in the first point. For example, fry diced chicken with the onion and garlic then add the peppers and mushrooms. You can skip the edamame beans in this case.

Chorizo, Feta, and Tomato Salad

The sweet tomatoes with salty and spicy chorizo make an awesome combination.

Prep: 5 mins
Cooking: 5 mins
Serves 2
Nutrition per serving: 350 kcals, 19 g protein, 13 g carbs, 25 g fat

What you need:
- 3 tomatoes, cut into wedges
- 3 cups (100 g) baby spinach
- 2 oz (60 g) feta cheese, crumbled
- ½ red onion, thinly sliced
- 8 basil leaves, roughly chopped
- 1 tbsp vinegar
- 1¾ oz (50 g) chorizo, sliced
- Salt and pepper

What you need to do:
1. Put the tomatoes, spinach, onion, feta, and basil in a bowl. Season with salt and pepper, and drizzle with the vinegar.
2. In a hot dry pan, fry the chorizo slices until browned on both sides.
3. Add cooked chorizo to the salad and mix well.
4. Serve immediately or store in the fridge for later.

Broccoli Pizza Crust

This veggie-powered pizza needs to make its way into your kitchen!

Prep: 10 mins
Cooking: 25 mins
Serves 2
Nutrition per serving (crust only): 182 kcals, 10 g protein, 22 g carbs, 7 g fat

What you need:
- 1 small broccoli head (around 11 oz/300 g)
- 2 onions, chopped
- 4 garlic cloves, crushed
- 1 egg
- 2 tbsp flaxseeds
- Salt and pepper

What you need to do:
1. Preheat oven to 390°F (200°C).
2. In a food processor, combine the onions, broccoli, and garlic.
3. Add the egg and flaxseeds and season with salt and pepper. Pulse until well combined.
4. Place the broccoli dough on a baking sheet covered with waxed paper, and spread out until you have an even crust (about ¼ inch (65 mm) thick). Make sure the edges are a bit thicker; this will prevent them from burning.
5. Bake for 15 mins, until starting to turn golden.
6. Top with your favorite toppings and bake for another 8–10 mins.
7. Serve with homemade sauces and side salad.

HPL Bonus: Simple Garlic Oil

You can prepare a garlic oil that is great for topping your pizza.

What you need: 2 garlic cloves, crushed; ⅓ cup (80 ml) olive oil; 1 tsp white wine vinegar; pinch of salt.

What you need to do: combine all ingredients together and serve as a side to drizzle over your pizza.

Nutrition per tbsp: 123 kcals, 0 protein, 0 carbs, 14 g fat

Zucchini Pizza Crust

What's this? Veggie pizza base? Yep—give this healthy twist on a carryout classic a go (you'll be glad you did).

Prep: 20 mins
Cooking: 20 mins
Serves: 2
Nutrition per serving (crust only): 242 kcals, 16 g protein, 12 g carbs, 16 g fat

What you need:
- 3 medium zucchini (courgettes) (about 19–21 oz/550–600 g), grated
- 1 oz (30 g) mozzarella, grated
- 1 oz (30 g) parmesan, grated
- 3 tbsp ground almonds
- 1 egg white
- 1 tsp oregano
- ½ tsp garlic granules
- Salt and pepper

HPL Bonus
How to make the tomato base sauce:

What you need: ¾ cup (200 g) chopped tomatoes, 1 crushed garlic clove, ½ tsp dried herbs, salt and pepper.

What you need to do: combine the ingredients together in a pan and heat through. Then just spread onto the pizza before topping with your favorite ingredients.

What you need to do:
1. Preheat the oven to 390°F (200°C).
2. Grate the zucchini using a food processor or hand grater and transfer into a bowl. Place in the microwave on high for 5 mins.
3. Remove from the bowl onto a clean dish towel to cool.
4. Once cool, twist the dish towel around the zucchini to wring out as much water as possible. It is very important you remove as much water as you can, otherwise the crust will be soggy.
5. Transfer the zucchini back into the bowl and add mozzarella, ground almonds, parmesan cheese, oregano, garlic, egg white, salt, and pepper. Mix well until combined.
6. Shape the crust into two balls, for two personalized pizzas, or one big ball, for a big pizza.
7. Place the ball on a baking sheet covered with waxed paper, and press out into a circle until the dough is about ¼ inch (65 mm) thick.
8. Bake the crust for 10 mins, or until it starts to turn golden.

Cauliflower Pizza Crust

You will never guess this pizza crust is made with cauliflower (and nor will your guests... if you can bear to share it!).

Prep: 20 mins
Cooking: 20 mins
Serves 2
Nutrition per serving (crust only): 208 kcals, 15 g protein, 16 g carbs, 10 g fat

What you need:
- 1 medium cauliflower (20 oz/580 g)
- 1 oz (30 g) parmesan, grated
- 1 oz (30 g) mozzarella, grated
- 1 tbsp ground almonds
- ½ tsp oregano
- ½ tsp basil
- ½ tsp red pepper flakes
- 1 egg white
- 1 garlic clove, crushed
- Salt and pepper
- Toppings of your choice

What you need to do:
1. Preheat the oven to 390°F (200°C).
2. In a food processor, pulse the cauliflower until it's a sand-like texture. Place in a bowl and microwave on high for 4 mins.
3. Remove from the bowl onto a clean dish towel to cool.
4. Once cool, twist the dish towel around the cauliflower to wring out as much water as possible. It is very important you remove as much water as you can, otherwise the crust will be soggy.
5. Place the cauliflower back into the bowl and stir in the parmesan, mozzarella, ground almonds, salt and pepper, herbs, and egg white. Stir well until combined.
6. Shape the crust into two balls, for two personalized pizzas, or one big ball, for a big pizza.
7. Place the ball on a baking tray covered with baking paper, and press out into a circle until the dough is about ¼ inch (65mm) thick.
8. Bake the crust for 10 mins, or until it starts to turn golden.
9. Top with your favorite toppings and place back into the oven for 8–10 mins.
10. Serve with homemade ketchup and side salad.

Asparagus Wraps

An extremely easy starter, side or lunch that tastes awesome, and reaps the many benefits of asparagus.

Prep: 5mins
Cooking: 15 mins
Serves 2
Nutrition per serving: 268 kcals, 23 g protein, 11 g carbs, 15 g fat

What you need:
- 12 asparagus tips
- 4 slices of ham
- Scant ½ cup (100 g) low-fat soft cheese (or you can use normal soft cheese, or a dairy-free alternative)
- 1 tbsp coconut flour
- 1 oz (30 g) parmesan, grated
- 3 tbsp coconut milk
- 2 tbsp chives, chopped

What you need to do:
1. Bring a small pot of water to the boil and cook the asparagus for 4–5 mins, until just tender.
2. In a small bowl, mix the soft cheese, coconut flour and two-thirds of the parmesan. Add the milk and beat until combined, then set aside.
3. Wrap three asparagus tips in a slice of ham and place in a baking dish. Wrap the others in the same way.
4. Top the wraps with the cheese mixture. Sprinkle the remaining parmesan on top and bake for 10 mins, until the cheese has browned.
5. Serve sprinkled with chives.

Food Fact—Asparagus
Asparagus is a natural diuretic; it helps the body flush the toxins out of its system. It stimulates the kidneys, bladder, and liver, making it a powerful detoxifier.

Mackerel Paste

This light and fluffy paste is extremely quick to prepare, which makes it a perfect breakfast or snack.

Prep: 5 mins
Serves 2
Nutrition per serving: 311 kcals, 20 g protein, 2.5 g carbs, 24 g fat

What you need:
- 5½ oz (150 g) smoked mackerel fillets
- Scant ½ cup (100 g) low-fat soft cheese (or a dairy-free alternative)
- 1 small garlic clove, crushed
- Juice and zest of half a lemon
- 1 scallion (spring onion)
- 2 tbsp dill, chopped
- Ground black pepper

What you need to do:
1. In a bowl, mash the mackerel with a fork and season with ground pepper.
2. Add the soft cheese, garlic, lemon, and dill, and mix.
3. Separate into two portions and sprinkle with the scallions to serve.

HPL Bonus Tip
You can make a bigger portion of this paste and keep it in the freezer for up to two months.

Mushroom and Sun-Dried Tomato Side

This quick and easy side is full of fiber and can be served hot or cold.

Prep: 5 mins
Cooking: 5 mins
Serves 2
Nutrition per serving: 47 kcals, 4 g protein, 6 g carbs, 2 g fat

What you need:
- 2⅔ cups (200 g) brown (chestnut) mushrooms, halved
- 6 sun-dried tomatoes, drained, rinsed, and chopped
- 1 garlic clove, crushed
- 1 tbsp fresh parsley, chopped
- 1 tsp coconut oil
- Salt and pepper
- Lemon wedges, to serve (optional)

What you need to do:
1. Heat the coconut oil in a pan. Add the garlic and fry for 1 min on high heat.
2. Next, add the mushrooms and cook for 4–5 mins, stirring occasionally.
3. Lastly, add the tomatoes and parsley, season with salt and pepper, and cook for 1 more min.
4. Serve with lemon wedges.

HPL Food Fact—Mushrooms
Mushrooms are rich in selenium, a powerful antioxidant that helps prevent heart disease and cancer. They are also full of folic acid that benefits the circulation system.

Balsamic Glazed Carrots

This is the perfect side for a classic Sunday roast.

Prep: 10 mins
Cooking: 30 mins
Serves 4
Nutrition per serving: 103 kcals, 1 g protein, 18 g carbs, 4 g fat

What you need:
- 1 lb (500 g) carrots, peeled and halved lengthways
- 1 tbsp coconut oil, melted
- 2 tbsp balsamic vinegar
- 1 tbsp honey
- Salt and pepper

What you need to do:
1. Preheat oven to 350°F (180°C).
2. Cook the carrots in boiling water for 10 mins, until they are starting to soften. Drain and spread in a roasting pan.
3. Drizzle with the coconut oil, vinegar, and honey. Season with salt and pepper.
4. Roast for about 30 mins, turning occasionally, until carrots are soft and tender.

Sesame Broccoli and Bell Peppers

Need a quick and easy side dish? Try these oriental veggies, they're one of my favorite go-to recipes!

Prep: 10 mins
Cooking: 10 mins
Serves 2
Nutrition per serving: 95 kcals, 3 g protein, 7 g carbs, 7 g fat

What you need:
- 2 tsp sesame oil
- 1 bell pepper, sliced
- ¾ cup (75 g) broccoli, divided into small florets
- 1 small garlic clove, crushed
- ½ tsp ginger, grated
- 1 tbsp soy sauce
- 1 tbsp sesame seeds

What you need to do:
1. In a pan, heat 1 tsp sesame oil. Add the bell pepper and broccoli and cook for 8 mins, until the pepper is softened and browned.
2. Then add the garlic, ginger, soy sauce, and sesame seeds, and season with salt and pepper. Cook, stirring often, for 1 more minute.
3. Drizzle with the remaining sesame oil and sprinkle with some more sesame seeds, and serve as a side.

HPL Food Fact—Sesame Seeds
These little seeds are rich in zinc and antioxidant vitamin E. They are also a good source of calcium and magnesium, minerals necessary for bone and heart health. All of this makes them a perfect non-dairy bone-builder for vegans and vegetarians (although meat-eaters should eat them, too!).

Sweet Potato Fries

I'm convinced these taste better than traditional deep-fried fries, and I think you will be too.

Prep: 10 mins
Cooking: 30–40 mins
Serves 2
Nutrition per serving: 149 kcals, 2 g protein, 30 g carbs, 2 g fat

What you need:
- 10 oz (300 g) sweet potato, scrubbed and cut into large fries
- 1 tsp coconut oil, melted
- Salt and pepper

What you need to do:
1. Heat the oven to 390°F (200°C).
2. In a large bowl, toss the sweet potato fries with oil and salt and pepper.
3. Transfer to a shallow roasting pan and bake for 30–40 mins, until crisp.

HPL Food Fact—Sweet Potato
Sweet potatoes are rich in antioxidants, especially beta-carotene, vitamin A, and vitamin C, for boosting immunity. The skin is full of fiber, which helps the digestive system.

Cauliflower Rice

A delicious recipe for making "rice" from cauliflower (yes, really—give it a try!) Ideal for "low carb" days, helping you meet your macros!

Prep: 10 mins
Cooking: 10 mins
Serves 2
Nutrition per serving: 115 kcals, 6 g protein, 20 g carbs, 3 g fat

What you need:
- 1 medium cauliflower (20 oz/580 g)
- 1 garlic clove, crushed
- 1 tsp coconut oil
- 1 small onion, chopped
- Salt and pepper

What you need to do:
1. Rinse the cauliflower and divide into florets.
2. Using a food processor, pulse the cauliflower until evenly chopped, and set aside.
3. Heat the coconut oil in a pan and add the onion and garlic. Cook for 4 mins, until soft and golden.
4. Add the cauliflower rice and continue to cook for another 5 mins.
5. Season with salt and pepper, and serve.

HPL Food Fact—Cauliflower

Cauliflower has the ability to aid cell detoxification. It is full of antioxidants; however, its most powerful effects come from glucosinolates, which fuel and strengthen the liver during detoxification.

Greek Salad Omelet

Who said eggs have to be boring? Not me—try this Greek salad recipe and I think you'll agree.

Prep: 5 mins
Cooking: 15 mins
Serves 2
Nutrition per serving: 235 kcals, 19 g protein, 3 g carbs, 15 g fat

What you need:
- 5 eggs, beaten
- 1 small red onion, cut into wedges
- 6 cherry tomatoes, halved
- 10 black olives, sliced
- 2 oz (60 g) low-fat feta cheese, crumbled
- Handful of parsley leaves, chopped
- ½ tsp coconut oil
- Salt and pepper

What you need to do:
1. Preheat the broiler (grill) to high. In a large bowl, combine the eggs with the parsley. Season with salt and pepper.
2. Heat the coconut oil in a large pan, and fry the onions for 2–3 mins, until browned.
3. Add the tomatoes and olives and cook for another 2 mins.
4. Turn the heat down and pour in the eggs. Cook them for 2–3 mins, stirring as they begin to set.
5. Leaving the eggs still runny in places, scatter over the feta.
6. Place the pan under the broiler (keep it slightly opened) for 5–6 mins until the eggs have set and start to turn golden.
7. Cut into wedges and serve.

HPL Food Fact—Olives
Olives contain a substance called squalene, which has protective properties against cancer.

Baked Eggs in Spicy Tomato and Bell Pepper Sauce

This is set to become a firm favorite for a hearty mid-morning brunch on a lazy weekend.

Prep: 10 mins
Cooking: 25–30 mins
Serves 2
Nutrition per serving: 275 kcals, 18 g protein, 25 g carbs, 11 g fat

What you need:
- 1 red onion, sliced
- 2 red/yellow bell peppers, diced
- 1 tbsp harissa paste
- 1 tsp tomato paste
- 4 garlic cloves, crushed
- 1 red chili, chopped
- 1 tsp smoked paprika
- 1½ cups (100 g) kale
- 1½ cups (400 g) chopped tomatoes
- Salt and pepper
- 4 eggs
- 1 tbsp fresh parsley, chopped

What you need to do:
1. Heat the oil in a pan and cook the onions and bell peppers for 5 mins, until softened.
2. Add the chili, harissa paste, tomato paste, garlic, and smoked paprika, then cook for another 5 mins.
3. Add the kale and cook for another minute. Then add the chopped tomatoes and season with salt and pepper. Simmer for 10 mins.
4. Make four little wells in the sauce and break one egg in each. Simmer for another 10 mins or until the eggs have set.
5. Sprinkle with parsley and serve.

Salmon and Eggs

This partnership of smoked salmon and eggs is the perfect weekend option (breakfast in bed, if you're lucky!).

Prep: 2 mins
Cooking: 5 mins
Serves 2
Nutrition per serving: 236 kcals, 18 g protein, 1 g carbs, 16 g fat

What you need:
- 2 oz (60 g) smoked salmon, shredded
- 4 large eggs
- 1 tbsp parsley, chopped
- ½ tbsp butter
- Salt and pepper

What you need to do:
1. In a large bowl, beat the eggs, and add salt and pepper.
2. Heat the butter in a pan and add the eggs. Cook for about 2–3 mins.
3. Add the salmon and herbs while the eggs are still runny and mix together until set.
4. Serve immediately with freshly ground black pepper.

HPL Food Fact—Eggs

Many people worry about the high cholesterol content of eggs, but studies have shown that this is an unfounded fear, as the cholesterol that you eat does not circulate in the blood.

Herby Omelet with Asparagus

There are a lot of omelet recipes out there. I've tried most of them, and this one wins hands down. Try it and you will find out why.

Prep: 7 mins
Cooking: 5 mins
Serves 1
Nutrition info per serving: 196 kcal, 12 g protein, 1 g carbs, 14 g fat

What you need:
- 4 asparagus spears
- 2 eggs
- 2 tbsp chopped dill
- 5g butter

What you need to do:
1. Remove the hard ends of the asparagus stalks and place the rest of the spears in a pot pan of boiling water. Bring the heat down and simmer for 4–5 mins, until the asparagus is soft. Then drain and set aside.
2. In a bowl, combine the eggs with the dill and ½ tbsp of water and dill.
3. Heat half the butter in a pan to a high temperature. Pour in the eggs and fry for a few minutes.
4. When the omelet is nearly ready, place the asparagus spears on top of it and fold in half. Gently transfer onto a plate and serve.

HPL Bonus Tip

If you are a fan of salmon, why not add 1 oz (25 g) torn smoked salmon to each portion. Just place the salmon on top of the omelet before adding the asparagus.

The nutrition for a smoked salmon and asparagus omelet will be: 241 kcals, 17 g protein, 1 g carbs, 17 g fat.

Spinach and Feta Frittatas

These make the perfect breakfast when on the go. Cook them up the night before and you can just grab them and go the following morning.

Prep: 8 mins
Cooking: 15 mins
Serves 2
Nutrition per serving: 235 kcals, 10 g protein, 3 g carbs, 15 g fat

What you need:
- 3 cups (80 g) spinach leaves
- 1 garlic clove, crushed
- 3 eggs
- 2 egg whites
- 4 tbsp coconut milk
- 2 oz (60 g) low-fat feta cheese, cut into cubes
- Salt and pepper

What you need to do:
1. Heat oven to 390°F (200°C).
2. Place the spinach leaves and garlic in a pan, cover and steam for 2–5mins, or until wilted.
3. Cool the spinach and squeeze out the excess water, then roughly chop.
4. Place the eggs, egg whites, and coconut milk in a bowl, and whisk to combine. Stir in the spinach and season with salt and pepper.
5. Spoon the spinach mixture into the dips in a nonstick muffin pan, filling each three-quarters full. Place 3–4 cubes of feta cheese on top of each frittata and press lightly into the mixture.
6. Bake for 15 mins, until the frittatas are golden and set. Serve hot.

Mexican Baked Eggs

Bring some Mexican flavor to your breakfast table.

Prep: 20 mins
Cooking: 15 mins
Serves 4
Nutrition per serving: 202 kcals, 20 g protein, 9 g carbs, 9 g fat

What you need:

- 8 oz (225 g) ground (minced) lean beef
- 1 tsp coconut oil
- 2 garlic cloves, crushed
- 1 small red onion
- 1½ cups (400 g can) chopped tomatoes
- ½ red bell pepper, diced
- 1 celery stick, chopped
- 1 tbsp tomato paste
- 1 tsp smoked paprika
- 4 whole eggs
- Chili powder, to taste

What you need to do:

1. Preheat the oven to 350°F (180°C).
2. In a large saucepan, heat the coconut oil and add the onion and garlic. Fry for 5 mins over a medium heat until soft.
3. Add the beef and cook until starting to brown.
4. Stir in the tomatoes, bell pepper, celery, paste, and spices. Cook for 10 mins.
5. Spoon into four ramekins about three-quarters full and break an egg into each. Bake in the oven for 5–10 mins, until the egg is set.
6. Serve hot.

HPL Bonus Tip

If you haven't got much time in the mornings, make up the meat and vegetables the night before, then in the morning just break in the eggs and bake.

HPL Food Fact—Beef

Beef can help protect against chronic fatigue syndrome, weak digestion, eye disease, depression, and mood swings. All thanks to being a rich source of the B-vitamins.

Breakfast Veg and Egg

Try an HPL version of the traditional breakfast with this totally healthy and nutritious twist.

Prep: 10 mins
Cooking: 20 mins
Serves 2
Nutrition per serving: 230 kcals, 16 g protein, 12 g carbs, 13 g fat

What you need:
- 1 cup (100 g) snap (green) beans
- 2 tomatoes, halved
- 4 eggs
- 8 brown (chestnut) mushrooms
- 1 tsp coconut oil, melted
- ½ tsp dried mixed herbs
- 1 tbsp chives, chopped
- 1 tbsp parsley, chopped
- Salt and pepper

What you need to do:
1. Heat the broiler (grill) to high.
2. In a pot, bring water to the boil and simmer the beans for 5 mins. Then set aside.
3. Mix the coconut oil with the garlic and herbs.
4. Place the mushrooms and tomatoes on a baking tray, and rub them in half of the oil mixture. Broil for 6 mins.
5. Place the beans under the broiler for the last 2 mins, to heat them up.
6. In the meantime, heat the remaining oil in a pan and fry the eggs.
7. Plate the veg and egg and sprinkle with parsley and chives to serve.

Stuffed Mushrooms

These stuffed mushrooms are a perfect choice if you want something interesting and tasty for breakfast or lunch.

Prep: 5 mins
Cooking: 15 mins
Makes 4 mushrooms
Nutrition per mushroom: 309 kcals, 37 g protein, 24 g carbs, 8 g fat

What you need:
- 4 chicken-breast sausages, with the casing removed
- 4 Portobello flat mushrooms
- 3 cups (100 g) spinach, chopped
- ½ onion, diced
- 1 egg
- 1 tbsp coconut flour
- Salt and pepper
- 1 tsp coconut oil

What you need to do:
1. Heat the oven to 375°F (190°C) and prepare a baking sheet lined with foil.
2. Remove the stalks from the mushrooms and, using a sharp knife, cut an "X" on the top of each one. Place them on the baking sheet and oven bake for 10 mins.
3. In the meantime, heat the coconut oil in a pan and add the onion. Cook for 3 mins.
4. Then add the sausage and cook for another 5 mins. Transfer to a bowl and leave to cool.
5. Once sausage is cooled, add the egg, spinach, coconut flour, and salt and pepper and combine.
6. Stuff the mushrooms with the mixture and place back in the oven for 5 mins, until browned.
7. Serve topped with homemade tomato sauce.

Spinach, Cottage Cheese, and Bacon Quiche

Eggs, Canadian bacon, and some greens combine to make the perfect breakfast.

Prep: 5 mins
Cooking: 15–20 mins
Serves 2
Nutrition per serving: 197 kcals, 18 g protein, 4 g carbs, 12 g fat

What you need:
- 1½ cups (50 g) spinach, torn
- 2 scallions (spring onions), chopped
- 2 eggs, beaten
- ½ cup (100 g) cottage cheese
- 2 smoked Canadian bacon rashers
- Salt and pepper

What you need to do:
1. Preheat the oven to 390°F (180°C). Put in the bacon and cook for 5 mins while you prepare the rest of the ingredients.
2. In a medium bowl, beat the eggs and add the scallions and spinach.
3. Once the bacon is done, chop it into pieces.
4. Add the veg, cottage cheese, bacon, and salt and pepper to the beaten eggs and combine.
5. Transfer the mixture into a round baking dish, and bake for about 15–20 mins, until eggs are browned and set.
6. Serve immediately or store in the refrigerator for later.

Guacamole

This quick and healthy side dish can be used as a dip for your favorite veggies. Oh, and it tastes amazing spread on a broiled (grilled) chicken breast, too!

Prep: 10 mins
Serves 8
Nutrition per serving: 85 kcals, 1 g protein, 5 g carbs, 7 g fat

What you need:
- 2 ripe avocados
- 1 small tomato, finely chopped
- 1 tbsp lemon juice
- ½ red chili, deseeded and chopped
- ½ small red onion, finely chopped
- Salt and pepper

What you need to do:
1. Scoop the avocado flesh into a bowl and add the rest of the ingredients.
2. Season with salt and pepper, and combine everything, using a potato masher.
3. Serve as a side with vegetables or meats.

HPL Food Fact—Avocado
Containing twenty vitamins, minerals, and phytonutrients, avocados are a true superfood and a great dietary addition for anyone aiming to get fit.

Hummus

This traditional Middle Eastern spread is delicious, and pairs well with... just about everything!

Prep: 10 mins
Serves 8
Nutrition per serving: 162 kcals, 6 g protein, 19 g carbs, 7 g fats

What you need:
- 1 cup (240 g) chickpeas, drained
- 6 mint leaves, chopped
- 1 small garlic clove, crushed
- 2 tbsp tahini (sesame paste)
- 2 tbsp olive oil
- 1 celery stick, chopped
- Zest of 1 lemon
- Juice of half a lemon
- Salt and pepper

What you need to do:
1. In a food processor, mix together the chickpeas, mint, garlic, and tahini.
2. Continue mixing the paste and pour in the olive oil.
3. Still mixing, add the celery and lemon zest and juice. Season with salt and pepper (to taste) and blend well.
4. Serve as a dip with carrot sticks, celery, and pita bread.

HPL Bonus Tips
- If the paste is too thick, add a bit of water until the desired consistency is reached.
- You can store this dip in the fridge up to three days.
- To make a tomato hummus: in point 3, add 4 sun-dried tomatoes, drained and chopped. Instead of the mint, add 6 basil leaves. Leave to set for 30 mins and mix before serving.

Pesto

I'll show you how to make your own delicious pesto in just 10 mins. Add it to wraps, salads, or meats, or simply serve as a side.

Prep: 10 mins
Serves 8
Nutrition per serving: 115 kcals, 3 g protein, 2 g carbs, 9 g fat

What you need:
- 1 oz (30 g) parmesan, roughly chopped
- 1 small garlic clove, crushed
- ½ cup (50 g) walnuts
- 10 g basil leaves
- 4 tbsp olive oil

What you need to do:
1. In a food processor, combine the parmesan, walnuts, and basil until a paste has formed.
2. Keep the processor running and add the olive oil. Mix until all is combined.
3. Serve as a side or an addition to any wraps or salads.

HPL Bonus Tip

To make a traditional pesto, instead of walnuts use 50 g pine nuts.

HPL Food Fact—Walnuts

Walnuts are unique amongst other nuts as they contain alpha-linolenic acid as well as linoleic acid, the two essential fatty acids that the body cannot make itself. These provide cardiovascular protection, aid brain function, and support positive mood.

Healthy Ketchup

Traditional ketchup is packed with sugar. Not the HPL version! This easy-to-prepare tomato sauce will be a great addition to homemade sweet potato fries.

Prep: 5 mins
Makes 15 servings
Nutrition per serving (2 tsp): 10 kcals, 0 g protein, 2 g carbs, 0 g fat

What you need:
- ½ cup (140 g) tomato paste
- 2 tbsp vinegar
- ½ tsp dry mustard powder
- ¼ tsp cinnamon
- 1 pinch ground cloves
- 1 pinch ground allspice
- 1 pinch cayenne pepper
- ½ tsp stevia (a natural sweetener)

What you need to do:
Combine all ingredients together and blend until smooth. Add a bit of water if necessary. It will make over ½ cup (150 ml) of ketchup.

HPL Food Fact—Tomatoes
Tomatoes contain a versatile carotenoid called lycopene, which fights free radicals before they can cause damage to our bodies.

Healthy Mayo

This homemade mayonnaise is packed with healthy fats and tastes incredible, too!

Prep: 10 mins
Makes 1 cup (250 ml)
Nutrition per tbsp: 123 kcals, 0 g protein, 0 g carbs, 12 g fat

What you need:
- 1 egg yolk
- 1 tsp Dijon mustard
- 1 cup (250 ml) mixed oils (see HLP Bonus Tip below)
- 1 tbsp white wine vinegar
- 1 tbsp lemon juice
- Salt

What you need to do:
1. Using an electric hand whisk, beat the egg yolk in a bowl, then add the mustard and beat together.
2. Gradually add about half the oil, very slowly at first, beating continuously for around 3–5 mins, until thickened.
3. Once you have added half the oil, beat in 1 tbsp of vinegar (this will loosen the mixture slightly and give it a paler color).
4. Continue to gradually add the remaining oil, beating continuously.
5. Season with a pinch of salt, and lemon juice. Store in the refrigerator for up to one week.

HPL Bonus Tip
You can use a mixture of different oils such as olive oil, coconut oil, avocado oil, or macadamia oil.

Thousand Island Dressing

This homemade dressing tastes a thousand times better than the store-bought version, and is much better for you, too!

Prep: 5 mins
Makes over ½ cup (150 ml)
Nutrition info per tbsp: 129 kcals, 0 g protein, 1 g carbs, 12 g fats

What you need:
- ½ cup (115 ml) homemade mayo (see earlier recipe)
- 2 tbsp homemade ketchup (see earlier recipe)
- 2 tbsp sweet pickle relish
- 2 tsp red onion, finely diced
- ¼ tsp crushed garlic
- 1 tsp white wine vinegar
- 2–3 dashes Tabasco (optional)
- Pinch of salt

What you need to do:
Put all ingredients in a small bowl and mix well. Store in the refrigerator for up to five days.

Smooth Bell Pepper and Tomato Sauce

A fresh and filling sauce that can be served as a dip, side, or addition to any meat.

Prep: 10 mins
Cooking: 6 mins
Serves 4
Nutrition per serving: 74 kcals, 3 g protein, 7 g carbs, 5 g fat

What you need:
- 1 onion, finely diced
- 2 red bell peppers, diced
- 2 garlic cloves, crushed
- 1 scant cup (200 ml) tomato juice
- Scant ½ cup (50 g) ground almonds
- 1 tsp coconut oil

What you need to do:
1. Heat the coconut oil in a pan. Add the onion and peppers, and cook for 5 mins.
2. Add the garlic and cook for another minute.
3. Transfer the sauce into a blender, add the tomato juice, and blend.
4. Add the ground almonds and blend again.
5. Transfer back to the pan and heat, but do not bring to the boil.
6. Season with salt and pepper, and serve as a dip or side with your meals.

HPL Bonus Tip
If you want this sauce to have a dip consistency then only use ¾ cup (175 ml) tomato juice.

22. FISH AND SEAFOOD

Eating fish and seafood is great for your heart, joints, and brain. In this chapter, you will find recipes I've created to capture the wonderful taste of fresh fish and seafood, while retaining all the health benefits they have to offer.

White Fish in Citrus Sauce with Braised Vegetables

This recipe is an excellent way to serve delicate white fish. Accompanied with aromatic vegetables and a unique orange sauce, serve this up for a taste sensation.

Prep: 15 mins
Cooking: 15 mins
Serves 2
Nutrition per serving: 253 kcals, 37 g protein, 16 g carbs, 4 g fat

What you need:
- 14 oz (400 g) fresh or frozen white fish (try cod or sea bass), cut into chunks
- 1 leek, sliced
- 1 zucchini (courgette), sliced
- 2 celery sticks, chopped
- 1 tsp coconut oil
- 1 garlic clove, sliced
- Juice and zest of 1 small orange
- Salt and pepper

What you need to do:
1. Heat ½ tsp coconut oil in a pan, add the zucchini, and fry for 4 mins.
2. Then add the leek, celery, and garlic and cook for another 3–4 mins. Once all vegetables are soft, set aside.
3. In the same pan, heat the rest of the coconut oil and place the fish with the orange zest into it. Fry it for 2 mins each side and then add the orange juice.
4. Turn the heat and braise until fish is cooked.
5. Plate the vegetables and fish, leaving the sauce in the pan for an extra 30 seconds. Season the sauce with salt and pepper, pour it over the fish, and serve.

HPL Bonus Tip
This dish goes perfectly with a side of jacket potato.

HPL Food Fact—Oranges
Oranges are one of the top sources of vitamin C, which is crucial for strong immunity, fighting viruses, and producing disease-fighting cells to tackle bacteria. A medium-sized orange provides around 50–70 mg of vitamin C. Eating oranges can also help to reduce post-exercise muscle soreness.

Fish in Oat Coating with Avocado Salsa

The oats create a coating that is rich in fiber, light, and crisp—a great alternative to the typical heavily battered version.

Prep: 10 mins
Cooking: 12 mins
Serves 2
Nutrition per serving: 345 kcals, 43 g protein, 16 g carbs, 12 g fat

What you need:
- 2 tbsp cartoned coconut milk, or any alternative
- 4 tbsp oats (gluten free or normal)
- 2 cod fillets, fresh
- 1 tsp coconut oil
- Salt and pepper
- Lemon wedges, to serve

For the salsa:
- 1 tomato, diced
- ½ avocado, diced
- ½ green bell pepper, diced
- 1 scallion (spring onion), chopped
- 1 small garlic clove, crushed
- Tabasco, to taste

What you need to do:
1. Mix all the salsa ingredients together and set aside.
2. Season the cod fillets with salt and pepper.
3. Pour the milk into a flat container and dip the fish into it.
4. Spread the oats in a separate dish and dip the fish into them, until they are covered on both sides.
5. Heat the coconut oil in a pan. Fry the fish for 3 mins each side until the batter is crispy and browned and fish is cooked.
6. Serve with a side of your salsa and lemon wedges.

Tomato and Thyme Cod

If it's one of those nights where you'd rather be on the sofa than in the kitchen, this is the recipe for you. Low in fat, healthy... and ready in 20 minutes.

Prep: 5 mins
Cooking: 15 mins
Serves 2
Nutrition per serving: 243 kcals, 34 g protein, 13 g carbs, 6 g fats

What you need:
- 12 oz (350 g) cod fillets, frozen or fresh
- 1½ cups (400 g can) chopped tomatoes
- 1 onion, chopped
- ¼ cup (30 g) black olives, sliced
- 1 tbsp soy sauce
- 1 tsp coconut oil
- Pinch of stevia (a natural sweetener)
- 2 tbsp basil leaves, chopped
- 1 tbsp thyme leaves
- Salt and pepper, to taste

What you need to do:
1. Preheat the oven to 350°F (180°C). Heat the coconut oil in the frying pan and add the onion; fry until lightly browned.
2. Stir in the tomatoes, olives, stevia, herbs, and soy sauce, season with salt and pepper, then bring to boil and simmer for 5 mins.
3. Place the cod fillets into an ovenproof dish and cover with the sauce.
4. Bake for 15 mins until fish is cooked. Serve with sides of choice.

HPL Food Fact—Tomatoes

Tomatoes are rich in beta-carotene, which aids the production of vitamin A. This helps maintain a healthy thymus gland, which is important within the immune system. The potassium in tomatoes helps regulate fluid balance in the body.

Herby Cod with Crispy Walnuts

Walnuts, herbs, and ground almonds create a very interesting and crispy coating, a perfect partner for delicate cod.

Prep: 10 mins
Cooking: 20 mins
Serves 2
Nutrition per serving: 316 kcals, 32 g protein, 3 g carbs, 19 g fat

What you need:
- 11 oz (300 g) fresh Atlantic cod fillets
- ¼ cup (30 g) walnuts, chopped
- 3 tbsp ground almonds
- 3 tbsp fresh parsley, chopped
- 1 tbsp chives, chopped
- 1 tsp coconut oil, melted
- Lemon wedges, to serve

What you need to do:
1. Heat the oven to 375°F (190°C) and prepare an ovenproof dish for the fish.
2. Mix together the walnuts, ground almonds, parsley, and chives. Add the melted coconut oil and rub it in the mixture.
3. Place the mixture on top of the fillets and press gently.
4. Bake in the oven for 20 mins, until the coating is browned and fish is cooked.
5. Serve with lemon wedges.

HPL Bonus Tips

To make this recipe even more interesting, place a few slices of tomato sprinkled with crushed garlic on top of each fillet before spreading the coating.

To create a more zesty-flavored coating, add the zest of 1 lemon and 1 chopped chili pepper to the mixture.

Fish and Chips" with Mushy Peas

Here is the British nation's favorite Friday-night supper, with a healthier and lighter twist, of course! See, nothing is off limits when you live the HPL way.

Prep: 5 mins
Cooking: 30–45 mins
Serves 2
Nutrition per serving: 514 kcals, 41 g protein, 48 g carbs, 19 g fat

What you need:
- 2 × 5 oz (150 g) haddock fillets
- 14 oz (400 g) sweet potatoes, chopped into fries
- 3 tbsp ground almonds
- 1 egg white
- 2 tsp coconut oil
- 1 tbsp butter, melted
- 1 cup (150 g) frozen peas
- Salt and pepper
- Lemon wedges, to serve (optional)

What you need to do:
1. Preheat the oven to 350°F (180°C).
2. Place the chopped sweet potatoes on a baking sheet and rub with 1 tsp coconut oil, season with salt and pepper, and place in the oven. Bake for 30–45 mins.
3. In the meantime, season the fish with salt and pepper.
4. Place the ground almonds and egg whites in two separate bowls.
5. Heat the remaining coconut oil in a pan. Dip the fish into the egg and then coat in the ground almonds, then fry the fish for 2–3 mins each side, until golden.
6. Next, place the fish in an ovenproof dish and cook in the oven (alongside the fries) for 10–15 mins.
7. Steam the frozen peas for 5 mins until soft, then put them in a bowl and add the butter. Mash until creamy.
8. Serve with lemon wedges.

Kedgeree with Corn and Broccoli

This old colonial dish is a great combination of British and Indian cultures, perfect for any time of the day.

Prep: 15 mins
Cooking: 25 mins
Serves 2
Nutrition per serving: 481 kcals, 30 g protein, 56 g carbs, 12 g fats

What you need:
- 10 oz (280 g) smoked haddock fillets, cut into ¾ inch (2 cm) chunks
- ½ cup (100 g) long-grain rice, uncooked
- 1 onion, chopped
- ½ tsp cumin seeds
- 1 tsp turmeric
- 2½ cups (600 ml) fish stock, hot
- ½ heaping cup (100 g) corn (sweet corn), drained
- 2 eggs, boiled
- 1 cup (100 g) broccoli florets
- Zest of ½ lemon
- 1 tbsp fresh parsley, chopped
- 1 tsp coconut oil

What you need to do:
1. In a big pan, heat the coconut oil and cook the onion for 2 mins until soft.
2. Lower the heat and add the rice, cumin, and turmeric, stirring everything well.
3. Pour in the stock and bring to the boil, then simmer for 5 mins.
4. Add the fish, stir, and cover the pan, leaving to simmer for 15 mins, until the stock is absorbed. In the meantime, boil the eggs.
5. Put the broccoli into a pot of boiling water, bring back to the boil and cook for 3 mins.
6. Peel the eggs and cut into quarters. Drain the broccoli and add on top of the rice along with the boiled eggs.
7. Sprinkle with lemon zest and parsley, and serve.

Tuna Steak with Bean Salad

This salad is an excellent source of heart-healthy omega-3 fatty acids. Light and simple, it's a good lunch choice.

Prep: 20 mins
Cooking: 1 min
Serves 2
Nutrition per serving: 268 kcals, 38 g protein, 14 g carbs, 7 g fat

What you need:
- 11 oz (300 g) fresh tuna steak
- ½ cup (120 g) lima (butter) beans, drained
- 1 small red onion, sliced
- 1 garlic clove, chopped
- Zest of ½ lemon
- 2 tbsp fresh parsley, chopped
- 8 basil leaves, chopped
- 2 tsp olive oil
- Lemon wedges, to serve

What you need to do:
1. Mix together the beans, garlic, lemon zest, basil, parsley, and olive oil. Set aside.
2. Cut the tuna into thin slices. Heat a nonstick pan to a very high heat, and add the tuna. Fry it for about 30 seconds each side.
3. Serve with the salad and lemon wedges.

HPL Food Fact—Tuna
Tuna is a perfect high-protein, low-fat choice. It's packed with omega-3 fatty acids, which are important when it comes to energy production and burning excess fat.

Avocado and Tuna Wraps

These lettuce wraps, or "creative sandwiches" as I call them, are a perfect lunch if you need something quick.

Prep: 10 mins
Cooking: 0 min
Serves 1
Nutrition per serving: 197 kcal, 29 g protein, 4 g carbs, 8 g fat

What you need:
- 5½ oz (160 g) canned tuna in brine, (4 oz (112 g) drained weight)
- 1 scallion (spring onion), finely chopped
- ½ avocado
- Juice of ½ a lime
- Salt and pepper
- Red chili, to taste
- 3–4 baby gem (baby cos or romaine) lettuce leaves

What you need to do:
1. In a bowl, mash up the avocado with a fork.
2. Then add the tuna, spring onions, lime juice, and chili.
3. Season with salt and pepper and combine.
4. Divide the tuna mix onto the lettuce leaves and serve.

HPL Bonus Tip
This dish is a healthy sandwich alternative, which means you could add in any traditional sandwich filling between the lettuce leaves.

Baby Spinach and Salmon Salad

This super-healthy and quick salad is packed with protein, vitamins, and minerals. It will keep you going for hours.

Prep: 10 mins
Cooking: 5 mins
Serves 2
Nutrition per serving: 364 kcal, 32 g protein, 4 g carbs, 23 g fat

What you need:
- 11 oz (300 g) fresh salmon fillets, cut into chunks
- 2½ tbsp (20 g) green olives, halved
- 1 scallion (spring onion), chopped
- 12–15 cherry tomatoes, halved
- 3 cups (100 g) baby spinach
- 1 tsp coconut oil
- 10 basil leaves
- Zest and juice of 1 lemon

What you need to do:
1. Divide the spinach leaves between two plates and place 5 basil leaves on top of each.
2. Heat the coconut oil in a pan and fry the salmon for 4 mins each side, turning occasionally.
3. Add the olives, scallions, and lemon zest and juice and heat for a few seconds.
4. Now throw in the cherry tomatoes and stir everything for about 30 seconds until the tomatoes are warm.
5. Plate the salmon and veg on top of the spinach, sprinkle with the juices from the pan, and serve.

HPL Food Fact—Spinach
This type of leafy green is a powerhouse of nutrients that protect the body from numerous diseases. It's loaded with an extensive list of vitamins and minerals, such as iron, vitamin C, B-vitamins, zinc, calcium, magnesium... and loads more. No wonder Popeye was so fit and strong!

Salmon Burgers

These great-tasting oriental-style salmon burgers are an easy and light option—perfect for a fishcake lover.

Prep: 20 mins
Cooking: 10 mins
Makes 4 burgers
Nutrition per burger: 115 kcals, 20 g protein, 1 g carbs, 3 g fat

What you need:
- 4 boneless, skinless salmon fillets, cut into chunks
- 2 tbsp Thai red curry paste
- ¾ inch (2 cm) fresh ginger, grated
- 1 tbsp soy sauce
- Handful cilantro (coriander leaf), chopped
- 1 tsp coconut oil
- 1 tbsp coconut flour
- Lemon wedges, to serve

What you need to do:
1. Put the salmon into a food processor (or blender) with the curry paste, ginger, soy sauce, and chopped cilantro, and blend together.
2. Shape 4 burgers and cover in a thin layer of coconut flour.
3. Heat the coconut oil in a pan and fry the burgers for 4–5 mins on each side, until cooked throughout.
4. Serve with lemon wedges.

Wasabi Salmon Skewers

Salmon and wasabi are a match made in heaven.

Prep: 10 mins + 10 mins marinating
Cooking: 15mins
Serves 2
Nutrition per serving: 384 kcals, 33 g protein, 7 g carbs, 23 g fat

What you need:
- 11 oz (300 g) salmon fillet, cut into chunks
- 2 scallions (spring onions), cut into small lengths
- 2 tbsp sesame seeds

For the marinade:
- 2 tbsp dark soy sauce
- 1 tsp wasabi paste
- 1 tsp honey

What you need to do:
1. Thread skewers with alternating pieces of salmon and scallion.
2. In a shallow dish, whisk together the marinade ingredients and place the skewers in it, marinating for at least 10 mins. Turn the skewers occasionally.
3. Meanwhile, preheat the oven to 390°F (200°C).
4. Cook in the oven for 15 mins, brushing the marinade over the salmon a few times and turning the skewers occasionally.
5. Sprinkle with sesame seeds and leave in the hot oven for an additional 1 min.
6. Serve with green salad, hot or cold.

HPL Bonus Tip
If you are using wooden skewers, you need to soak them in water for 10–15 mins prior to cooking, to prevent them from burning when in the oven.

Pomegranate-Glazed Salmon

The pomegranate juice turns this salmon into a very special dish.

Prep: 10 mins + 15 mins marinating
Cooking: 15–20 mins
Serves: 2
Nutrition per serving: 348 kcals, 31 g protein, 7 g carbs, 20 g fats

What you need:
- Scant ½ cup (100 ml) pomegranate juice
- 2 tbsp soy sauce
- 1 garlic clove, sliced
- 11 oz (300 g) fresh salmon fillets
- Seeds of ½ pomegranate

What you need to do:
1. Make the marinade by mixing the pomegranate juice, soy sauce, and garlic, and pour it into a shallow dish.
2. Add the salmon and turn a few times, leave to marinate for 15 minutes.
3. Heat the oven to 375°F (190°C) and prepare a baking sheet covered in foil. Place the salmon on the sheet.
4. Pour the marinade into a small pan and heat for 2–3 mins, until it thickens.
5. When the marinade is ready, pour it over the salmon and oven bake for 5 mins, then turn and sprinkle the fish with the marinade from the baking tray. Repeat two more times, baking it 15–20 mins in total, until salmon is cooked throughout.
6. Serve sprinkled with pomegranate seeds.

HPL Food Fact—Pomegranate
Pomegranate juice has three times as many antioxidants as the same amount of green tea, red wine, or orange juice.

Salmon Risotto

The delicate salmon makes a great base for this smooth and creamy risotto with added asparagus.

Prep: 10 mins
Cooking: 35 mins
Serves 2
Nutrition per serving: 508 kcals, 31 g protein, 50 g carbs, 20 g fat

What you need:
- 11 oz (300 g) fresh salmon fillets, cut into chunks
- ¾ cup (150 g) risotto rice, uncooked
- 8 spears asparagus, chopped into ¾ inch (2 cm) pieces*
- 1 medium onion, chopped
- 2 garlic cloves, crushed
- 2½ cups (600 ml) fish stock, hot
- 1 tsp coconut oil
- 1 oz (30 g) parmesan, grated
- 1 tbsp fresh parsley, chopped

*You can replace the asparagus with broccoli or peas, either works just as well.

What you need to do:
1. Heat the coconut oil in a pan and fry the onion until browned.
2. Add the garlic and uncooked rice, and stir well.
3. Pour in one third of the fish stock and stir.
4. When the rice has absorbed the stock, pour in another third and add the salmon. Repeat with the rest of the stock; this should take about 25 mins.
5. Now add the asparagus and cook for a further 5 mins or until the salmon and asparagus are cooked. The rice should have absorbed the stock and have a creamy texture.
6. At the end of cooking, add the parmesan and stir well.
7. Serve sprinkled with parsley on top.

HPL Food Fact—Salmon
This fish is an excellent source of omega-3 fatty acids in the form of EPA and DHA, which help to reduce post-exercise joint stiffness. DHA also plays an important role in keeping the brain and nervous system functioning optimally. Salmon is also a valuable source of B-vitamins and selenium.

Fish Pie

This fish pie is simple to prepare, which makes it a perfect recipe for those busy nights and an ideal midweek supper.

Prep: 10 mins
Cooking: 25 mins
Serves 4
Nutrition per serving: 370 kcals, 26 g protein, 50 g carbs, 7 g fat

What you need:
- 2¼ lb (1 kg) potatoes
- 12 oz (350 g) mixed seafood
- 1½ cups (400 g) chopped tomatoes
- 1 leek, chopped
- 1 clove garlic, crushed
- ¼ tsp dried oregano
- 1 oz (30 g) parmesan, grated
- 1 tsp coconut oil

What you need to do:
1. Peel the potatoes and cut them into smaller pieces. Boil in a pot until tender.
2. Heat the broiler (grill) to high. Heat the coconut oil in a pan and cook the leek and garlic for 2–3 mins, stirring occasionally, until soft.
3. Add the tomatoes and oregano and bring to the boil. Turn the heat down and cook for 2 mins.
4. Add the seafood and bring to the boil. Stir and cook for another 2 mins, then season with salt and pepper to taste and transfer into a baking dish.
5. Mash the potatoes and spread in an even layer on top of the seafood mix. Sprinkle with parmesan and broil for 12–15 mins, until browned.
6. Serve with a side salad.

Quick and Easy Prawn Stir Fry

This quick and healthy dish is so simple you won't believe how fast it all comes together. It makes a great a light lunch or acts as a more meaningful meal when served with egg noodles.

Prep: 10 mins
Cooking: 6 mins
Serves 2
Nutrition per serving: 204 kcals, 23 g protein, 17 g carbs, 6 g fat

What you need:
- 7 oz (200 g) jumbo shrimp (king prawns), cooked and peeled
- 1 cup (150 g) frozen peas
- 3 cups (200 g) white cabbage, shredded
- ½–¾ inch (1–2 cm) fresh ginger, peeled and grated
- 1 red chili, chopped*
- 2 tbsp cilantro (fresh coriander), chopped
- 1 tsp sesame oil
- 1 tsp coconut oil

*If you don't like your food too hot remove or deseed the chili.

What you need to do:
1. Heat both oils in a pan. Add the ginger and chili and cook for a few seconds.
2. Then add the cabbage and cook for a further 2 mins.
3. Now add the peas and cook for another 3 mins until they are heated through.
4. Lastly add the prawns and cook for 1 min.
5. Season with salt and pepper, add coriander, and serve with egg noodles or on its own.

HPL Food Fact—Chili
Even one small chili contains high levels of the antiviral, anticancer, and antioxidant carotenoid beta-carotene, some of which is converted by the body into vitamin A. Both these nutrients help to prevent damage caused by toxins in the body, stave off cancer, and delay premature ageing.

Shrimp Thai Curry Stew

Perfect Friday-night food, this warming low-fat shrimp curry is on your plate and ready to eat in just 25 minutes.

Prep: 15 mins
Cooking: 10 mins
Serves 2
Nutrition per serving: 429 kcals, 24 g protein, 35 g carbs, 24 g fat

What you need:

- 7 oz (200 g) cooked and peeled jumbo shrimps (king prawns)
- 1½ oz (45 g) rice noodles
- 2 cups (150 g) Chinese leaf cabbage, shredded
- 1 cup (100 g) bean sprouts
- 1 onion, chopped
- Around 1 inch (2–3 cm) ginger, peeled and grated
- 1 red chili, chopped
- 1 garlic clove, crushed
- ½ tsp turmeric
- 6 leaves fresh mint, chopped
- 2 tbsp Thai green curry paste
- 1 tsp coconut oil
- 1¾ cups (400 ml) fish stock, hot
- 1 scant cup (200 ml) canned coconut milk, light
- ½ cup (50 g) cucumber, cut into strips, to serve
- 1 scallion (spring onion), to serve

What you need to do:

1. Heat the coconut oil in a pan. Add the garlic, onion, and chili and cook for about 2 mins.
2. Next add the ginger, turmeric, fish stock, coconut milk, and curry paste, stir and bring to the boil. Simmer for 5 mins.
3. Then add the noodles, cabbage, and bean sprouts and cook for another minute before adding the shrimp.
4. Cook until shrimps are heated through, but do not bring back to the boil.
5. Serve in bowls with sprinkled cucumber and scallion on top.

Sushi

Always wanted to make sushi at home? It doesn't have to be complicated: this is the simplest recipe you will ever find.

Prep: 10 mins
Cooking: 20 mins
Serves 2
Nutrition per serving: 149 kcals, 3 g protein, 23 g carbs, 5 g fat

What you need:
- ¼ cup (50 g) sushi rice, uncooked
- 6 or 7 spears (100 g) asparagus
- 2 sushi nori sheets
- 1 tbsp rice vinegar
- ¼ tsp salt
- 1 tsp sugar
- 1 tsp coconut oil
- 2 oz (50 g) shiitake mushrooms, sliced
- 1 tbsp sake or dry sherry
- 1 tsp soy sauce

What you need to do:
1. Cook the sushi rice according to the instructions on the packaging.
2. Cut the seaweed sheets into small strips and set aside.
3. Mix together the vinegar, salt, and sugar and pour into the cooked rice, stir and set aside.
4. Heat the coconut oil in a pan and fry the asparagus until soft (about 3 mins), set aside.
5. In the same pan, fry the mushrooms for 2 mins. Then pour in the sake and soy sauce, and stir well. Sprinkle the seaweed over the mushrooms.
6. Plate the rice, forming it into a rectangular shape and put the asparagus on top.
7. Place the mushrooms on the side and serve with a portion of your favorite meat.

HPL Food Fact—Nori
Seaweed and sea vegetables are rich in fiber, which helps the digestive system function optimally. They are also a source of protein, iron, vitamin B12, potassium, and iodine, which help fight anemia and regulate blood pressure. Nori is also packed with powerful antioxidants called carotenoids.

23. POULTRY

Chicken and turkey are protein packed and very low in fat. This is probably why poultry is the second most widely eaten type of meat in the world. It is very simple to cook and tastes great combined with various herbs and vegetables—broiled (grilled), fried, or stir-fried. Find your favorite recipe from this fantastic bunch...

Chicken, Lima Bean, and Walnut Salad

This quick, light, and easy salad is a treat for your taste buds.

Prep: 10 mins
Cooking: 20 mins
Serves 2
Nutrition per serving: 300 kcals, 27 g protein, 17 g carbs, 15 g fat

What you need:
- 7 oz (200 g) chicken breast (about 1 large breast), diced
- 1½ cups (150 g) snap (green) beans
- 2 oz (50 g) can lima (butter) beans (about ¼ cup), rinsed and drained
- ½ red onion, thinly sliced
- ¼ cup (30 g) walnuts, chopped
- 1 clove garlic, crushed
- ½ tsp coconut oil
- ½ tbsp rosemary leaves
- ½ tbsp lemon thyme leaves

For the dressing:
- 1 tsp olive oil
- Juice of ½ lemon
- 2 tsp wholegrain mustard
- 1 tsp honey
- 1 small garlic clove, crushed

What you need to do:
1. Place the chicken, rosemary, lemon thyme, and garlic in a bowl and mix together.
2. Heat the coconut oil in a large nonstick pan and fry the chicken for 5 mins until cooked throughout.
3. In the meantime, bring a large pan of water to the boil, add the snap beans, and cook for 5–7 mins.
4. Then add the lima beans and cook for a further 2–3 mins until the snap beans are tender.
5. Make the dressing by mixing together the olive oil, lemon juice, mustard, honey, and crushed garlic.
6. Mix together the warm chicken, beans, red onion, and walnuts.
7. Pour over the dressing. Serve warm or cold.

HPL Food Fact—Chicken

Chicken contains magnesium, which reduces the risk of cramps, and potassium, which helps balance the fluid levels in the body. It is also rich in selenium, to prevent wrinkles and keep hair glossy.

Stuffed Chicken Breast with Parma Ham, Pesto, and Sun-Dried Tomato

This easy yet so tasty recipe is my all-time favorite. Served with some rice and a side salad, it makes a great dinner or lunch.

Prep: 8 mins
Cooking: 30 mins
Serves: 4
Nutrition per serving: 317 kcals, 49 g protein, 5 g carbs, 10 g fat

What you need:
- 4 × 7 oz (200 g) chicken breasts, slit
- 2 oz (50 g) homemade pesto (or store bought)
- 8 sun-dried tomatoes, drained
- 8 green olives, sliced
- 4 slices Parma ham

What you need to do:
1. Preheat the oven to 390°F (200°C).
2. Spread chicken breast onto a board and with a knife make a small slit in each to create a "pocket."
3. Stuff each chicken breast with pesto, sun-dried tomatoes, and green olives.
4. Wrap each breast in a slice of Parma ham and place on a baking sheet.
5. Bake the chicken breasts for about 30 mins, until cooked and browned.
6. Serve hot with side salad and rice, or store in the fridge for later.

HPL Bonus Tip

You can do exactly the same with fish instead of chicken. Just spread some pesto over a fillet of cod or halibut, top it with olives and sun-dried tomatoes, then wrap in Parma ham. Reduce cooking time to 20–25 mins for white fish.

Light Chicken, Bacon, and Avocado Salad

This fresh and light salad is high in protein and full of healthy fats. It will keep you full for longer than a regular salad, without feeling as heavy as a traditional lunch dish.

Prep: 10 mins
Cooking: 5 mins
Serves 2
Nutrition per serving: 428 kcals, 39 g protein, 11 g carbs, 19 g fat

What you need:
- 11 oz (300 g) skinless chicken breast, cut into strips
- 4 smoked Canadian (back) bacon rashers
- ½ fresh avocado, sliced
- 4½ cups (150 g) baby spinach
- 5 cups (100 g) arugula (rocket)
- 2 tbsp (10 g) parmesan, grated
- Salt and pepper
- ¼ tsp coconut oil

For the dressing:
- 1 tbsp olive oil
- 1 tbsp cider vinegar
- 1 tbsp lemon juice
- 1 heaped tsp wholegrain mustard
- 1 small clove garlic, crushed
- Salt and pepper

What you need to do:
1. Light the broiler (grill) and place the bacon under it to cook.
2. In the meantime, heat the coconut oil in a pan and fry the chicken until brown. Season with salt and pepper.
3. Divide the salad leaves onto two plates and place the avocado on top of the leaves.
4. When the bacon is crispy, cut into pieces and divide between the two plates. Do the same with the chicken. Then top with the parmesan.
5. To make the dressing, mix all the ingredients together, and drizzle on top.

HPL Food Fact—Avocado
Avocados are one of the few fruits that contain fat. They provide healthy monounsaturated fat, which raises levels of "good" cholesterol while slightly lowering fatty triglycerides.

Marinades for Chicken Drumsticks

The marinades below are perfect for chicken thighs or drumsticks, but can also be used with other meats and fish.

Balsamic Barbecue

Prep: 5 mins
Cooking: 25 mins
Makes 8 drumsticks
Nutrition per drumstick (skin removed):
96 kcals, 10 g protein, 3 g carbs, 4 g fats

What you need:
- 8 chicken drumsticks
- 6 tbsp balsamic vinegar
- 1 tsp Dijon mustard
- ½ tbsp honey
- ½ tsp salt
- 1 tsp ground black pepper

What you need to do:
1. Heat the oven to 350°F (180°C).
2. In a bowl, mix all the ingredients together.
3. Coat the drumsticks, and place in a baking dish.
4. Oven bake (or grill on a BBQ) for about 25 mins, turning a few times.

Sweet and Sour

Prep: 5 mins
Cooking: 25 mins
Makes 8 drumsticks
Nutrition per drumstick (skin removed):
159 kcals, 11 g protein, 14 g carbs, 8 g fats

What you need:
- 8 chicken drumsticks
- 4 tbsp honey
- 2 tbsp sesame oil
- 6 tbsp soy sauce
- 4 tbsp lemon juice
- 4 tsp wholegrain mustard

What you need to do:
1. Heat the oven to 350°F (180°C).
2. In a bowl, mix all the ingredients together.
3. Coat the drumsticks, and place in a baking dish.
4. Oven bake (or grill on a BBQ) for about 25 mins, turning a few times.

HPL Bonus Tip
It is best to marinate the meat and chill it in the fridge for 1–2 hours before cooking. This way the meat will absorb the marinade and taste even better.

Herby Chicken Breast with Homemade Cranberry Coleslaw

The cranberries in this recipe have an intense taste, the perfect partner for the creamy coleslaw and herby chicken.
Ideal as a lunch option, or a dinner served alongside roasted potatoes.

Prep: 15 mins
Cooking: 12 mins
Serves 2
Nutrition per serving: 371 kcals, 46 g protein, 21 g carbs, 12 g fat

What you need:
- 2 chicken breasts (7 oz/200 g each), skinless and boneless
- 4 sprigs thyme, leaves picked
- 3 sage leaves, chopped
- 2 tsps coconut oil
- 2 cups (150 g) white cabbage, shredded
- 1 small carrot, grated
- ½ onion, sliced thinly
- 1 tbsp mayonnaise
- 1 tbsp 0% fat yogurt
- 3 tbsp (25 g) dried cranberries

What you need to do:
1. Melt 1 tsp coconut oil in a bowl (microwave for 10–20 sec) and mix it with the herbs.
2. Place the chicken in the bowl and rub the herbs in, then set aside.
3. Place the shredded cabbage, grated carrot, and thinly sliced onion in another bowl, add the mayo, and season with salt and pepper. Add the cranberries and mix well.
4. Heat 1 tsp coconut oil in a pan and fry the chicken for about 12 mins, until cooked throughout and browned on each side.
5. Serve hot or cold with a side of coleslaw.

HPL Food Fact—Cranberries
Dried cranberries actually have a lot more nutritional value than the fresh berries. These tart, tangy berries are high in the antioxidant vitamin C, making them great immunity boosters.

Chicken in a Spicy Tarragon and Apricot Sauce

This is an ambitious choice of flavors, combining the tastes of apricots, pine nuts, oranges, and tarragon. It would be the ideal recipe for an HPL dinner party! Goes perfectly with green snap beans and baby potatoes.

Prep: 5 mins
Cooking: 25 mins
Serves 2
Nutrition per serving: 277 kcals, 46 g protein, 15 g carbs, 4 g fat

What you need:
- 2 chicken breasts (7 oz/200 g each)
- 2 tbsp Dijon mustard
- 1 oz (25 g) dried apricots, chopped
- 1 tbsp dried tarragon
- Juice of 1 orange
- 2 tbsp pine nuts

What you need to do:
1. Heat the broiler (grill) up to the highest temperature. Cover the chicken breasts in mustard and place in an ovenproof dish. Broil for 10 mins.
2. In the meantime, chop the apricots.
3. Turn the chicken over and broil for another 5 mins, or until cooked.
4. Next pour in the orange juice and sprinkle with tarragon and apricots. Broil for another 5 mins.
5. Finally, sprinkle with pine nuts and leave under the broiler for 1 min to warm them up.
6. Serve with the apricots, nuts, and sauce.

HPL Food Fact—Pine Nuts
Pine nuts are actually the small seeds of the pine tree. Pine nuts are nature's only source of pinolenic acid, which stimulates the secretion of a hormone in the gut that sends signals to tell the brain that you are full.

Coconut Chicken

This is a very simple and effective combination of delicate coconut and the distinctive taste of black olives, which are just perfect together.

Prep: 5 mins
Cooking: 25 mins
Serves 2
Nutrition per serving: 418 kcals, 47 g protein, 16 g carbs, 20 g fat

What you need:
- 14 oz (400 g) chicken breast, diced
- ½ cup (50 g) desiccated coconut
- 3 medium tomatoes, cut into wedges
- 10 black olives, cut into halves
- Salt and pepper, to taste

What you need to do:
1. Heat oven to 350°F (180°C) and dice the chicken.
2. Mix all ingredients together and place in a baking dish.
3. Oven bake for 25–30 mins or until chicken is cooked throughout and browned.
4. Serve hot or cold, either with rice or on its own.

Oriental Chicken and Cashew Stir-Fry

The cashews in this recipe are sweet and crunchy and contain a lot of fiber, antioxidants, vitamins, and minerals. A great addition to this chicken- and vegetable-based meal.

Prep: 20 mins
Cooking: 10 mins
Serves 2
Nutrition per serving: 310 kcals, 41 g protein, 17 g carbs, 12 g fat

What you need:
- 11 oz (300 g) chicken breast, diced
- 11 oz (300 g) vegetable stir-fry, fresh or frozen
- 2 oz (50 g) shiitake mushrooms, chopped
- 3 tbsp (25 g) cashews
- 1 garlic clove, crushed
- 1 tsp sesame oil
- 1 tsp coconut oil
- 1 tbsp coconut flour
- 2 tbsp soy sauce

What you need to do:
1. In a small bowl, combine the coconut flour with 1 tbsp of cold water until you have a smooth paste. Add the soy sauce and sesame oil and mix well.
2. In a pan, toast the cashews until browned and then set aside (do not use any fat).
3. In the same pan, heat the coconut oil and cook the chicken until browned.
4. Add the vegetables and cook 2–3 mins until soft and heated through.
5. Add the cashews and mushrooms and cook for a further 2 mins.
6. Then add 100 ml boiling water and the earlier-prepared paste.
7. Mix all the ingredients well and cook 2–3 mins, until the sauce thickens.
8. Season with salt and pepper to taste.
9. Serve hot with rice or noodles.

HPL Food Fact—Cashews
These nuts are rich in omega-6 essential fatty acids, which protect against heart disease by helping to keep cholesterol levels down. They are also a source of B-vitamins, which aid the maintenance of nerves and muscle tissue, and boost resistance to stress.

Spanish Chicken Pot

Because this one-pot dish uses only whole foods, it's packed full of Mediterranean flavors.

Prep: 15 mins
Cooking: 23 mins
Serves 2
Nutrition per serving: 524 kcals, 51 g protein, 64 g carbs, 7 g fat

What you need:
- 14 oz (400 g) chicken breast, cut into long strips
- 1 medium onion, diced
- 2 bell peppers (red and green), cut into squares
- 1 garlic clove, crushed
- 1¼ cups (300 ml) chicken stock, hot
- ¾ cup (200 g) chopped tomatoes
- ⅔ cup (125 g) uncooked long grain rice
- 10 black olives, halved
- 1 tsp coconut oil
- 1 tbsp parsley, chopped

What you need to do:
1. Heat half the coconut oil in a pan and cook the chicken until browned, then set aside.
2. In the same pan, heat the remaining coconut oil and cook the onion, peppers, and garlic for 5 mins, until softened.
3. Then put the chicken back in the pan and add the rice.
4. Add the stock and chopped tomatoes and bring to the boil. Stir well, cover and simmer for 15 mins, until the rice is cooked.
5. Take the pan off the stove and add the olives.
6. Season with salt and pepper to taste.
7. Sprinkle with parsley and serve.

Kung Pao Chicken

This is an easy re-creation of the popular Chinese dish typically served in restaurants. It is perfect for a weekend night in: you get all the flavor without derailing your diet!

Prep: 12 mins
Cooking: 20 mins
Serves 2
Nutrition per serving (without rice): 440 kcal, 56 g protein, 19 g carbs, 18 g fat

What you need:
- 2 chicken breasts, diced
- 1 garlic clove, crushed
- 2½ tbsp (25 g) peanuts, roasted
- 1 red onion, cut into wedges
- 1 green bell pepper, sliced
- 1 chili pepper, chopped
- Small can chestnuts, halved
- ¾ cup (200 ml) chicken stock
- 1 tbsp soy sauce
- 2 tbsp (30 g) peanut butter
- 1 tsp coconut oil
- Salt and pepper

What you need to do:
1. Heat ½ tsp coconut oil in a large pan and roast the peanuts, then set aside.
2. Make the sauce by mixing the peanut butter, soy sauce, garlic, and chicken stock together and set aside.
3. In the same pan, use the rest of the coconut oil and cook the chicken until browned and set aside.
4. Now cook the onions, peppers, and chestnuts until soft.
5. Add the chicken back to the pan and add the chili, pour in the peanut butter sauce, and stir so everything is covered in the sauce. Cook for a few minutes.
6. At the end of cooking, stir in the roasted peanuts and serve with rice.

Chicken Risotto

This might just sound like plain old chicken, rice, and peas, but believe me when I say it's far more than the sum of its parts!

Prep: 20 mins + 5 mins
Cooking: 30 mins
Serves: 2
Nutrition per serving: 444 kcals, 37 g protein, 61 g carbs, 5 g fat

What you need:
- 1 onion, chopped
- 11 oz (300 g) chicken breast, diced
- 1½ cups (200 g) frozen peas
- 1 tsp coconut oil
- ⅔ cup (125 g) uncooked risotto rice
- 2 cups (450 ml) chicken stock, hot
- Salt and pepper
- Parmesan, to serve (optional)

What you need to do:
1. Heat the coconut oil in a large pan. Fry the onion until browned and then add the chicken and cook for about 5 mins.
2. Put in the rice and mix well so that it is all covered in oil.
3. Pour in 1¼ cups (300 ml) of the stock and stir. Cover and cook on a low heat for 10 mins.
4. Add the remaining stock and bring to the boil. Cover and cook on la ow heat for another 10 mins.
5. Add the frozen peas and stir well. Cook for another 2–3 mins or until peas are cooked.
6. Season with salt and pepper and take off the heat.
7. Cover the pan and leave for an additional 5 mins. All the stock should be absorbed, leaving the rice thick and creamy.
8. Serve topped with grated parmesan and freshly ground pepper.

HPL Food Fact—Peas
Peas are rich in soluble fiber, which means they will stay in the stomach for longer, giving a more gradual rise and fall of blood sugar levels and thus helping keep energy levels steady.

Simple Turkey Burgers

Turkey burgers are here to save the day! You might be able to tell... I love burgers. And with the HPL way of cooking, there's never any reason to avoid them!

Prep: 10 mins
Cooking: 20 mins
Makes: 8 burgers
Nutrition per burger: 90 kcals, 15 g protein, 3 g carbs, 2 g fat

What you need:
- 1 lb (500 g) ground (minced) turkey
- 1 egg
- 1 red onion, chopped
- 1 green bell pepper, chopped
- 3 cups (100 g) fresh baby spinach, chopped
- 2 tbsp tomato paste
- 1 tbsp fresh parsley, chopped
- 1 tsp coconut oil
- Salt and pepper

What you need to do:
1. In a large bowl, mix together the turkey, onion, pepper, spinach, parsley, egg, and tomato paste.
2. Season with salt and pepper and shape into 8 burgers.
3. Heat the coconut oil in a large pan and fry the burgers for about 6–8 mins on each side until cooked throughout and browned each side, turning them frequently.
4. Serve immediately or cool and store in the fridge until required. Serve with a side salad of own choice.

HPL Bonus Tip

You can add almost any type of veggies into your burgers. Try mushrooms, carrots, zucchini (courgettes)—keep it interesting.

Burgers are great if you are preparing yourself for the week ahead, and they can be eaten for practically any meal. Perfect for on the go when travelling too.

Broiled Turkey and Sweet Peppers

A high-protein hit packed with flavor and ready in minutes.

Prep: 10 mins
Cooking: 15 mins
Serves 2
Nutrition per serving: 243 kcals, 40 g protein, 12 g carbs, 5 g fat

What you need:
- 2 turkey breast fillets (4½ oz/125 g each)
- 1 red bell pepper, sliced
- 1 tbsp honey
- 1 tbsp cider vinegar
- 2 slices cooked ham
- 2 sage leaves
- 1 oz (25 g) cheddar cheese (or dairy-free alternative), grated

What you need to do:
1. Heat the broiler (grill) to a very high temperature. Place the fillets on a baking sheet and broil for 6 mins.
2. Turn the fillets and place the slices of pepper on top. Broil for a further 6 mins, until the turkey is cooked.
3. Mix the honey and vinegar. Drizzle it onto the fillets and top them with a slice of ham, a sage leaf and half the cheese.
4. Broil for another 3–6 mins, until cheese has melted and browned.
5. Serve with the juice made whilst cooking, and a side salad.

HPL Food Fact—Turkey

Turkey is rich in immunity-fortifying zinc and contains significant amounts of selenium. This mineral helps repair cell DNA and may lower the risk of cancer. Studies have shown that turkey contains one of the highest concentrations of muscle-building dipeptides.

Lemon and Thyme Turkey Burgers

These healthy burgers are chock-full of taste and very low in fat. Turkey burgers are great for lunches or dinners. Serve hot or cold, with a side salad.

Prep: 15 mins
Cooking: 30 mins
Makes 4 burgers
Nutrition per burger: 282 kcal, 49 g protein, 3 g carbs, 6 g fat

What you need:
- 1 lb (500 g) ground (minced) lean turkey breast
- 1 onion, finely chopped
- Zest of 1 lemon
- 1 tsp dried thyme or 2 tsp fresh
- 2 tbsp fresh parsley, chopped
- 4 smoked Canadian bacon rashers
- 1 tsp coconut oil
- Salt and pepper, to taste

What you need to do:
1. Heat the oven to 390°F (200°C).
2. Melt the coconut oil in a pan and fry the onion until golden brown.
3. Mix the turkey, lemon zest, thyme, parsley, onion, and seasoning until all is well combined.
4. Shape into 4 burgers and wrap a rash of bacon around each.
5. Place on a baking sheet and bake for 25–30 mins.
6. When cooked through, use the pan in which you fried the onion to fry the burgers on each side (to crisp up the bacon).
7. Serve straight away or store in the fridge for later.

HPL Food Fact—Lemon
Often overlooked as merely a flavoring, lemons are a powerhouse of antioxidant vitamin C, which is an immune booster but also assists in healing of wounds and strengthening the walls of blood capillaries.

Turkey Chili

This lighter version of chili is made with ground lean turkey, which is low in fat and high in protein.

Prep: 10 mins
Cooking: 30 mins
Serves 4
Nutrition per serving: 300 kcals, 37 g protein, 29 g carbs, 4 g fat

What you need:
- 1 lb (500 g) ground (minced) lean turkey
- 1 onion, diced
- 1 red bell pepper, cut in squares
- 2 medium carrots, chopped into squares
- 1⅓ cups (100 g) mushrooms, chopped
- 2 garlic cloves, crushed
- 1½ cups (400 g) chopped tomatoes
- 1 cup (240 g) red kidney beans, drained
- 1½ cups (200 g) frozen peas
- 2 tsp cumin seeds
- 2 tsp smoked paprika
- 1 tsp coconut oil
- Chili, to taste

What you need to do:
1. Heat the coconut oil in a pan and cook the turkey, cumin seeds, and chili on a medium heat for 5 mins, stirring occasionally, until meat is browned. Turn the heat up toward the end of cooking.
2. Add the onion, peppers, garlic, carrots, and mushrooms and cook together with the turkey for another 5 mins.
3. Add the chopped tomatoes and scant ½ cup (100 ml) water, as well as the smoked paprika and chili, and stir well. Cook for 15 mins on a low heat, stirring occasionally.
4. Add the peas and cook for another couple of minutes until peas are cooked.
5. Serve on its own or with rice.

HPL Bonus Tip
This dish goes well with a side of rice or spooned onto a jacket potato. Don't forget your greens: serve with a side salad.

Turkey Cottage Pie

This cottage pie alternative shows you that low-fat meals don't have to be boring. This dish is full of the sort of goodness a high-performance body needs.

Prep: 15 mins
Cooking: 30 mins
Serves: 4
Nutrition per serving: 425 kcals, 35 g protein, 54 g carbs, 9 g fat

What you need:
- 1 lb (500 g) ground (minced) turkey breast
- 2¼ lb (1 kg) white potatoes, chopped
- 2 tbsp (25 g) butter
- 1 onion, chopped
- 1 garlic clove, crushed
- 2 carrots, peeled and finely chopped
- 2 celery sticks, chopped
- 1 tbsp Worcester sauce
- 1½ cups (400 g) chopped tomatoes
- ⅔ cup (100 g) bell peppers, chopped
- 1 tbsp tomato paste
- Cayenne pepper, to taste
- 1 tsp fresh thyme leaves, chopped
- 1 tsp coconut oil
- Salt and pepper

What you need to do:
1. Cook the potatoes in a large pan of salted water until tender. Drain well. Season with salt and pepper and add butter, mash, and set aside.
2. In the meantime, heat the oven to 390°F (200°C).
3. Heat half the coconut oil in a pan and cook the onion, peppers, carrots, and celery for a few minutes until browned, and set aside.
4. In the same pan, heat the remaining coconut oil and cook the turkey until browned.
5. Add back the vegetables, plus the chopped tomatoes, tomato paste, garlic, and Worcester sauce. Stir well, bring to the boil, and season with the herbs and spices.
6. Transfer the turkey into a large ovenproof dish, top with the mash and cook for 30 mins or until golden.
7. Serve with a side green salad.

24. MEATS

It's time to say goodbye to bland chicken salad and hello to a world of variety: one full of delicious-flavored meats. All of the meats you'll see featured are high in protein, containing all of the essential amino acids, and in most cases are a good source of zinc, vitamin B, and iron.

Stuffed Tomatoes

These juicy tomatoes stuffed with lamb, dill, and rice are packed with flavor and offer a very distinctive taste. They are perfect as a small meal or starter, or double them up if you're extra hungry.

Prep: 20 mins
Cooking: 35 mins
Serves 4
Nutrition per tomato: 297 kcals, 25 g protein, 11 g carbs, 19 g fat

What you need:
- 4 beefsteak (beef) tomatoes
- Pinch of sugar/stevia
- ½ tsp coconut oil
- 1 red onion, finely chopped
- 2 garlic cloves, finely chopped
- 14 oz (400 g) ground (minced) lamb
- 1½ tsp ground cinnamon
- 3 tbsp tomato paste
- 4 tbsp chopped dill
- 2 tbsp chopped flat-leaf parsley
- 1 tbsp chopped mint

What you need to do:
1. Heat oven to 350°F (180°C).
2. Slice the tops off the tomatoes and scoop out most of the pulp with a teaspoon, being careful not to break the skin. Finely chop the pulp.
3. Sprinkle the insides of the tomatoes with a little sugar or stevia, then place them on a baking sheet.
4. Heat the coconut oil in a large pan, add the onion and garlic, and cook for about 10 mins until soft.
5. Add the lamb, cinnamon, and tomato paste, and fry until the meat is browned.
6. Add half of the tomato pulp and season with salt and pepper. Bring to the boil, then simmer for 15 mins. Set aside to cool a little, then stir in the fresh herbs.
7. Stuff the tomatoes up to the brim, top them with their lids and place in an ovenproof dish. Sprinkle 3 tbsp water into the dish and bake for 35 mins.
8. Serve with a side salad, hot or cold.

Indian Lamb with Apricots

This korma-style curry is quick and easy to make but retains all the unique tastes and textures of the traditional Indian dish.

Prep: 15 mins
Cooking: 12 mins
Serves 2
Nutrition per serving: 339 kcals, 36 g protein, 14 g carbs, 16 g fats

What you need:
- 9 oz (250 g) lean lamb medallions, diced*
- 6 or 7 (about 2 oz/50 g) dried apricots, chopped
- 1 tbsp curry powder
- 1 onion, chopped
- 3 tbsp (15 g) almond flakes
- 1 garlic clove, crushed
- 2½ tbsp (20 g) ground almonds
- 1 tbsp cilantro (fresh coriander), chopped
- 1 tsp coconut oil
- Scant ½ cup (100 ml) natural yogurt, to serve (or a non-dairy alternative)
- Salt and pepper

*When making this dish you could also use chicken or beef.

What you need to do:
1. Toast the almond flakes in a dry pan, stirring often, until browned, then set aside.
2. Now heat the coconut oil and fry the lamb for 4 mins, until browned.
3. Add the onion and garlic and cook for a further 2 mins.
4. Lower the heat and add the apricots, ground almonds, and curry. Cook for another 2–3 mins.
5. Gently pour in the yogurt and cook for 1–2 mins, stirring, until the sauce thickens.
6. Season with salt and pepper, sprinkle with the almond flakes and cilantro, and plate. Rice would be a perfect addition to this dish.

HPL Food Fact—Apricots
Dried apricots are packed with potassium, helping regulate blood pressure. They are also rich in soluble fiber, which steadies blood sugar levels and helps with constipation.

Punjabi Lamb with Peas

Another great-tasting Indian dish that is perfect for a quiet weekend night in.

Prep: 10 mins
Cooking: 30 mins
Serves 2
Nutrition per serving: 415 kcals, 31 g protein, 15 g carbs, 24 g fat

What you need:
- 1 onion, chopped
- 5 tbsp (30 g) ginger, grated
- 1 chili, chopped
- 1 garlic clove, grated
- 9 oz (250 g) ground (minced) lamb
- 1 tsp turmeric
- ¾ cup (200 g) chopped tomatoes
- 1 heaping cup (150 g) frozen peas
- Scant ½ cup (100 ml) yogurt
- 1 tbsp cilantro (coriander leaf), chopped
- ½ tsp coconut oil

What you need to do:
1. Blend together the onion, ginger, chili, and garlic, until a paste has formed (use a food processor or hand blender).
2. Heat the coconut oil in a large pan and add the paste. Cook it on a medium heat for 2–3 mins.
3. Add the ground lamb and turmeric. Cook for a further 5 mins until browned.
4. Now add the chopped tomatoes, bring to the boil, and simmer for 10 mins.
5. In a small bowl, mix the yogurt with the cilantro and set aside.
6. Add the frozen peas to the pan and cook for another 5 mins.
7. Season with salt and pepper.
8. Serve with a side of earlier-prepared yogurt and white rice.

HPL Food Fact—Lamb

Lamb is rich in protein, as well as a great source of two vital minerals: iron and zinc. Iron helps boost the oxygen-carrying capability of blood, preventing fatigue, and zinc is needed for optimum functioning of the immune system.

Mustard Steak with Roasted Bell Peppers

This quick recipe will transform your steaks forever!

Prep: 15 mins
Cooking: 10 mins
Serves 2
Nutrition per serving: 430 kcals, 63 g protein, 18 g carbs, 11 g fat

What you need:
- 2 beef steaks (7 oz/200 g each)*
- 2 tbsp wholegrain mustard
- 1 tbsp tomato paste
- Pinch cayenne pepper, to taste†
- 3 tbsp (15 g) oats (normal or gluten-free)
- ½ red bell pepper, sliced into wedges
- ½ yellow bell pepper, sliced into wedges
- 1 onion, sliced into wedges
- 1 tsp coconut oil

*If you prefer white meat, you can also prepare this dish with chicken or turkey steaks.

†If you like your food spicy, add 1 crushed garlic clove and a pinch of chili to the tomato sauce—this will make it more fiery.

What you need to do:
1. Mix the tomato paste, mustard, and cayenne pepper together in a bowl.
2. Cover one side of the steak in the mixture and sprinkle with oats; do the same for the other side.
3. Heat the coconut oil in a large nonstick pan. Place the steaks in the middle of the pan and the vegetables around them.
4. Fry the steak 3 mins each side until the oats are browned and crispy.
5. Stir the vegetables from time to time and cook the meat until it's as well done as you like.
6. Serve hot with vegetables on the side.

HPL Food Fact—Red Bell Peppers
Bell peppers give a powerful nutritional punch, as they are rich in vitamins A, B3, B6, C, E, and K as well as minerals such as zinc, potassium, calcium, and magnesium.

Bolognese Sauce

These simple ingredients come together to create a tasty dish that the whole family can enjoy…

Prep: 10 mins
Cooking: 25 mins
Serves 4
Nutrition per serving: 282 kcals, 36 g protein, 10 g carbs, 10 g fat

What you need:
- 1 lb (500 g) ground (minced) lean beef
- 1 onion, chopped
- 2 celery sticks, chopped
- 1 carrot, chopped
- 1 garlic clove, crushed
- 1½ cups (400 g) chopped tomatoes
- 1 scant cup (200 ml) beef stock, hot
- 1 tsp dried mixed herbs
- 1 tsp coconut oil
- Pinch of stevia
- Salt and pepper

What you need to do:
1. Heat ½ tsp coconut oil in a large pan and add the onion, carrot, and celery. Cook for 5 mins, until the onion is soft, and set aside.
2. To the same pan, add the beef and cook for 2–3 mins, until browned.
3. Return the vegetables to the pan, along with the garlic and herbs.
4. Pour in the chopped tomatoes and beef stock, bring to the boil, and simmer for 10 mins.
5. Season with stevia and salt and pepper to taste.
6. Serve with spaghetti.

HPL Food Fact—Celery
This vegetable is packed with vitamin K, which helps blood clotting and building strong bones, has vitamin A, which helps the immune system and promotes good eyesight, and vitamin C for boosting immunity. It also acts as a detoxifier, cleansing the liver, and has anti-inflammatory properties, aiding painful joints.

Beef Burgers

These homemade burgers are perfect for the BBQ or a light lunch. They are very aromatic and packed with nutrients.

Prep: 15 mins
Cooking: 15 mins
Makes 4 burgers
Nutrition per burger: 209 kcals, 21 g protein, 14 g carbs, 9 g fat

What you need:
- 9 oz (250 g) ground (minced) lean beef, 5% fat
- 2 carrots, grated
- 1 small red bell pepper, thinly sliced
- 2 scallions (spring onions), chopped
- 1 egg
- 2 garlic cloves, crushed
- 1 tsp oregano
- 2 tbsp tomato paste
- ⅔ cup (50 g) oats, gluten-free or normal
- 1 tsp coconut oil
- Salt and pepper

What you need to do:
1. Beat the egg in a medium-sized bowl.
2. Add the carrot, scallion, pepper, garlic, oregano, and tomato paste, and mix well.
3. Now add the oats and beef and season with salt and pepper. Combine all ingredients using your hands. Form 4 burgers.
4. Heat the coconut oil in a nonstick pan and cook the burgers for about 7 mins each side, turning occasionally, until cooked throughout.
5. Serve with a side salad.

HPL Bonus Tip
If it's BBQ season and the weather is nice, get yourself outside and grill these burgers on the BBQ.

Beef and Spinach Stir-Fry

This superfood dish makes for a quick yet nutritious meal. Have your rice or noodles ready and you can feast in fewer than 30 mins…

Prep: 7 mins
Cooking: 20 mins
Serves 2
Nutrition per serving: 226 kcals, 36 g protein, 3 g carbs, 8 g fats

What you need:
- 14 oz (400 g) beef sirloin (rump steak), thinly sliced
- 2 cups (150 g) brown (chestnut) mushrooms, chopped
- 6 cups (200 g) fresh baby spinach
- 4 tbsp oyster sauce
- 2 tbsp soy sauce
- ½ inch (1 cm) fresh root ginger, grated
- 1 garlic clove, crushed
- 1 tsp coconut oil
- Red chili, to taste

What you need to do:
1. Heat ½ tsp coconut oil in a large pan and stir-fry the beef until browned, then set aside.
2. Heat the rest of the coconut oil, add the ginger and garlic, and cook until golden, then add the mushrooms. Cook for 3–4 mins, stirring often.
3. Add the beef, the sauces, and chili and cook for another 4–5 mins until sauce has thickened and is warmed through.
4. Lastly add the spinach and cook 1–2 mins, until wilted.
5. Serve hot with rice or rice noodles.

Indonesian Satay Wraps

Ever since I first tasted this recipe, it has become one of my favorites. Why? It could be something to do with pouring peanut butter over beef...!

Prep: 15 mins
Cooking: 12 mins
Serves 2
Nutrition per serving: 395 kcals, 39 g protein, 10 g carbs, 19 g fat

What you need:
- 9 oz (250 g) ground (minced) lean beef, 5% fat
- ½ red bell pepper, sliced
- ½ yellow bell pepper, sliced
- 1 small onion, sliced
- 2 small garlic cloves, crushed
- 1 tsp dried coriander
- 1 tbsp soy sauce
- 2 scallions (spring onions), chopped
- 8 leaves baby gem (baby cos or romaine) lettuce
- 1 tsp coconut oil

For the sauce:
- 2 tbsp (30 g) natural peanut butter, smooth
- ½ garlic clove, crushed
- 1 tsp sesame oil
- 1 tsp soy sauce

What you need to do:
1. Firstly, prepare the sauce. In a small bowl, mix the peanut butter, garlic, and sesame oil. Still mixing, gradually add 3 tbsp of boiling water. The sauce will become thick, and after a minute or so will become thinner and pale. At this point pour in the soy sauce, mix, and set aside.
2. Heat ½ tsp coconut oil in a pan and cook the beef for about 5 mins, stirring occasionally, until browned. Set aside.
3. Heat the remaining coconut oil in the same pan and add the onion and garlic, and cook for 2 mins.
4. Now add the peppers and coriander, and cook for a further 5 mins.
5. Lastly, return the meat to the pan and pour in the soy sauce, mix, and take off the heat.
6. To serve, place the beef and veg in the lettuce leaves, dress with the sauce, and sprinkle with the scallions.

Beef and Sweet Potato Bake

I'm willing to bet that this simple beef bake will quickly become one of your favorite recipes, just like it has mine.

Prep: 10 mins
Cooking: 45 mins
Serves 4
Nutrition per serving: 505 kcals, 40 g protein, 49 g carbs, 16 g fat

What you need:
- 1 lb 12 oz (800 g) sweet potatoes
- 1 lb (500 g) ground (minced) lean beef, 5% fat
- 1 onion, chopped
- 1 carrot, chopped
- 2 cups (150 g) mushrooms, sliced
- 1½ cups (400 g) chopped tomatoes
- 1 tsp dried mixed herbs
- 2 tbsp tomato paste
- 1 scant cup (200 ml) beef stock, hot
- 2 tbsp (25 g) butter
- Salt and pepper

What you need to do:
1. Bake the potatoes in the oven or microwave. When done, scoop out the innards, place the pulp in a bowl and set aside.
2. Heat the oven to 375°F (190°C).
3. Heat the coconut oil in a pan and add the onion and carrot. Cook for 5 mins and then add the beef. Cook for a further 2–3 mins, until browned.
4. Next add the mushrooms, chopped tomatoes, herbs, tomato paste, and stock, and stir well. Bring to the boil and simmer for 10 mins. Season with salt and pepper.
5. In the meantime, prepare the mashed potatoes by adding the butter and seasoning with salt and pepper.
6. Transfer the beef into an ovenproof dish and cover with the sweet potato mash.
7. Oven bake for 25 mins or until browned.
8. Serve with your favorite side salad.

Moroccan Meatballs

Everybody loves meatballs, and this has got to be the best recipe I have created to make them taste even better.

Prep: 10 mins
Cooking: 30 mins
Serves 2
Nutrition per serving: 345 kcals, 40 g protein, 15 g carbs, 12 g fats

What you need:
- 1 red onion, chopped
- 2 garlic cloves, crushed
- ½ tsp cumin seeds
- ½ tsp coriander seeds
- ¾ cup (200 g) chopped tomatoes
- 1 egg, beaten
- 9 oz (250 g) ground (minced) lean beef, 5% fat
- 1 tsp honey
- 2 tbsp fresh mint, chopped
- 1 tsp coconut oil
- 2 tbsp natural yogurt, to serve

What you need to do:
1. Heat ½ tsp coconut oil in a pan and cook the onions, garlic, cumin, and coriander and cook for 2–3 mins. Put half of this mixture in a bowl and set aside.
2. Add the tomatoes and honey to the remaining onions in the pan, season with salt and pepper, and simmer for about 15 mins.
3. In the meantime, add the egg, ground beef, and half the mint to the cooled onions, then season with salt and pepper, and mix everything well with your hands.
4. Shape into walnut-sized balls.
5. Heat the rest of the coconut oil and fry the meatballs until golden.
6. Add the meatballs to the sauce and simmer for a few minutes until they're cooked through.
7. In a small bowl, mix the yogurt with the remaining mint.
8. Serve with couscous and a spoonful of yogurt.

HPL Food Fact—Onions
Onions are rich in flavonoid quercetin, a very strong antioxidant.

Veal Escallops in Mushroom and Prune Sauce

My amazing mushroom and prune sauce is the perfect match for these delicate veal escallops…

Prep: 10 mins
Cooking: 10 mins
Serves 2
Nutrition per serving: 261 kcals, 33 g protein, 17 g carbs, 9 g fat

What you need:
- 2 veal escallops (5 oz/140 g each)
- 1 onion, thinly sliced
- 1⅔ cups (120 g) brown (chestnut) mushrooms, halved
- 1 garlic clove, crushed
- 1 tsp coconut oil
- 2–3 prunes (1 oz/25 g), chopped
- Scant ½ cup (100 ml) chicken stock, hot
- 2 tbsp fresh parsley, chopped
- Salt and ground pepper

What you need to do:
1. Heat ½ tsp coconut oil in a pan and fry the onion and garlic until soft.
2. Add the mushrooms and cook for an extra few minutes. Then set aside in a bowl.
3. Season the veal with salt and pepper.
4. Place the rest of the coconut oil in the pan and fry the veal on each side until browned and cooked throughout. Set aside.
5. Place the mushrooms and onions back into the pan, add the hot stock and prunes, season with ground pepper. Cook for a few minutes, until the sauce thickens.
6. Place the cooked veal back in the pan to heat through with the sauce.
7. Sprinkle each portion with fresh parsley to serve.

HPL Food Fact—Prunes
Prunes contain a laxative that is helpful for keeping the bowels regular.
(Don't say I didn't warn you!)

Pork Steak with Apple and Blackberry Relish

This nutrient-packed dish is full of vitamins and minerals, which will keep you strong and healthy—and your taste buds happy.

Prep: 10 mins
Cooking: 18 mins
Serves 2
Nutrition per serving: 430 kcals, 52 g protein, 24 g carbs, 14 g fat

What you need:
- 2 pork loin steaks, fat removed (5 oz/145 g each)
- 1 leek, chopped
- 2 cups (150 g) savoy cabbage, shredded
- 1 apple, peeled and grated, core removed
- ⅔ cup (100 g) blackberries, fresh or frozen
- Pinch of sugar/stevia
- 1 tsp coconut oil
- Salt and pepper

What you need to do:
1. Braise the apples and blackberries with the sugar for about 5 mins and set aside.
2. Heat the coconut oil in a pan and fry the steaks for 4–5mins each side, until browned and cooked through. Set aside.
3. In the same pan, add the cabbage and cook for 3 mins then add the leek and cook for another few mins, adding 1–2 tbsp water if necessary, until all is tender.
4. Divide the vegetables and steaks between two plates and serve with the apple and blackberry relish. Season with salt and pepper, to taste.

Spicy Meatball Skewers

No introduction is needed to this simple combination of lean meat and veggies, and it really doesn't get much easier than this.

Prep: 10 mins
Cooking: 20 mins
Serves 2
Nutrition per serving: 179 kcals, 27 g protein, 5 g carbs, 6 g fat

What you need:
- 9 oz (250 g) ground (minced) lean pork
- 1 zucchini (courgette), thickly sliced
- ½ green bell pepper, cut into chunks
- ½ red bell pepper, cut into chunks
- 1 garlic clove, crushed
- 1 bird's eye chili, chopped
- 1 tbsp fresh parsley, chopped
- 1 tsp turmeric
- 1 tsp cumin
- Salt and pepper

What you need to do:
1. Heat the oven to 350°F (180°C).
2. In a small bowl, mix together the pork, parsley, turmeric, garlic, chili, and cumin. Season with salt and pepper, and form into twelve small balls.
3. Thread alternating zucchini, pepper, and meatballs onto the skewers until you've filled four skewers.
4. Cook in the oven for 20 mins, turning occasionally, until cooked through and browned.
5. Serve hot with side salad or store in the refrigerator for later.

Herby Sausages

It's easy to make your own sausages with this super-simple recipe. These are lean and tasty too.

Prep: 5 mins
Cooking: 15 mins
Makes 6 sausages
Nutrition per sausage: 59 kcals, 9 g protein, 0 g carbs, 3 g fat

What you need:
- 9 oz (250 g) ground (minced) lean pork
- ½ tsp salt
- ½ tsp black pepper
- 2 tsp fresh sage, chopped
- 2 tsp fresh basil, chopped
- ½ tsp coconut oil

What you need to do:
1. In a large bowl, mix together the pork with the salt, pepper, sage, and basil.
2. Combine well and shape into six sausages.
3. Melt the coconut oil in large nonstick frying pan and cook the sausages on medium heat until well browned and thoroughly cooked.
4. Serve hot or store in the refrigerator for later.

HPL Food Fact—Sage
Sage has antiseptic, antiviral and antibacterial properties. Studies have also shown that it can improve brainpower, specifically short-term memory.

Bacon and Cranberry Pilaf

This light, fluffy, and nutritious pilaf might just surprise you. It's a great way to get all the benefits of these amazing ingredients.

Prep: 15 mins
Cooking: 25 mins
Serves 2
Nutrition per serving: 486 kcals, 25 g protein, 54 g carbs, 21 g fat

What you need:
- 5 rashers smoked Canadian bacon, cut into pieces
- ¼ cup (30 g) walnuts, chopped
- 1 onion, chopped
- 1 celery stick, chopped
- 2 cups (150 g) savoy cabbage, shredded
- 1¼ cups (250 g) cooked brown rice
- 3 tbsp (25 g) dried cranberries
- 2 tbsp chives, chopped
- 1 tsp coconut oil

What you need to do:
1. Heat ½ tsp coconut oil a large pan and fry the bacon for 5 mins.
2. Add the walnuts and cook for a further 1 min, then set aside.
3. Heat the remaining coconut oil and add the onion and celery. Cook for 2–3 mins, until soft.
4. Now add the cabbage and cook for a further 10 mins until softened.
5. Add the rice, chopped bacon, walnuts, and cranberries and stir well. Season with salt and pepper.
6. Sprinkle with chives and serve.

HPL Food Fact—Brown Rice
Brown rice contains ample amounts of fiber, which promotes healthy digestion. It is a complex carbohydrate, so it releases energy slowly, and keeps you satisfied for longer.

25. BARS, SNACKS, AND SHAKES

As a busy person, you'll sometimes need some very quick and easy high-performance foods to keep you going until your next meal. The items in this chapter will be the perfect addition to all the other great-tasting meals you're about to create: bars, snacks, and shakes to grab when time is tight.

Dark Chocolate Islands

Everybody loves these little islands of goodness.

Prep: 10 mins + chilling time
Makes 8
Nutrition per serving: 75 kcals, 1 g protein, 5 g carbs, 6 g fats

What you need:
- 1½ oz (40 g) 85% cocoa dark chocolate, melted
- 8 almonds
- 4 brazil nuts, halved
- 4 walnuts
- 1½ tbsp (14 g) raisins
- 2 tbsp (14 g) dried cranberries

What you need to do:
1. Melt the chocolate using a bain-marie or in the microwave, and prepare a sheet of waxed paper.
2. With a spoon, form eight "islands" of chocolate on the waxed paper. Set aside for 5 mins.
3. Place the fruit and nuts on the chocolate islands.
4. Chill them in the refrigerator for 20–30 mins before serving.

HPL Food Fact—Almonds
Almonds are one of the top sources of the cancer-preventing antioxidant vitamin E, containing 24 mg per 100 g. This plays an important role in protecting cells from free radicals.

Homemade Granola

Granola is a moreish treat, but shop-bought versions tend to be full of sugar and oils. HPL's own granola recipe is easy and customizable. Just add your favorite dried fruits, nuts, or seeds.

Prep: 5 mins
Cooking: 40 mins
Makes over 3 lb (1.5 kg)
Nutrition per serving (1½ oz/40 g): 166 kcals, 5 g protein, 28 g carbs, 4 g fat

What you need:
- Apple compote (from 4 big apples; see HLP Bonus Tip below)
- ⅓ cup (120 g) honey
- 1½ tsp vanilla extract
- 2 tsp cinnamon
- ¾ tsp salt
- 2¼ lb (1 kg) oats (normal or gluten free)
- ¾ cup (100 g) brazil nuts, chopped
- ¾ cup (60 g) flaked almonds
- Scant ½ cup (80 g) dates, chopped
- 10 (80 g) dried apricots, chopped
- ⅔ cup (100 g) golden raisins (sultanas)

What you need to do:
1. Preheat oven to 320°F (160°C).
2. In a large bowl, beat together the apple compote, honey, vanilla, cinnamon, and salt.
3. Add the oats and stir well to combine.
4. Spread the mixture onto two large baking sheets; bake for 10 mins.
5. Remove from the oven and stir well, then return to the oven and bake for another 10 mins.
6. Repeat, but this time, add the nuts. Return to the oven for another 10 mins.
7. Then stir again and bake for a final 10 mins.
8. Remove from the oven and mix in the fruit.
9. Store in an airtight jar.

HPL Bonus Tip
To make apple compote, stew four big, peeled, cored, and chopped cooking apples in a little water until they turn into mush. Then mash them with a fork (or use a food processor).

Dark Chocolate Macaroons

If you've ever fancied trying coconut macaroons, but thought they were too unhealthy, give in and just bake these ones up already! They're HPL approved!

Prep: 10 mins
Cooking: 10–15 mins
Makes: approx. 10
Nutrition per serving: 163 kcals, 3 g protein, 9 g carbs, 12 g fat

What you need:
- 1 egg white
- 1½ cups (150 g) desiccated coconut
- Scant ½ cup (3½ oz/100 ml) condensed milk
- 1½ oz (40 g) dark chocolate, melted

What you need to do:
1. Preheat oven to 350°F (180°C) and prepare a baking sheet lined with waxed paper.
2. Mix the coconut and egg white together.
3. Then pour in the milk slowly until you reach a clumpy consistency.
4. Take a tablespoon of the mixture and form a pyramid on the baking sheet.
5. Bake in the oven for 10–15 mins, until the edges are golden brown; leave to cool.
6. Melt the dark chocolate in a bain-marie or in the microwave, and dip the base of the pyramids in the melted chocolate before placing back on the baking paper.
7. Wait for the chocolate to cool and set before serving.

HPL Food Fact—Coconut

The medium-chain fatty acids in coconut oil are soluble and easily digested by the body. They have also been show to help the body absorb some of the commonly deficient minerals such as calcium and magnesium.

Bakewell Tart Bar

I created this recipe spontaneously one day when I was craving a classic cherry Bakewell cake slice. It's a keeper!

Prep: 10 mins + overnight soaking
Makes 10 bars
Nutrition per bar: 83 kcals, 2 g protein, 10 g carbs, 4 g fat

What you need:
- ¾ cup (100 g) cashews
- ½ cup (100 g) dates, pitted
- 1 tsp almond extract

What you need to do:
1. Soak the cashews in water overnight.
2. In a food processor, blend all ingredients together until a smooth paste has formed; this may take 5–10 mins.
3. Shape into 10 small bars and serve.

HPL Food Fact—Cashews
Cashew nuts are the perfect choice for active people. A serving of thirty nuts provides one-fifth of a woman's recommended daily iron intake.

Orange Chocolate Soufflé

You'll be sure to impress guests with this easy yet so tasty dessert.

Prep: 10 mins
Cooking: 12 mins
Serves 2
Nutrition per serving: 165 kcals, 6 g protein, 26 g carbs, 5 g fat

What you need:
- 1 cup (150 g) blueberries, frozen
- 1 egg
- 2 tsp brown sugar (or stevia, to taste)
- 1 ½ tbsp coconut flour
- 1 tbsp unsweetened cocoa powder
- Juice and zest of half an orange
- Powdered (castor) sugar, to serve (optional)

What you need to do:
1. Preheat the oven to 430°F (220°C).
2. Divide the blueberries into two ramekins and place in the oven.
3. Separate the egg into two bowls.
4. Add the brown sugar, flour, cocoa powder, and orange into the yolk and mix until well combined.
5. Beat the egg white into froth and combine with the mixture in the other bowl.
6. Pour the mixture over the blueberries and bake for 12 mins.
7. Sprinkle some powdered sugar over the top and serve hot.

Carrot Cake

Carrot cake is a classic favorite. This raw, no-bake, no-cook version is easy to make and will wow anyone lucky enough to sample it.

Prep: 25 mins + chilling time
Serves 12
Nutrition per serving: 265 kcals, 4 g protein, 22 g carbs, 20 g fat

What you need:

For the cake:
- 4 carrots (around 250 g), grated (about 2 cups)
- 1 cup (100 g) walnuts, chopped
- ¾ heaping cup (150 g) dates, pitted
- Scant ½ cup (40 g) desiccated coconut
- 1 tsp cinnamon
- ½ tsp nutmeg
- Pinch of salt

For the frosting:
- 1¼ cups (170 g) cashews, soaked overnight
- 3 tbsp honey
- 1 tsp vanilla extract
- Juice of ½ lemon
- 2½ oz (70 g) coconut oil, melted
- Pinch of salt

What you need to do:
1. Grate the carrots in the food processor (or by hand), place in a large bowl and set aside.
2. Blend together the walnuts, dates, coconut, spices, and salt in a food processor.
3. Add the carrots and combine.
4. Transfer the mixture into a 9-inch spring-form pan or an 8-inch square pan lined with waxed paper and chill in the refrigerator.
5. Now make the frosting by blending the cashews, honey, vanilla, lemon, and salt, adding water to achieve a very smooth paste. This may take up to 10 mins.
6. Add the melted coconut oil and blend again.
7. Transfer the frosting onto the chilled cake and smooth the top, then freeze for about 2 hours.
8. Remove from the freezer and wait about 30 mins before removing the cake from the tray.
9. Decorate with additional walnuts and cinnamon, and serve.

Vanilla Cheese Cake

This is a beautiful, simple vanilla cheesecake recipe with a fresh raspberry topping.

Prep: 5 mins + chilling time
Cooking: 30–45 mins
Serves 8
Nutrition per serving (0% fat products):
150 kcals, 13 g protein, 12 g carbs, 5 g fat

What you need:

For the base layer:
- 2 tbsp almond butter
- 4 tbsp (30 g) ground almonds
- 1 tbsp honey

For the cheesecake layer:
- ⅔ cup (150 g) 0% fat Greek yogurt (or full fat)
- 1 cup (250 g) 0% fat (or full fat) quark (a kind of curd cheese)
- 2 scoops vanilla whey powder
- 3 egg whites
- 1 tsp vanilla extract

For the top layer/side sauce:
- 2 cups (250 g) raspberries, fresh or frozen
- 2 tbsp honey
- 1 tbsp chia seeds

What you need to do:
1. Heat the oven to 320°F (160°C).
2. Put all the base-layer ingredients in a bowl and mix well with your hands to form a crumbly mix. Then press it down into a spring-form cake pan.
3. Put all the cheesecake-layer ingredients in a clean bowl and combine. Pour the mixture onto the base.
4. Bake in the oven for about 30–45 mins, being careful to not over bake. You need to remove it from the oven when it is still a little bit wobbly in the middle. Leave to cool—the cheesecake will set while it cools.
5. In a medium bowl, blend together the top-layer ingredients until it forms a smooth sauce.
6. Once the cheesecake has cooled completely, pour the top layer over it, or serve the sauce as a side and drizzle over the cheesecake slices.

HPL Food Fact—Raspberries
Raspberries are high in anthocyanins, powerful antioxidants that reduce the risk of cardiovascular disease, have various roles in fighting cancer, and may improve memory and slow age-related loss of cognitive function.

HPL "Snickers"

You're going to love this High Performance take on this classic chocolate bar.

Prep: 30 mins + chilling time
Serves 12
Nutrition per serving: 315 kcals, 8 g protein, 26 g carbs, 18 g fat

What you need:

For the base:
- 2 cups (230 g) ground almonds
- 1 oz (30 g) coconut oil, melted
- 2 tbsp honey
- 2 tbsp (30 g) natural smooth peanut butter
- 1 tsp vanilla extract
- Pinch of salt

For the caramel layer:
- 1½ cups (300 g) dates, pitted
- 3½ oz (100 g) coconut oil, melted
- 2 tbsp (30 g) peanut butter
- 3 tbsp (30 g) peanuts

For the chocolate layer:
- 3 oz (80 g) 85% cocoa dark chocolate, melted
- 1½ tbsp (15 g) peanuts

What you need to do:
1. Place all the base ingredients into a food processor and blend until a dough layer is formed.
2. Transfer into an 8 inch square silicon tray and press evenly onto the base. Place into the freezer.
3. Prepare the caramel layer in the food processor by blending together the dates, coconut oil, and peanut butter, until very smooth.
4. Add the peanuts and pulse for a few seconds. Spread the caramel over the top of the base. Place back in the freezer for 1 hour.
5. After the caramel has set, prepare the top layer.
6. Melt the chocolate in a bain-marie or microwave, and add the peanuts.
7. Spread over the caramel layer and return to refrigerator for 20–30 mins until the chocolate has set.
8. Cut into twelve squares and serve.

Apple and Raspberry Crumble

A classic and delicious pairing of raspberries and apples topped with buttery crumble.

Prep: 10 mins
Cooking: 30 mins
Serves 10
Nutrition per serving: 169 kcals, 2 g protein, 19 g carbs, 11 g fat

What you need:
- 4 medium apples, sliced
- 1¼ cups (150 g) raspberries
- 2½ tbsp (25 g) raisins
- 1 tbsp cinnamon

For the crumble:
- ½ heaping cup (60 g) desiccated coconut
- ¼ cup (30 g) walnuts, chopped
- ½ cup (50 g) ground almonds
- 1 tbsp honey
- 2 tbsp (30 g) soft butter

What you need to do:
1. Preheat the oven to 350°F (180°C).
2. In a pot, heat the apples on a low heat until softened.
3. Mix in the raspberries, raisins, and cinnamon, and transfer into a baking dish.
4. Mix together the coconut, ground almonds, honey, and butter, using your hands.
5. Add the walnuts and combine.
6. Top the fruit with an even layer of the crumble and bake for 30 mins, until golden brown.
7. Serve hot.

HPL Food Fact—Apple
Apples are rich in both soluble and insoluble fiber, which help food to pass at a healthy rate through the digestive system.

Protein Banana Bread

Who doesn't love banana bread, warm from the oven and smelling delicious? This is a super easy protein-packed recipe that gives perfect and tasty results every time.

Prep: 5 mins
Cooking: 45 mins
Serves 10
Nutrition per serving: 77 kcals, 4 g protein, 8 g carbs, 2 g fat

What you need:
- 1 scoop vanilla whey powder (or chocolate if you want a choc/banana bread)
- 2 ripe bananas, mashed
- 3 egg whites
- 3 tbsp coconut flour
- 1 tbsp vanilla extract
- 6 dates, chopped
- ¼ cup (30 g) walnuts, chopped
- ½ tsp baking powder

What you need to do:
1. Preheat oven to 340°F (170°C).
2. Mix all ingredients together until well combined.
3. Pour the batter into a 9 × 5 inch (23 × 12 cm) loaf pan, and bake for about 45 mins, until an inserted knife comes out clean.
4. Allow to cool before serving.

HPL Food Fact—Banana
Bananas contain high levels of B vitamins, which the body needs to produce energy. They are also a good source of immunity-enhancing vitamin C, and contain manganese, which works with vitamin C to produce the virus-fighting substance interferon.

Protein Brownies

These are super-quick brownies that can be in the oven in just minutes.

Prep: 5 mins
Cooking: 20 mins
Serves 9
Nutrition per serving: 108 kcals, 7 g protein, 3 g carbs, 5 g fat

What you need:
- ⅓ cup (40 g) chocolate whey powder
- 1½ oz (45 g) 85% cocoa dark chocolate
- 4 egg whites
- ½ tsp baking powder
- 2 tbsp (30 g) butter
- 2 tbsp unsweetened cocoa powder
- 4 oz (115 g) 0% fat cream cheese (or a dairy-free alternative)
- Stevia, to taste

What you need to do:
1. Preheat oven to 350°F (180°C). Mix all the ingredients in a large bowl, using a hand blender, until smooth.
2. Pour the batter into a brownie pan and bake for 20 mins.
3. Allow to cool before cutting into nine squares and serving.

Lemon and Poppy Seed Protein Loaf

This lemony fresh and delicious bread is perfect with a cup of good coffee. It's full of protein too (bonus!)

Prep: 5 mins
Cooking: 30 mins
Serves 8
Nutrition per serving: 68 kcals, 7.5 g protein, 6 g carbs, 1 g fat

What you need:
- 6 egg whites
- 1½ scoops vanilla whey powder
- 2 tbsp coconut flour
- ¼ cup (25 g) quinoa flakes
- 1 tbsp poppy seeds
- ½ tbsp vanilla essence
- ½ tsp baking powder
- Zest of 1 lemon
- 2 tbsp apple sauce

What you need to do:
1. Preheat oven to 340°F (170°C).
2. In a bowl, combine all the ingredients.
3. Transfer into a 9 × 5 inch (23 × 12 cm) loaf pan and bake for 30 mins, until browned.
4. Allow to cool before serving.

Protein Ice Cream

Who said you can't have ice cream on a healthy diet? This unbelievably simple recipe will show you how.

Prep: 5 mins + freezing time
Serves 2
Nutrition per serving: 178 kcals, 11 g protein, 32 g carbs, 2 g fat

What you need:
- 2 medium bananas, chopped and frozen
- ⅓ cup (50 g) blueberries, frozen
- Scant ½ cup (100 ml) coconut milk
- ¼ cup (25 g) vanilla whey powder

What you need to do:
1. Prepare the bananas by peeling, chopping, and freezing in a container.
2. Once they are frozen, add all ingredients to a food processor and blend until combined. Keep blending until your desired consistency is reached.
3. Serve immediately with your favorite toppings.

HPL Bonus Tip
Some of my favorite topping suggestions:
- Nuts
- Dried berries
- Fresh berries
- Honey
- Flax seeds
- Chia seeds

HPL Food Fact—Blueberries
This superfood ranks top for antioxidant activity compared to forty other fresh fruit and vegetables. Eat blueberries three or four times a week for their full immunity-boosting benefits.

Protein Panna Cotta

This gorgeous dessert is deliciously light and creamy.

Prep: 10 mins + chilling time
Serves 2
Nutrition per serving: 183 kcals, 12 g protein, 25 g carbs, 2.5 g fat

What you need:
- ¼ cup (25 g) whey powder
- 1¾ cups (220 g) raspberries
- 1 cup (235 ml) coconut milk
- 1 banana, chopped
- 2 tbsp (12 g) gelatin

What you need to do:
1. In a bowl, dissolve the gelatin in hot coconut milk.
2. Add the whey, raspberries, and banana, and mix with a hand blender until smooth.
3. Transfer into two ramekins and chill for a few hours until set.
4. Serve with fresh berries.

HPL Food Fact—Whey Protein
Whey is a very effective source of protein for increasing muscle protein synthesis, the process in muscle cells that results in muscle growth.

Protein Pancakes

I reckon these are the easiest and tastiest pancakes in the universe!

Prep: 5 mins
Cooking: 5 mins
Serves 1
Nutrition per serving: 240 kcals, 25 g protein, 29 g carbs, 4 g fat

What you need:
- 1 medium banana, mashed
- ¼ cup (25 g) vanilla whey powder
- 1 egg
- ½ tsp coconut oil

What you need to do:
1. In a bowl, mash the banana with a fork.
2. Add the egg and whey, and blend until well combined.
3. Heat the coconut oil in a pan and fry three small pancakes over a medium heat, for about 2 mins each side.
4. Serve with your favorite toppings.

HPL Bonus Tip
Some of my favorite pancake toppings:
- Apple pie topping: cook 1 chopped apple in maple syrup and cinnamon.
- HPL chocolate sauce: melt 1 tsp coconut oil, add raw cocoa, and a dash of coconut milk.
- Top with your favorite nuts and seeds and a side of natural yogurt.

Bounty Protein Balls

Seriously, who wouldn't love these bounty balls? They're the perfect pre- and post-workout snack.

Prep: 10 mins
Makes 5 balls
Nutrition per ball: 89 kcals, 5 g protein, 5 g carbs, 5 g fat

What you need:
- ¼ cup (25 g) desiccated coconut
- ¼ cup (25 g) vanilla whey powder
- ¼ cup (25 g) quinoa flakes
- 2 tbsp coconut flour
- 3 or 4 tbsp (50 ml) coconut milk, or as required

What you need to do:
1. Combine all ingredients together, add coconut milk until a desired dough texture is achieved.
2. Shape batter into five balls.
3. Roll the balls in some more coconut (optional).

HPL Food Fact—Quinoa
Quinoa contains significantly more protein than other grains, and it is also particularly rich in the amino acid lysine, which the body needs to grow and repair tissue.

Fiery Orange and Goji Berry Protein Bars

Let these orange and goji berry bars fire you up with some extra protein.

Prep: 15 mins
Makes 5 bars
Nutrition per bar: 161 kcals, 9 g protein, 14 g carbs, 8 g fat

What you need:
- ¼ cup (25 g) vanilla whey powder
- ⅓ cup (35 g) ground almonds
- 2 tbsp coconut flour
- ½ cup (60 g) goji berries
- 2 tbsp (25 ml) coconut milk, or as required
- 1 tbsp vanilla essence
- 1 tbsp orange zest
- Pinch or two cayenne pepper
- 1½ oz (40 g) 85% cocoa dark chocolate, melted

What you need to do:
1. Combine all ingredients (except the chocolate), add coconut milk until a desired dough texture is achieved.
2. Shape batter into five bars.
3. Melt the chocolate in a bain-marie or microwave and cover the bars.
4. Refrigerate before serving until chocolate has set.

Chocolate and Cinnamon Protein Balls

Just in case you haven't had enough chocolate yet, these should do the trick nicely.

Prep: 15 mins
Makes 6 balls
Nutrition per ball: 87 kcals, 9 g protein, 4 g carbs, 6 g fat

What you need:
- 2 scoops chocolate whey powder
- 2 dates, finely chopped
- 1 tsp cinnamon
- 2 tbsp peanut butter
- 1 tbsp coconut flour
- 1 tsp vanilla/almond extract
- 1 tbsp coconut flakes
- 2 tbsp (25 ml) coconut milk, or as required
- ⅔ oz (20 g) 85% cocoa dark chocolate, melted

What you need to do:
1. Combine all ingredients (except the chocolate), and add coconut milk until a desired dough texture is achieved.
2. Shape batter into five balls.
3. Melt the chocolate in a bain-marie or in the microwave, and use it to top each ball.
4. Chill the balls in the refrigerator before serving.

Red Velvet Protein Bars

These protein bars get their gorgeous color (and nutrients) from a surprising source... beets! Discover how amazing they are.

Prep: 15 mins
Makes 4 bars
Nutrition per serving: 140 kcals, 9 g protein, 7 g carbs, 8 g fat

What you need:
- 1 small beet (beetroot), cooked
- ¼ cup (25 g) vanilla whey powder
- ¼ cup (25 g) coconut flour
- 2 tbsp (25 ml) coconut milk, cartoned
- 1 tbsp nut butter
- 1½ oz (40 g) 85% dark chocolate, melted (optional)

What you need to do:
1. In a bowl, mix together the protein powder and coconut flour.
2. Grate the beet on the smallest setting of your grater.
3. Add the nut butter and beet to the powder and combine with milk. You need to add enough liquid to make the batter come together like dough, so you can roll it into bars using your hands.
4. Shape the batter into four bars.
5. Melt the chocolate and use it to top the bars—this step is optional.
6. Place the bars in the freezer for 30 mins, then take out and store in the refrigerator until you're ready to eat them!

HPL Food Fact—Beets
Beets are the perfect pre-workout food because of their high levels of nitrates, thought to be a source of nitric oxide, which improves the supply of oxygen to cells.

Strawberries and Cream Protein Bars

I can't tell how many times I've made these; they are little bites of heavenly delight!

Prep: 15 mins
Makes 4 bars
Nutrition per bar: 98 kcals, 7 g protein, 6 g carbs, 5 g fat

What you need:
- 1 scoop strawberries and cream whey powder
- 2 tbsp coconut flour
- 1 tsp coconut oil, melted
- 2 tbsp (25 ml) coconut milk, or as required
- ⅔ oz (20 g) dark chocolate
- 2 strawberries, halved

What you need to do:
1. Combine all ingredients (except the chocolate), and add coconut milk until a desired dough texture is achieved.
2. Shape into four bars.
3. Melt the dark chocolate in a bain-marie or in the microwave and coat each bar. Place half a strawberry on top.
4. Chill in the refrigerator until chocolate has set.

HPL Food Fact—Strawberries
Packed with vitamin C, an average serving (1 cup/150 g) of strawberries gives all the recommended daily adult intake of this immunity-boosting vitamin.

Almond Protein Bars

A sweet and simple way top up your protein levels.

Prep: 25 mins
Makes 6 bars
Nutrition per bar: 139 kcals, 6 g protein, 7 g carbs, 7 g fat

What you need:
- ¼ cup (25 g) vanilla whey powder
- 2 tbsp (10 g) flaked almonds
- 4 cup (30 g) ground almonds
- 1½ tbsp (10 g) coconut flour
- ¼ cup (60 ml) coconut milk
- 2 oz (60 g) white chocolate, melted
- ⅔ oz (20 g) dark chocolate, melted

What you need to do:
1. Combine all ingredients (except the chocolate), and add coconut milk until the desired dough texture is achieved.
2. Shape into six bars.
3. Melt the white chocolate (in a bain-marie or microwave) and coat each bar in a thin layer and allow to set.
4. Melt the dark chocolate in the same way, and drizzle it over the top of the bars, then sprinkle with almond flakes (optional).
5. Chill the bars in the refrigerator before serving.

Lemon Protein Balls

These energy balls are packed with zesty flavor and are perfect for a "pick me up" moment.

Prep: 20 mins
Makes 8
Nutrition per ball: 177 kcals, 7 g protein, 12 g carbs, 9 g fat

What you need:
- 1 heaping cup (150 g) cashews, soaked overnight
- 3 tbsp (20 g) coconut flour
- 2 tbsp honey
- 2 tbsp lemon juice
- 1 tsp vanilla extract
- 1 tbsp lemon zest
- ¼ cup (25 g) vanilla whey powder
- 1¾ oz (50 g) 85% cocoa dark chocolate

What you need to do:
1. In a food processor, combine all the ingredients (except the chocolate) until a dough-like texture is achieved.
2. Form into eight balls.
3. Melt the dark chocolate (using a bain-marie, or in the microwave) and coat the balls.
4. Chill the balls in the refrigerator before serving.

Smoothies

Raspberry Cheesecake Smoothie

All the taste of a cheesecake in a high-protein and nutritious smoothie—it doesn't get much better than this.

Prep: 5 mins
Serves 1
Nutrition per serving: 280 kcals, 36 g protein, 21 g carbs, 7 g fat

What you need:
- 1 scant cup (200 ml) cartoned coconut milk
- 1 cup (150 g) fat-free cottage cheese
- ½ cup (60 g) raspberries, fresh or frozen
- 1 scoop vanilla or raspberry whey powder
- ½ tsp vanilla extract
- Stevia, to taste

What you need to do:
Place all the ingredients in a blender and blend until texture is smooth.

HPL Bonus Tip
- If you are using fresh berries, add 2–3 ice cubes.
- If you want to eliminate dairy from your diet, just omit the cottage cheese from this recipe.

Banana and Peanut Butter Smoothie

A classic combination of ingredients that never fails to impress the taste buds.

Prep: 5 mins
Serves 1
Nutrition per serving: 228 kcals, 35 g protein, 8 g carbs, 7 g fat

What you need:
- 1 scant cup (200 ml) cartoned coconut milk
- 1 tbsp natural peanut butter
- ½ medium banana
- 1 scoop vanilla whey powder
- ½ tsp vanilla essence
- 2–3 ice cubes

What you need to do:
Place all the ingredients in a blender and blend until texture is smooth.

Greek Chocolate Smoothie

The smoothie of the Gods. Try it to find out why.

Prep: 5 mins
Serves 1
Nutrition per serving: 256 kcals, 37 g protein, 24 g carbs, 4 g fat

What you need:
- 3½ tbsp (50 ml) cartoned coconut milk
- ⅔ cup (150 g) 0% fat Greek yogurt
- ½ medium banana
- 1 tsp cocoa powder, unsweetened
- 1 scoop chocolate whey powder
- 2 handfuls of spinach
- 2–3 ice cubes

What you need to do:
Place all the ingredients in a blender and blend until texture is smooth.

HPL Bonus Tip
If you want to eliminate dairy from your diet, just use ⅔ cup (150 ml) extra coconut milk instead of the yogurt.

Fresh Peach Smoothie

If you are in need of something fresh and sweet, then this is the smoothie for you.

Prep: 5 mins
Serves 1
Nutrition per serving: 217 kcals, 26 g protein, 24 g carbs, 2 g fat

What you need:
- Scant ½ cup (100 ml) coconut water
- 1 fresh peach, flesh only
- 1 slice cantaloupe melon
- 1 scoop vanilla whey powder
- 2–3 ice cubes

What you need to do:
Place all the ingredients in a blender and blend until texture is smooth.

Purple Thunder Smoothie

Don't let the color of this one put you off, it's full of flavor and packed with nutrients too.

Prep: 5 mins
Serves 1
Nutrition per serving: 263 kcals, 30 g protein, 29 g carbs, 3 g fat

What you need:
- Scant ½ cup (100 ml) cartoned coconut milk
- Scant ½ cup (100 g) 0% fat Greek yogurt
- 1 tbsp flax seeds
- ½ medium banana
- ½ cup blueberries
- ½ tsp almond essence
- ½ tsp stevia (optional)
- 1 scoop vanilla whey powder

What you need to do:
Place all the ingredients in a blender and blend until texture is smooth.

Ginger Kick Smoothie

This is my favorite smoothie, as I just love that little kick from the fresh ginger.

Prep: 5 mins
Serves 1
Nutrition per serving: 251 kcals, 21 g protein, 23 g carbs, 6 g fat

What you need:
- ½ cup (70 g) fresh strawberries
- ½ medium banana
- 1 scant cup (200 ml) cartoned coconut milk
- 1 tbsp fresh ginger, grated
- 2 handfuls baby spinach
- 1 scoop vanilla whey

What you need to do:
Place all the ingredients in a blender and blend until texture is smooth.

The Hulk Smoothie

Warning: do NOT make this smoothie angry.

Prep: 5 mins
Serves 1
Nutrition per serving: 173 kcals, 21 g protein, 10 g carbs, 6 g fat

What you need:
- ½ medium banana
- 1 scoop vanilla whey powder
- 1 tsp cinnamon
- 1 scant cup (200 ml) cartoned coconut milk
- 2 handfuls fresh baby spinach
- 2–3 ice cubes

What you need to do:
Place all the ingredients in a blender and blend until texture is smooth.

PART IV
YOUR
TRAINING
PROGRAM

The first three parts of the book were all about nutrition and how it will be your primary factor to achieving HPL. Of course, I'd be lying if I said nutrition was the only part of the equation to becoming your best. Your training program is also a vital part of ensuring your success with this system.

Just like with my own nutrition in the past, I used to truly underestimate how a good training program could dramatically enhance my results. I believed that if I just did what the "big guys" did and put some effort in, results would come my way. Of course, this wasn't the case, and I had to reach out further, stretch myself, and learn alternative methods and techniques to finally get the results I wanted.

Over the years, I tried lots of training programs and learnt from many coaches. Today, I think I've found the winning combination. And that's what you're about to discover in Part IV of the HPL book. These days, I listen to—and trust—just a few strength and conditioning coaches. One of these coaches is Jack Lovett.

I met Jack a few years ago and we quickly became friends. We share the same passion for great coaching. Just as I have spent years becoming an expert in the field of nutrition, Jack has done the same in strength and conditioning. He is a true expert in his work and, despite our specializing in different areas of fitness, we're both driven by getting our clients the best possible results. Oh yeah, Jack is also a two-times British Natural Strongman Champion.

That's why I was delighted when Jack said he would write the training section coming up. I wanted to make this book a complete resource that will serve you forever. With Jack kindly unlocking his advanced training knowledge for us, I can be confident that your training will be as good as your nutrition.

Like the nutritional information you've just read, the training advice and program here aren't what you will find in mainstream publications. Chances are, it's unlike anything you have ever tried before, and that's good news for you, because that means better results. Have confidence in it: this is how I train, it's how Jack trains, and it's how all of the HPL clients train, too. I know you will love the results.

It's now over to Jack.

ABOUT JACK

Jack Lovett is the owner of Spartan Performance. A strength and conditioning specialist, Jack works with athletes and individuals of all levels and disciplines. Jack's ethos is simple—maximize athletic performance and results in all clients.

Jack's training system is the result of years of constant learning, hands-on "in the trenches" experience, and frequent collaboration with elite-level coaches across the world, including Joe Defranco, Martin Rooney, Dan John, and Mike Mahler. Having mentored in the US with Joe, Jack Lovett is the UK's only Defranco-Approved Performance Specialist.

As a writer, Jack is a regular contributor to numerous international publications, including *Men's Fitness, IronLife, Muscle & Fitness, Train Hard Fight Easy*, and the *Daily Mail*. Also a competitive athlete, Jack is a two-times British Natural Strongman Champion and World Natural Strongman competitor.

26. TRAINING FOR HIGH PERFORMANCE LIVING

We've already established that you're a High Performance Living (HPL) individual; someone who wants to:

- Perform better
- Build strength
- Increase muscle mass
- Reduce body fat more consistently.

Now you've read the nutritional and lifestyle changes in parts I and II of this book, and started to put them into practice, it's time to talk about training!

What Is High Performance Living Training?

Certain athletes have always fascinated me. You know the ones, they don't just perform incredible feats but look almost superhuman, too. In 1992 it was Linford Christie, and in 1996 it was Michael Johnson and Pyrros Dimas. In the 2000s I loved watching Mariusz Pudzianowski compete. More recently, I've been captivated by Dmitry Klokov and Rich Froning. All of these athletes are a rare breed: that combination of performance and aesthetics. As Ru would put it: they look and perform awesome!

And it's not just me that's captivated by this potent partnership of performance and aesthetics. My clients say they find it appealing, too. Yes, my clients all want to look better naked (who doesn't?), but a growing number of everyday people are seeking more than just fat loss. They want to challenge themselves, and to perform better in sport, fitness, and activity, too. Many men and women can name a particular athlete that inspires them, with names like Jessica Ennis cropping up frequently.

As a coach, how do I go about addressing my clients' performance goals? By looking to the very people who inspire us. Athletes.

Some common elements underpin the training of almost all the world's best athletes: they lift, sprint, jump, and throw. The ways in which they implement these factors may differ, but the foundation remains the same. They all strength-train on the basic lifts (squat, deadlift, press, etc.), they increase explosive power through various jumps and throws, and they top it all off with the ultimate in power development and fat loss—sprinting.

It sounds pretty simple when you compare it to the latest, in-vogue, "revolutionary" training system in the media and online. But don't be fooled. It works incredibly well. Even non-athletes (people just like my clients) should focus their training on these basics to get stronger, leaner, faster, and more powerful. Like you, my clients aren't professional athletes. No, they are results-oriented people who want to look better and perform better, too. And this is exactly why I've designed this program. For driven individuals who won't accept mediocrity. For people who want to take control of their nutrition, lifestyle, and training. All whilst holding down busy lives, careers, relationships, and social lives.

Does HPL Training Differ for Females?

Notice I say "individuals," not men and not women. HPL is not gender specific and neither is the training. I want females to lift, sprint, jump, and throw (women have so much to gain from adding these elements into their training). But there are certain recommendations I'd like to make to females following this program. These will help you get the best results.

- The front squat is my preferred squat variation for females. The range of motion is greater, placing a greater emphasis upon mobility and form, whilst engaging the rectus abdominis more than during a back squat. Front squats are also kinder on the knees than back squats.
- In general, I like females to perform the bench press with a slightly narrow grip. This places more stress on the triceps, an area in which females tend to be comparatively weaker.
- Great glutes are of paramount importance to the female lifter. (We have Miley Cyrus, and her untrained posterior, to thank for the recent increased interest in good glute training!) Whilst heavy leg training will address this to a certain extent, I strongly recommend women dedicate more lifting time to glute-specific exercises. In the HPL program, you'll see direct glute work (hip thrusts, 45 degree back extensions, swings, etc.) On conditioning days, I suggest females stay off the bike and instead focus on prowler pushes (both high and low handle).
- Conventional deadlifts work just fine for females, though if you are new to strength training I strongly recommend beginning with the trap bar version. This makes it easier to get into the

start position and places less stress on the lower back owing to the neutral position of the bar. This is not a lifting law, but is certainly sound advice for the novice lifter (and equally applicable to males).

Please note these are suggestions based upon my own experience with athletes and clients. It doesn't mean the female lifter can't back squat or deadlift conventionally. The choice remains with the individual.

HPL training is a simple and effective method of achieving a very specific set of results. But what exactly will you find in the program and, most importantly, why?

How do us mere mortals train like our heroes and see appreciable results? Read on, and I'll break the whole thing down for you.

27. THE SEVEN COMPONENTS OF HIGH PERFORMANCE LIVING TRAINING

These seven distinct components form the blueprint for our training success. So let's explore them properly.

1. Warm-Up

You must warm up effectively before every training session. An optimal warm-up improves performance and recovery and, most importantly, reduces the chance of injury. We want consistent long-term gains, not a stop/start approach plagued by annoying injuries that a good warm-up could help prevent. Warm-ups are also a great opportunity to focus on the task at hand. They act as a bridge between arriving at the gym with life's baggage and starting the main workout.

Warm-ups are hugely beneficial, but please don't become the person who turns the warm-up into a workout in itself. Remember the HPL way: simple, direct, and effective. So, what exactly constitutes an appropriate warm-up? Well, here's what not to do (I can't tell you how often I see athletes warming up before strength sessions, skill sessions, and even competitions with these!):

- Skip briefly
- Do a few half-assed arm circles
- Maybe a few push-ups and squats with shabby form
- A quick jog on the spot then you're good to go.

No, no, no! I'll teach you how to warm up properly.

In my opinion, a well-structured and efficient warm up is the foundation of a successful session. Here's what I recommend for you:

SMR

Self-myofacial release (SMR), or self massage performed with foam rollers and lacrosse balls. This improves the quality of your soft tissue whilst working to reduce scar tissue, adhesions, and trigger points. My preference is to keep this to a minimum pre workout, using it for longer in the post-workout cooldown (more on this in the "recovery" section).

General

Begin raising the core temperature with basic movements that raise heart rate and increase circulation. This helps prepare your body for the stresses of the main workout. Try the Concept2 rower, a bike such as an Airdyne, or skipping. You also need to start increasing the range of motion of the joints. Most people will benefit from exercises targeting the glutes and hip mobility.

General Specific

Now bring in movements focusing on the muscle groups and movement patterns specific to the upcoming workout. You should include dynamic flexibility and mobility drills. These help to improve strength and power potential and further reduce the potential for injury.

Specific

Move on to movements specific to the upcoming workout. For example, if we will be squatting as a primary movement in the workout then we will begin repping out lighter sets of the squat in preparation for the "work sets." I go into more detail in the FAQ section.

Lovett Tip

I recommend that the warm-ups up to this point are performed barefoot (provided that you are training on a suitable surface). This helps to improve both ankle mobility and toe dexterity. As HPL individuals, we want to be strong and mobile from the ground up.

2. Explode

Conclude the warm-up by progressively introducing central nervous system (CNS)-activating movements. The CNS is composed of the brain and the spinal cord. Its job, particularly in regard to training, is to control movement, coordinate reflexes, and allow you to perform exercises at specific intensities.

Exciting your nervous system with exercises such as jumps, sprints, and med-ball throws enable it to become more efficient. The more neurologically efficient you are, the more you can get out of your muscles.

Here's how and why you should perform explosive warm-up movements.

Jumps

These are tremendous at developing explosive strength whilst helping you build a high rate of force development (and you'll need this if you want to be explosive in the core strength lifts—squat, press, and deadlift). Jumps are also an effective and simple way to strengthen the joint structures of the ankles, knees, hips, and lower back. Typically, jumping exercises can be performed one to two times per week, ideally before squat or deadlift training.

Lovett Tip
Because jumps are highly CNS intensive, full recovery between sets is recommended so you can perform at the highest intensity.

I've added three types of jump into the HPL training program:

1. Box jump
2. Broad jump
3. Hurdle jump

Lovett Tip
It is important to master the ability to land softly and safely when jumping. After all, a Bugatti Veyron may be the world's fastest and most powerful production car, but all those thousands of horsepower and boggling 0–180 mph stats would be immaterial if it did not have quality breaks to decelerate safely.

Of the three, the broad jump requires the least equipment. You simply need space and a practical level surface. However, it has the most potential for injury to the knee and shins, especially to those new to such exercises. Exercise caution, and make sure that your arms are incorporated into the movement, aiming to cover as much distance as possible with each jump. A soft landing after each jump is essential. Look to perform two to three consecutive jumps per set and between three and five sets.

Box jumps are the simplest to perform but are limited slightly by equipment

requirements. Thankfully, suppliers of foam plyo boxes are becoming more widespread. Any reputable gym should now be stocking these, as opposed to the shin- and confidence-destroying wooden boxes of old. Perform a powerful arm swing to aid greater jump height, making sure to finish each jump with a soft, controlled landing. This is the least stressful jump and the easiest to recover from, because there is minimal loading during the landing when compared to all other jumps. Look to perform between two and five reps and between three and six sets.

Hurdle jumps are my personal favorite. They are high-intensity plyometric movements that utilize the stretch shortening cycle (SSC) to enhance reactive strength potential, develop eccentric (deceleration) strength, and improve joint stability/integrity. If that seems like a lot to take in—simply, you get a lot of bang for your buck with hurdle jumps. They are very efficient but do require some equipment. If you don't have access to hurdles then standard gym benches will suffice. Two to five jumps in sets of three to five are optimal.

Med Ball Throws/Slams

So simple, yet very effective... the perfect HPL training exercise! Med ball throws/slams are easy to grasp with little or no technical skill required, so you can hit the ground running with them.

They are a great way to develop explosive power through the entire body, as throwing enables you to accelerate fully to an uninhibited triple extension. Unlike with a barbell, you don't need to slow down and control a bar at the end of the movement. Instead, you can release the ball at max velocity. Throws are also great for developing power from the ground up, transferring through the midsection and up to the arms for release.

Lovett Tip
Every slam/throw should be performed with "bad intentions." It's impossible to slam or throw a ball hard enough, so give it your all. Maximum application to every rep is key.

Here are my preferred med ball exercises:

Med Ball Slam

1. Stand with feet shoulder-width apart with a non-bounce slam ball held at the waist.
2. Reach the ball up high above your head, ensuring to extend up onto your toes.
3. Slam the ball down to the ground in front of your feet with as much force as possible.
4. Repeat as required.
5. Three to eight sets of three to five reps is my recommendation here.

Standing Med Ball Chest Launch

1. Start standing facing the direction you will launch.
2. Grasping the ball, hold it onto your abdomen.
3. Hinge the hips, tipping the torso slightly forward.
4. Reverse this motion as aggressively as possible, exploding up through the legs and driving the arms forward away from the body.
5. Release the ball at full extension with the intention to launch it over the maximum possible distance.
6. Three to six sets of one to three reps is my recommendation here.

Overhead Med Ball Throw (Backward)

1. Begin facing away from the direction you will throw.
2. Start position is with the ball in both hands held above the head, with arms extended.
3. With arms extended, swing the ball down between the legs whilst flexing the knees. Do so as fast as possible.
4. In one fluid motion, explode the ball back up and overhead, releasing the ball at maximum velocity. This is a perfect example of uninhibited triple extension.
5. Three to five sets of three to five reps is my recommendation here.

Lovett Tip
Whilst there are many med balls available on the market, I am currently a fan of "slam balls" for such exercises. These are filled with sand to reduce bounce, which is particularly useful with med ball slams (less bounce means less likelihood of the ball hitting you painfully on the way back up). Slam balls also come in a much greater weight range, so you can load accordingly.

Sprints

Providing a tremendous stimulus to the body, sprinting is the highest velocity the human body can achieve. It is a great way to recruit fast twitch muscle fibers and provide a fat-burning effect. Simply check out a sprinter's physique as testament—muscled lower body, shoulders, and back, with low levels of body fat.

Adding sprinting into your program is a sure fire way to accelerate power development and improve body composition. Should you decide to add sprint training into your program, then do so instead of one jumping session. If you want to sprint more than once a week, be aware that this comes at the expense of assistance work and additional recovery protocols. Remember, we are using sprints to excite the nervous system, which allows the body to generate force faster, not to become the next Olympic hundred meters champion. Sprinting is just one tool in the HPL training repertoire. Use it accordingly.

Quality, not quantity, is the goal of sprint training. For the noncompetitive sprinter, distances of 10–40 meters are sufficient, with complete recovery between sets. Total volume should not exceed 200 meters in a sprint session.

The downside to sprinting is that not many people have access to a running track. Even fewer have access to a facility with sufficient length of indoor turf. So, despite all the benefits of sprinting, I find both jumps and throws far easier for the majority to incorporate into their routine.

Lovett Tip

Don't fall into the trap of turning any of the explode exercises into a conditioning session. Perform every movement with maximal purpose and "bad intentions," with full recovery between sets.

3. Strength

What Is Strength?

In its simplest terms, strength is the ability to apply force to an external resistance. If you ask me, the foundation of any worthwhile training program is the pursuit of maximal strength development, whether you are a competitive powerlifter/strongman, new to training, or seventy-five years old.

Improving your strength has a positive effect on all other facets of fitness. It truly is our bread and butter. For every training trend and fitness fad, strength is the one constant. Simple. Direct. Proven.

Founding your program on strength training also has the added benefit of increased neural drive. Jumps, throws, and sprints excite the nervous system, as does strength training. Exciting the nervous system early in a workout enables you to recruit more motor units during subsequent assistance lifts. The result is you can lift heavier weights for more reps.

The Best Tool for Strength

Smart strength-training programming will progressively increase an individual's ability to apply force and get stronger. The best tool to achieve this goal is the barbell. Barbell training has a long and proven history. The strongest, largest, and most powerful individuals over the years are all products of smart and effective barbell training. Why? Because squats, presses, deadlifts, and the Olympic lifts all train the entire body at one time, enabling us to lift sufficient weight to bring about strength gains, muscle growth, and fat loss.

How to Load for Strength

I recommend three set/rep schemes to a lifter beginning their High Performance journey:

- 5 × 5
- 6 × 3
- Work up to a 1RM (1-rep max)

I find these to be the simplest and most effective loading parameters for the development of the novice lifter. The less experienced you are, the simpler your program should be. However, the principle of progression is the same: aim to add weight to the work sets used every session until you are unable to add more. This "progressive overload" is the most important aspect of strength training. You must try to use heavier loads and perform more reps over time.

5 × 5

The 5 × 5 loading scheme has a rich history. Its advocates include Bill Starr, Fred Hatfield, Mark Rippetoe, and the infamous Russian squat programs. The scheme worked for such esteemed company and, applied correctly, it will do so for you too. This method provides plenty of volume to stimulate muscle growth, challenges you to work at a high load, and allows for enough repeated efforts to continue getting stronger.

6 × 3

However, nothing works forever. Thus, it is important to experience higher loading with even fewer reps: meet 6 × 3! This will prepare you to ultimately work up to a heavy single or new PR/1RM (personal record/one-rep max).

1RM

When following the prescribed loading methods, always adhere to the principal of never missing a rep. Yes, your final sets (whether that be five, three, or one rep) must be a challenge, but I want it to contain the best quality rep(s) you can give, as opposed to the best attempt you can give. The aim of strength training is to never miss a rep. No one becomes stronger missing a rep. People improve by hitting all their reps as assertively as possible. Missed reps can lead to injury and damaged confidence.

Lovett Tip

The barbell is our tool of choice, but, like any tool, it must be mastered if you want to unlock its full potential. I can't stress enough the importance of quality technique over ever-increasing weight. I want you to load optimally, not maximally. Never add weight at the expense of form. If in any doubt, seek out a qualified and experienced coach to assist you with correct exercise technique. Such an investment will be repaid multiple times over your lifting lifetime.

4. Build

The strength component of your workout should receive your maximum effort and attention. Don't be the type of lifter who rushes the big lifts in order to spend hours hitting their biceps from fourteen different angles. Warm up smartly and efficiently. Get fast through appropriate CNS activation, then give everything you have to every rep of strength work. Results are forged through hard work. This is the time to give it your very best.

Assistance work enables us to build on the foundations laid by that day's strength work. But please note that assistance work is just that: assistance. I find a lot of value in the work of Jim Wendler, who lists the four main tasks of assistance work as:

Strengthening Weak Areas of the Body

The old adage that you are only as strong as your weakest link applies to HPL training. A powerful bench press is for nothing if it is supported by a weak shoulder girdle and underdeveloped upper back. A house built on foundations of sand will fail sooner rather than later.

Complementing and Helping the Four Basic Lifts

The stronger you become in the main lifts (squat, bench, deadlift, press) the greater your gains will be. Assistance lifts can be tailored to the strength lift of that day. For example, dips are an excellent assistance exercise to the press. Likewise heavy, high-rep dumbbell rows complement a deadlift well.

Providing Balance and Symmetry to Your Body and Training

This is important for both maximizing performance and aesthetics. The HPL individual wants both in equal measure.

Building Muscle Mass

Increasing lean muscle is a primary goal of the HPL individual. Increasing muscle mass alongside increased strength results in improved body composition, which is what we all want.

My personal preference is to get the most benefit out of the least amount of exercise. Less truly is more here. Assistance exercises should stimulate the muscle, not annihilate it. Stick to this emphasis on training economy whilst meeting the above criteria. I advocate larger, more compound-based movements, even as assistance. A chin/pull-up is far more effective and efficient than minor isolation exercises.

You will also see that I incorporate supersets: two separate exercises paired up and performed back to back with minimal rest, as shown in the example below:

- A1 Gym-ring push-up: 3–4 × 10–20
- A2 Inverted gym-ring row: 3–4 × 8–10 (60 s)

In the above example, you'd perform gym-ring push-ups (A1) for a set of between ten and twenty reps (dictated by individual ability). Rest minimally and then perform inverted gym-ring rows (A2) for a set of between eight and ten reps (again dictated by individual ability). Rest the prescribed 60 seconds, then repeat for three to four total sets.

Supersets are an excellent option for gaining muscle mass whilst decreasing body fat and building work capacity. They achieve this because the short rest intervals increase lactate production and decrease blood pH levels, resulting in increased growth hormone secretion. This lactate also stimulates testosterone release. Such anabolic hormone production is ideal for both muscle growth and reducing body fat simultaneously.

5. Challenge

Your daily HPL workouts will conclude with a challenge, the purpose of which is as mental as it is physical. Why? Because pursuing the high-performance lifestyle requires determination, dedication, and a willingness to do what others won't. To reap the rewards requires hard work and the ability to challenge yourself. Let's use these challenges to build strength and muscle whilst improving body composition and work capacity. There is nothing wrong with being able to look AND perform to a high standard, after all!

Challenge Tools

Effective challenges can be done using dumbbells (DB), kettlebells (KB), and your own body weight (B/W). What is even more effective is combining all three into a short and sharp complex. Such complexes will see various DB, KB, and B/W exercises performed back to back with short rest periods between them.

6. Condition

The HPL individual is not necessarily a competitive athlete, but a regular person wishing to train and perform to their very best. Conditioning offers us mortals a myriad of benefits including:

- Better health
- Improved sense of well-being
- Faster recovery time between sets
- More mental toughness
- Awesome body composition

Yes, our primary goal is to become as strong as we possibly can, but that is for nothing if we get out of breath foam rolling or consider anything above three reps "cardio." I recommend conditioning work to be done at least two to three times per week on non-strength-training days. This allows us to focus on one thing at a time. It also breaks the training week down and enables suitable recovery between strength sessions.

Anything from walking to cycling on the AirDyne for thirty minutes or so will suffice. However, my personal favorite conditioning sessions are the "prowler" and hill sprints. Whilst there is a place for steady-state cardio (as exhibited by walking or bike work) I find prowler/hill sprints to be far more effective and—most importantly—more mentally stimulating. They are demanding, task-orientated drills that are easier to avoid than complete, which automatically gets me interested! Anything hard fought is worthwhile, in my opinion.

Hill sprints provide all the benefits of short-distance sprints with the added bonus of more load and less stress due to the angle of incline. Ideally these are performed on grass to further soften the impact to the joints. The only catch is finding a suitable hill. If you can, then here is a solid plan:

10 × 10 m hill sprints (75–90 s)

working up to:

6 × 30 m (90–120 s)

Granted, no two hills are exactly the same. But you can grasp what I am prescribing here.

The prowler is quite simply one of the most effective conditioning devices available. More and more facilities have them, so they are becoming increasingly accessible. Due to the eccentric-less nature of the exercise you can really push hard whilst not inducing a great deal of muscle soreness. Work up to ten times twenty meters prowler sprints. Prowler use will limit the progress of maximal strength gains, but that's not what the HPL individual is after. You want better body composition as well as strength. The prowler gives the best of both worlds.

7. Recover

In its simplest terms (and I do like simple!), recovery can be described as shown in the figure.

Keep Your Glass Full

Sleep
Nutrition
Recovery

Your body

Training
Work/School
Stress

If you are truly dedicated to being your best and building the strongest, most capable, and most powerful body in the gym, then you must be equally zealous outside the gym by maximizing recovery. Optimizing effective restorative measures will make a huge difference to your results. It will:

- Increase your ability to train more frequently, intensely, and effectively
- Reduce the risk of injury
- Aid the management of minor aches and pains
- Ensure your body and mind are at their best for every workout.

Below is a list of recovery methods that my clients and I use weekly. This isn't an exhaustive list, but covers the methods I am familiar with and happy to recommend.

Optimize Your Nutrition/ Supplementation

You've already read all about this in parts I and II of Ru's book.

Sleep

Ru covered the topic of sleep in Chapter 8, but it is worth reiterating. I am frequently asked about the best miracle supplement. People will pay anything for a quick-fix tablet. My advice is simple: close your wallet and sleep more. It costs nothing, and no energy, equipment, or outside help is required. Eight (or a bit more) hours per day works for me. If possible, try and grab a "NASA nap" during the day. A 1995 study by NASA found a 26-minute nap improved performance by 34% and alertness by 54%. I have no way of quantifying the effect such naps have on me, but I feel fresher and can train harder and more frequently. That's good enough for me.

Active Recovery

I am a firm believer that individuals recover far more efficiently by staying active as opposed to sitting around idle. Numerous studies demonstrate that increased muscle blood flow via low-intensity exercise is highly beneficial for recovery purposes. It helps minimize the delayed onset of muscle soreness (DOMS), and promotes muscle healing.

My preferred methods for this are as follows:

- 30 minutes on the Airdyne bike, or similar
- 10–15 minutes continuous sled walks. Note this must be with a light sled.
- 20–30 minutes walk

Massage

Massage can help reduce inflammation, increase the elasticity of the ligaments and muscles, and has a general relaxing effect on the body.

Get a deep tissue massage from a qualified therapist, someone with a sound knowledge of anatomy and physiology. The more "hands-on experience" they have, the better. Find a practitioner who actively works with athletes as opposed to a beauty or "spa day" masseuse.

Foam Rolling

A quality massage therapist can be costly. Enter self myofacial release (SMR). More widely known as foam rolling (or as strength coach Mike Boyle calls it, a poor man's massage). This is a version of deep tissue massage that is far cheaper and easy to implement.

Whilst I have included limited use of SMR in the warm-up section, I prefer it during the post-workout cooldown and especially on "rest days" to promote recovery. Here's a sample SMR cool down:

Upper back
- Position the foam roller between the shoulder blades.
- Raise the hips up with the feet providing a solid base.
- Roll the length of the back in smooth strokes, focusing upon tighter areas.
- Ensure the arms are crossed over the chest and elbows directly above the shoulders.

Quadriceps
- Lie facing down with the foam roller between your hips
- Roll from the hip all the way down to the knee with long smooth strokes.
- Move from side to side as you do so, in order to cover as much of the muscle group as possible.
- Supporting your body with your hands, push up and place as much of your body weight as possible onto the roller.
- Slow down and focus upon any tight areas.

Adductors
- Lie facing down with the foam roller next to you in a parallel position.
- Place one leg over the roller so that you are lying over it with the roller positioned at the top inner part of your thigh.
- Support the upper body with your hands planted on the floor.
- Raise up and roll back and forth over the inside area of the thigh, focusing particularly on any tighter areas.

Glutes (note that I much prefer a lacrosse ball for SMR of this area)

- Place opposite foot onto opposite knee.
- Pivot and support the body whilst focusing on the glute with foot off the ground.
- Roll the glutes in small steady strokes, ensuring maximum body weight is on the foam roller.
- Focus upon tighter, more painful areas.

Electromyostimulation (EMS)

An effective method in reducing recovery time when utilized with a low-intensity pulse. This acts in a similar way to sports massage, stimulating blood flow and moving nutrients to the muscles. This is especially effective the day after intense training on the affected area.

The most popular model is the Compex unit, which has numerous settings to enhance strength, power, and endurance, and (most applicable here), an active recovery and potentiation setting.

EMS is effective, but costly compared to the other methods listed here. I do rate EMS but it's not essential to this program.

Cryotherapy (Ice Massage)

Ice massage is useful in reducing inflammation and decreasing pain. Simply massage the affected muscle in a circular fashion for between five and ten minutes with an icepack. Adding a small amount of baby oil to the area before icing can help.

Contrast Baths/Showers

These increase local blood circulation by vasodilatation via the warm water, followed by vasoconstriction from the cold water. Simply alternate between thirty seconds of cold water and two minutes of warm water. This cycle can be repeated three or four times. This contrast technique increases peripheral blood flow and thus enhances recovery.

The late, great sprint coach Charlie Francis was a fan. He advocated three minutes as hot as an individual could stand, followed immediately by one minute as cold as the individual could stand, repeating for two cycles. Experiment and find what works for you.

Epsom Salt Baths

A personal favorite of mine: take a red-hot bath for ten to twenty minutes with the addition of 500–600 g of Epsom salt (also known as magnesium sulfate). This is a very simple method to relax your muscles and help reduce inflammation, especially after a hard training session. Taking such a bath allows the magnesium to be absorbed transdermally, increasing mean blood magnesium levels. Magnesium is an important mineral for trained individuals, who are often deficient.

Charlie Francis used this technique with his sprinters to boost recovery from intense training.

In keeping with the HPL way, these recovery methods are all simple, easily implemented, and effective. Experiment and find what works best for you. Which method(s) can you implement consistently that will help you recover optimally and help keep your glass full?

28. TWELVE-WEEK TRAINING PROGRAM

Warm Up

Below is a sample warm-up that can be performed prior to any of the attached workouts.

Foam Rolling

Foam roll for 1–2 minutes each area with 30–45 seconds on painful/tender areas.

Upper Back
- Position the foam roller between the shoulder blades.
- Raise the hips up with the feet providing a solid base.
- Roll the length of the back in smooth strokes, focusing upon tighter areas.
- Ensure the arms are crossed over the chest and elbows directly above the shoulders.

Iliotibial Band (IT Band)
- Cross your feet for extra stability and roll from the knee (but not over it) to the hip in smooth strokes.
- Aim to place as much body weight on the foam roller as possible.
- Focus upon tighter, more painful areas.

Piriformis (I prefer the use of a lacrosse ball here but a foam roller will suffice.)
- Place opposite foot onto opposite knee.
- Pivot and support the body, whilst focusing on the glute, with foot off the ground.
- Roll the glutes in small steady strokes, ensuring maximum body weight is on the foam roller.
- Focus upon tighter, more painful areas.

Concept2 Rower OR Airdyne Bike

- For five to ten minutes; duration dictated by individual ability/condition. This must remain a warm-up and not a workout!

Blackburns × 10 reps

- Start in the prone position with the head looking forward.
- Place the backs of the hands onto the glutes, retracting the scapula and squeezing the shoulders together.
- Bring the arms into a "Y" position above the head, rotating the hands so that the thumbs are pointing upwards.

- Hold this position for a count of two seconds.
- Return the arms to the starting position in a controlled manner. At no time do the arms touch the floor.

Band Pull Apart × 10–15 reps

- Choose an appropriate level resistance band.
- Maintain tension on the band at all times, keeping the hands, elbows, and shoulders in line whilst pulling the band apart and squeezing the scapula.

Inch Worm × 5–10 reps (2-second pause)

- Start standing with feet shoulder-width apart.
- Reach down to the floor as close to the body as possible, whilst maintaining straight legs.
- Walk the hands out in a controlled manner as far as possible, whilst maintaining a braced core. Do not let the lower back sink. Hold this position for two seconds.
- Walk the hands back in towards the feet in small steps, ensuring the legs do not bend.
- Repeat.

Squat/Lunge combo × 5 reps

- Perform a body-weight squat.
- Perform a forward lunge off one leg.
- Perform a reverse lunge off the same leg.
- Perform forward and reverse lunges on opposite leg.
- This equals one rep. Repeat as required.

Cossack Squats × 10 reps each side

- Start with legs straight in a wide stance.
- Maintain an upright torso, squat down to one side, pulling up the toe of the straight leg.
- Move towards the opposite side, staying low whilst maintaining an upright torso.

Roll Over V-Sits × 10

- Roll backward with legs over the face, keeping them straight and together.
- Roll legs forward over the face towards the ground; bring them apart into a V-position.
- With legs straight, reach forward with the arms.

Explode

Box Jump: 3 × 5 (60 s)

- Feet in an athletic stance, jump onto the box, landing athletically.

The above is not set in stone. Rather, it is a sample of what I would look to use with the following workouts. If you have something else in your warm-up routine that you feel works, then by all means do it. Just remember this is a warm-up and not a workout.

HPL TRAINING: WEEKS ONE TO SIX

The goal of the sessions in weeks one to six is to master quality form on all exercises, whilst learning to progressively add weight to the main lifts each week. Remember we want quality repetitions at all times. Do not sacrifice form for poor reps and too much weight.

Pay attention to the rep scheme of the assistance exercises. As these drop each week, there should be a corresponding increase in weight lifted. Again, this must not be at the expense of form.

Each workout is separated into four sections:

1. Explode
2. Strength
3. Build
4. Challenge

The sessions are designed to be full body. I like this approach for HPL training because:

- Full-body sessions provide a greater training frequency per week, enabling you to train the same areas numerous times, stimulating your muscles more often. More stimulation will see an increase in muscle growth as well as strength and body composition.

- By nature, full-body training challenges numerous muscle groups at the same time. Not only does this provide a greater training efficiency, but also a greater anabolic hormonal response—the perfect environment for sustained muscle growth.
- Using multiple muscle groups in the same session allows for more total calories to be burned. An excellent stimulus for fat loss.

You will see that I have offered alternative exercises for females—these are in italics. In particular, these provide more glute work: something I've found successful for female clients. Please note these are only alternatives and not a direct requirement for the female lifter. The choice, as always, remains with the individual.

Week One

Day One
Explode:
A box jump: 3 × 5 (60 s)

Strength:
A back squat: 5 × 5 (90–120 s)
*Add warm-up sets as required

Build:
A1 45 raise: 3 × 15
A2 push-up plank: 3 × 45–60 s (75 s)—load
if applicable. The aim is to make 45–60 s as
challenging as possible.

Challenge:
A1 hip thrust: 2 × 15
A2 alt reverse lunge: 2 × 10 each leg
A3 dumbbell burpee: 2 × 10

Day Two
Explode:
A med ball slam: 5 × 2 (30 s)

Strength:
A deadlift: 5 × 5 (90–120 s)
*Add warm-up sets as required
B military press: 5 × 5 (90 s)
*Add warm-up sets as required

Build:
A1 pull-up: 3 × 5–10 (load if required)
A2 side plank (feet on floor): 3 × 30–60 s
each side (75 s)

Challenge:
A1 alternate dumbbell curl and press:
2 × 10 each arm
A2 band pull apart: 2 × 12
A3 band triceps pushdown: 2 × 15–20

Day Three
Explode:
A broad jump:
3 × 3 (60 s)

Strength:
A bench press: 5 × 5 (90 s)
*Add warm-up sets

Build:
A back squat: 3 × 10 (60 s)
*These should be light and snappy
*Alternative: dumbbell Romanian deadlift
3 × 15
B1 push-up: 3 × max
B2 chest-supported dumbbell row: 3 × 15
(75 s)

Challenge:
A1 barbell curl: 2 × 10
A2 dumbbell reverse fly: 2 × 12
A3 inch worm: 2 × 10

Challenge: Perform each exercise with
minimal rest between exercises and with
thirty to sixty seconds between sets. Two
total sets.

Week Two

Day One
Explode:
A box jumps: 3 × 5 (60 s)

Strength:
A back squat: 5 × 5 (90–120 s)
*Add warm-up sets as required.

Build:
A1 45 degree back extension: 3 × 12
A2 push-up plank: 3 × 45–60 s (75 s)
*Load as required.

Challenge:
A1 hip thrust: 3 × 15
A2 alt reverse lunge: 3 × 10 each leg
A3 dumbbell burpee: 3 × 10

Day Two
Explode:
A med ball slam: 5 × 2 (30 s)

Strength:
A deadlift: 5 × 5 (90–120 s)
*Add warm-up sets as required
B military press: 5 × 5 (90 s)
*Add warm-up sets as required

Build:
A1 pull-up: 3 × 5–10 (load if required)
A2 side plank (feet on floor): 3 × 30–60s
each side (75 s)

Challenge:
A1 alternate dumbbell curl and press:
3 × 10 each arm
A2 band pull apart: 3 × 12
A3 band triceps pushdown: 3 × 15–20

Day Three
Explode:
A broad jump: 3 × 3 (60 s)

Strength:
A bench press: 5 × 5 (90 s)
*Add warm-up sets as required

Build:
A back squat: 3 × 10 (60 s)
*These should be light and snappy
*Alternative: dumbbell Romanian deadlift
3 × 12
B1 push-up: 3 × max
*Aim to beat previous week's total.
B2 chest-supported dumbbell row:
3 × 12 (75 s)

Challenge:
A1 barbell curl: 3 × 10
A2 dumbbell reverse fly: 3 × 12
A3 inch worm: 3 × 10

Challenge: Perform each exercise with minimal rest between exercises and with thirty to sixty seconds between sets. Three total sets.

Week Three

Day One
Explode:
A box jump: 4 × 5 (60 s)

Strength:
A back squat: 5 × 5 (90–120 s)
*Add warm-up sets as required

Build:
A1 45 degree back extension: 3 × 10
A2 push-up plank: 3 × 45–60 s (75 s)
*Load as required

Challenge:
A1 hip thrust: 4 × 15
A2 alt reverse dumbbell lunge × 10 each leg
A3 dumbbell burpee: 4 × 10

Day Two
Explode:
A med ball slam: 5 × 3 (30 s)

Strength:
A deadlift: 5 × 5 (90–120 s)
*Add warm-up sets as required
B military press: 5 × 5 (90s)
*Add warm-up sets as required

Build:
A1 pull-up: 3 × 5–10
*Load as required
A2 side plank (feet elevated): 3 × 30–60 s each side (75 s)

Challenge:
A1 alternate dumbbell curl and press: 4 × 10 each arm
A2 band triceps pushdown: 4 × 15–20
A3 band triceps pushdown: 4 × 15–20

Day Three
Explode:
A broad jump: 4 × 3 (60 s)

Strength:
A bench press: 5 × 5 (90 s)
*Add warm-up sets as required

Build:
A back squat: 3 × 8 (60 s)
*Alternative: dumbbell Romanian deadlift 3 × 10
B1 push-up (feet elevated): 3 × max
B2 chest-supported dumbbell row: 3 × 10 (75 s)

Challenge:
A1 barbell curl: 4 × 10
A2 dumbbell reverse fly: 4 × 12
A3 inch worm: 4 × 10

Challenge: Perform each exercise with minimal rest between exercises and between thirty and sixty seconds between sets. Four total sets.

Week Four

Day One

Explode:
A box jump: 4 × 5 (60 s)

Strength:
A back squat: 5 × 5 (90–120 s)
*Add warm-up sets as required

Build:
A1 45 degree back extension: 3 × 8
A2 push-up plank: 3 × 45–60 s (75 s)
*Load as required

Challenge:
A1 dumbbell Romanian deadlift: 2 × 6
A2 dumbbell squat: 2 × 6
A3 dumbbell mountain climbers: 2 × 12
(6 each leg)

Day Two

Explode:
A med ball slam: 5 × 3 (30 s)

Strength:
A deadlift: 5 × 5 (90–120 s)
*Add warm-up sets as required
B military press: 5 × 5 (90 s)
*Add warm-up sets as required

Build:
A1 pull-up: 3 × 5–10
*Load as required.
A2 side plank (feet elevated): 3 × 30–60 s
each side (75 s)

Challenge:
A1 dumbbell squat jump: 2 × 6
A2 dumbbell curl and press: 2 × 6 (both
arms together)
A3 dumbbell squat thrust: 2 × 6

Challenge: Perform as a complex. No rest
between exercises. Do not put dumbbells
down between exercises. Thirty to sixty
seconds between complexes. Two total
complexes.

Day Three

Explode:
A broad jump: 4 × 3 (60 s)

Strength:
A bench press: 5 × 5 (90 s)
*Add warm-up sets as required

Build:
A back squat: 3 × 6 (60 s)
*Alternative: dumbbell Romanian deadlift
3 × 8
B1 push-up (feet elevated): 3 × max
*Aim to beat previous week's total
B2 chest-supported dumbbell row: 3 × 8
(75 s)

Challenge:
A1 dumbbell hammer curl: 2 × 12 each arm
A2 face pull: 2 × 10–12
A3 hanging knee raise: 2 × 10–12

Challenge: Perform each exercise with
minimal rest in between. Rest thirty to sixty
seconds between sets. Two total sets.

Week Five

Day One

Explode:
A box jump: 5 × 3 (60 s)

Strength:
A back squat: 5 × 5 (90–120 s)
*Add warm-up sets as required

Build:
A1 barbell hip thrust: 3 × 10–20
A2 incline dumbbell press: 3 × 12 (75 s)

Challenge:
A1 dumbbell Romanian deadlift: 3 × 6
A2 dumbbell squat: 3 × 6
A3 dumbbell mountain climbers: 3 × 12
(6 each leg)

Day Two

Explode:
A med ball slam: 3 × 5 (30 s)

Strength:
A deadlift: 5 × 5 (90–120 s)
*Add warm-up sets as required
B military press: 5 × 5 (90 s)
*Add warm-up sets as required

Build:
A1 pull-up: 30 total reps
A2 bench dips: sets of 10 in between pull-up sets (60 s)

Challenge:
A1 dumbbell squat jump: 3 × 6
A2 dumbbell curl and press: 3 × 6 (both arms together)
A3 dumbbell squat thrust: 3 × 6

Challenge: Perform as a complex. No rest between exercises. Do not put dumbbells down between exercises. Thirty to sixty seconds between complexes. Three total complexes.

Day Three

Explode:
A broad jump: 3 × 5 (60 s)

Strength:
A bench press: 5 × 5 (90 s)
*Add warm-up sets as required

Build:
A back squat: 3 × 5 (60 s)
*Alternative: dumbbell Romanian deadlift 3 × 8
B1 reverse-grip push-up: 3 × 10–20
B2 one-arm dumbbell row: 3 × 15 each arm (75 s)

Challenge:
A1 dumbbell hammer curl: 3 × 12 each arm
A2 face pull: 3 × 10–12
A3 hanging knee raise: 3 × 10–12

Challenge: Perform each exercise with minimal rest in between. Rest thirty to sixty seconds between sets. Three total sets.

Week Six

Day One
Explode:
A box jump: 6 × 3 (60 s)

Strength:
A back squat: 5 × 5 (90–120 s)
*Add warm-up sets as required

Build:
A1 barbell hip thrust: 3 × 10–20
A2 incline dumbbell press: 3 × 10 (75 s)

Challenge:
A1 dumbbell Romanian deadlift: 4 × 6
A2 dumbbell squat: 4 × 6
A3 dumbbell mountain climbers: 4 × 12
(6 each leg)

Day Two
Explode:
A med ball slam: 4 × 5 (30 s)

Strength:
A deadlift: 5 × 5 (90–120 s)
*Add warm-up sets as required
B military press: 5 × 5 (90 s)
*Add warm-up sets as required

Build:
A1 pull-up: 35 total reps
A2 bench dips: sets of 10 in between pull-up sets (60 s)

Challenge:
A1 dumbbell squat jump: 4 × 6
A2 dumbbell curl and press: 4 × 6 (both arms together)
A3 dumbbell squat thrust: 4 × 6

Challenge: Perform as a complex. No rest between exercises. Do not put dumbbells down between exercises. Thirty to sixty seconds between complexes. Four total complexes.

Day Three
Explode:
A broad jump: 3 × 5 (60 s)

Strength:
A bench press: 5 × 5 (90 s)
*Add warm-up sets as required

Build:
A back squat: 3 × 5 (60 s)
Alternative: dumbbell Romanian deadlift 3 × 8
B1 reverse-grip push-up: 3 × 10–20
B2 one-arm dumbbell row: 3 × 15 each arm (75 s)

Challenge:
A1 dumbbell hammer curl: 4 × 12 each arm
A2 face pull: 4 × 10–12
A3 hanging knee raise: 4 × 10–12

Challenge: Perform each exercise with minimal rest in between. Rest thirty to sixty seconds between sets. Four total sets.

WEEK SEVEN (DELOAD)

The goal of a deload is to recover both mentally and physically. Note the reduced volume on all exercises. Pay close attention to the main lifts. I specify that they should be performed with lighter weights so please make sure that you do so. The short sixty-second rest periods should help with this.

Day One
Explode:
A box jump: 2 × 5 (60 s)

Strength:
A back squat: 3 × 5 (60 s)
*Deload week—lighter weights

Build:
A barbell hip thrust: 2 × 10 (60 s)
B incline dumbbell press: 2 × 10 (60 s)

Challenge:
A1 push-up × 10
A2 burpee × 5
A3 mountain climbers × 10 total
(5 each leg)

Day Two
Explode:
A med ball slam: 2 × 5 (30 s)

Strength:
A deadlift: 3 × 5 (60 s)
*Deload week—lighter weights
B military press: 3 × 5 (60 s)
*Deload week—lighter weights

Build:
A pull-ups: 2 × 5–10 (60 s)

Challenge:
A1 goblet squat × 10
A2 underhand-grip band pull apart
A3 single-leg hip thrust (body weight only)
× 5 each leg

Day Three
Explode:
A broad jump: 2 × 5 (60 s)

Strength:
A bench press: 3 × 5 (90 s)
*Deload week—lighter weights

Build:
A back squat: 2 × 10 (60 s)
*Alternative: dumbbell Romanian deadlift
2 × 15

Challenge:
A1 push-up (feet elevated) × 10
A2 dumbbell renegade row × 10 (5 each arm)
A3 dumbbell squat thrust × 10

Challenge: Two to three times through the above circuits. Rest sixty seconds.

HPL TRAINING: WEEKS EIGHT TO ELEVEN

Fresh from your deload, you'll feel ready to meet the goal of the sessions over the next four weeks: to progressively add weight to your main lifts whilst not sacrificing quality form. The loading parameters have progressed from 5 × 5 to 6 × 3. This exposes you to higher loads with reduced reps and more work sets, all in preparation for setting a personal best and 1RM (one-rep max) in each of the main lifts in week twelve.

Again, pay close attention to the varying sets/reps of the assistance exercises. Reduction in reps indicates an increase in weight lifted, if possible.

You will notice pull-ups being performed on two separate days. This is not a typo! I am a huge proponent of not only developing maximal strength but also relative body weight strength. Any grip will suffice: fat grip, neutral, narrow grip, underhand, overhand, rings. They are all acceptable.

The "challenge" complexes/circuits are removed in week eleven. This reduces training volume slightly in preparation of the following week's 1RM testing.

Again, you will see alternative options for females—these are in italics. In particular, these provide more glute work, something I've found beneficial for my female clients. Please note these are only alternatives and not a direct requirement. The choice, as ever, remains with you.

Week Eight

Day One
Explode:
A box jump: 5 × 5 (60 s)

Strength:
A back squat: 6 × 3 (90–120 s)
*Add warm-up sets as required

Build:
A incline bench: 3 × 8 (75–90 s)
B pull-up (any variation): 40 total reps.
Feel free to superset some of these in with bench.

Challenge:
A1 dumbbell Romanian deadlift × 6
A2 dumbbell military press × 6
A3 dumbbell squat × 6
A4 dumbbell burpee × 6

Challenge: dumbbell in each hand at all times. Six reps per exercise, no rest between exercises, don't put dumbbells down until the completion of the complex. Rest thirty to sixty seconds between rounds. Perform three to five rounds.

Day Two
Explode:
A med ball chest launch (standing): 3 × 3 (60 s)

Strength:
A deadlift: 6 × 3 (90–120 s)
*Add warm-up sets as required
B military press: 6 × 3 (90 s)
*Add warm-up sets as required

Build:
A pull-ups (any variation): 40 total reps.
Superset in with military press if you wish.

Challenge:
A1 split squats × 8 each leg
A2 ab wheel roll out × 8
A3 45 degree back extension × 10–15
(body weight only)
A4 med ball slam × 10

Day Three
Explode:
A hurdle jump: 3 × 3 (60 s)

Strength:
A bench press: 6 × 3 (90 s)
*Add warm-up sets

Build:
A back squat: 3 × 5–10 (75 s)
*Alternative: barbell glute bridge 3 × 10–20
B1 ring push up: 3 × 10–20
B2 inverted ring row: 3 × 5–10 (75 s)

Challenge:
A1 swing × 15
A2 goblet squat × 10
A3 Russian kettlebell challenge (or normal) plank × 20 s
*Ensure a solid brace and squeeze
A4 band pull apart × 10

Challenge: Perform all exercises back to back with minimal rest. Perform two rounds with thirty to sixty seconds rest between rounds.

Week Nine

Day One
Explode:
A box jump: 4 × 4 (60 s)

Strength:
A back squat: 6 × 3 (90–120 s)
*Add warm-up sets as required

Build:
A incline bench: 3 × 6 (75–90 s)
B pull-up (any variation): 45 total reps.
Feel free to superset some of these in with bench.

Challenge:
A1 dumbbell Romanian deadlift × 8
A2 dumbbell military press × 8
A3 dumbbell squat × 8
A4 dumbbell burpee × 8

Challenge: dumbbell in each hand at all times. Eight reps per exercise, no rest between exercises, don't put dumbbells down until the completion of the complex. Rest thirty to sixty seconds between rounds. Perform three to five rounds.

Day Two
Explode:
A med ball chest launch (standing): 4 × 3 (60 s)

Strength:
A deadlift: 6 × 3 (90–120 s)
*Add warm-up sets as required
B military press: 6 × 3 (90 s)
*Add warm-up sets as required

Build:
A pull-ups (any variation): 45 total reps.
Superset in with military press if you wish.

Challenge:
A1 split squats × 8 each leg
A2 ab wheel roll out × 8
A3 45 degree back extension × 10–15 (body weight only)
A4 med ball slam × 10

Challenge: Perform all exercises back to back with minimal rest. Perform two rounds with thirty to sixty seconds rest between rounds.

Day Three
Explode:
A hurdle jump: 4 × 3 (60 s)

Strength:
A bench press: 6 × 3 (90 s)
*Add warm-up sets as required

Build:
A back squat: 3 × 5–10 (75 s)
*Alternative: barbell glute bridge 3 × 10–20
B1 ring push up: 3 × 10–20
B2 inverted ring row: 3 × 5–10 (75 s)

Challenge:
A1 swing × 15
A2 goblet squat × 10
A3 Russian kettlebell challenge (or normal) plank × 20 s
*Ensure a solid brace and squeeze
A4 band pull apart × 10

Challenge: Perform all exercises back to back with minimal rest. Perform three rounds with thirty to sixty seconds rest between rounds.

Week Ten

Day One
Explode:
A box jump: 5 × 4 (60 s)

Strength:
A back squat: 6 × 3 (90–120 s)
*Add warm-up sets as required

Build:
A incline bench: 4 × 6 (75–90 s)
B pull-up (any variation): 50 total reps.
Feel free to superset in with bench.

Challenge:
A1 dumbbell Romanian deadlift × 10
A2 dumbbell military press × 10
A3 dumbbell squat × 10
A4 dumbbell burpee × 10

Challenge: Ten reps per exercise, no rest between exercises, don't put dumbbells down until the completion of the complex. Rest thirty to sixty seconds between rounds. Perform three to five rounds.

Day Two
Explode:
A med ball chest launch (standing):
5 × 3 (60 s)

Strength:
A deadlift: 6 × 3 (90–120 s)
*Add warm-up sets accordingly
B military press: 6 × 3 (90 s)
*Add warm-up sets accordingly

Build:
A pull-up (any variation): 50 total reps.
Superset with press if you wish.

Challenge:
A1 split squats × 8 each leg
A2 ab wheel roll out × 8
A3 45 degree back extension × 10–15
(body weight only)
A4 med ball slam × 10

Challenge: Perform all exercises back to back with minimal rest. Perform four rounds with thirty to sixty seconds rest between rounds.

Day Three
Explode:
A hurdle jump: 5 × 3 (60 s)

Strength:
A bench press: 6 × 3 (90 s)
*Add warm-up sets as required

Build:
A back squat: 3 × 5–10 (75 s)
*Alternative: barbell glute bridge 3 × 10–20
B1 ring push up (feet elevated): 3 × 10–20
B2 inverted ring row (feet elevated):
3 × 5–10 (75 s)

Challenge:
A1 swing × 15
A2 goblet squat × 10
A3 Russian kettlebell challenge (or normal) plank × 20 s
*Ensure a solid brace and squeeze throughout
A4 band pull apart × 10

Challenge: Perform all exercises back to back with minimal rest. Perform four rounds with thirty to sixty seconds rest between rounds.

Week Eleven

Day One
Explode:
A box jump: 6 × 3 (60 s)

Strength:
A back squat: 6 × 3 (90–120 s)
*Add warm-up sets accordingly

Build:
A incline bench: 4 × 6 (75–90 s)
B pull-up (any variation): 50 total reps.
Superset with bench if you wish.
A farmer's walk: 3 × 60s (75 s)
*Use dumbbell or kettlebell in each hand

Day Two
Explode:
A med ball chest launch (standing):
6 × 3 (60 s)

Strength:
A deadlift: 6 × 3 (90–120 s)
*Add warm-up sets as required
B military press: 6 × 3 (90 s)
*Add warm-up sets as required

Build:
A pull-ups (any variation): 50 total reps.
Superset in with press if you wish.
B 1 arm farmer's walk: 3 × 30s each side
(75 s)

Day Three
Explode:
A hurdle jump: 5 × 4 (60 s)

Strength:
A bench press: 6 × 3 (90 s)
*Add warm-up sets as you wish

Build:
A back squat: 3 × 5–10 (75 s)
*Alternative: barbell glute bridge 3 × 10–20
B1 ring push up (feet elevated): 3 × 15–25
B2 inverted ring row (feet elevated):
3 × 10–15 (75 s)
C swing: 3 × 30 (45 s)

HPL TRAINING: WEEK TWELVE

Here we are at the culmination of the previous twelve weeks' hard work and progressive overload. The goal of these sessions is to set the very best 1-rep max (1RM) you can—the highest possible weight in each of the main lifts (squat, deadlift, press, and bench).

You will notice there is no set rest period for the main lifts. When setting a 1RM, rest periods are dictated only by how you feel and not by the clock. There is a greater body-weight theme to the assistance exercises here. I don't just want you to be strong maximally; I also want you to have impressive relative body-weight strength.

Again, there is an absence of the "challenge" complex/circuits. Training efficiency is always a key component of HPL training. The priority of these sessions remains the 1RM testing of the main lifts. Any remaining time in each session is used for complementary assistance exercises. Female lifters may consider the alternative exercises in italics to increase the volume of direct glute work.

Week Twelve

Day One
Explode:
A box jump: 3 × 5 (60 s)

Strength (1RM)
A back squat: work up to a 1RM. Rest as long as required.

Build:
A split squat: 3 × 10 each leg (60 s)
B swing: 3 × 10–15 (60 s)
C farmer's walk: 4 × 45 s (75 s)
*Reduced time here indicates a rise in load carried

Day Two
Explode:
A overhead med ball throw (backward): 3 × 5 (60 s)

Strength (1RM):
A deadlift: work up to a 1RM. Rest as long as required.
B military press: work up to a 1RM. Rest as long as required.

Build:
A pull-ups (any variation): 50 total reps
B glute ham raise: 3 × 10–15 (75 s)

Day Three
Explode:
A hurdle jump: 3 × 5 (60 s)

Strength (1RM):
A bench press: work up to a 1RM. Rest as long as required.

Build:
A back squat: 3 × 5–10
*Alternative: American hip thrust: 3 × 10–20
B pull-up (any variation): 50 total reps (load if required)
C dips: 100 total reps (body weight only)

29. FREQUENTLY ASKED QUESTIONS

Why Only Three Strength Sessions/Week?

Performed correctly, that is all you need to improve. Remember we are looking for the minimum effect dose: getting the most out of the least. Applied correctly, three strength days/week along with two to three conditioning days is more than sufficient.

Why No Olympic Lifts?

The Olympic lifts are an excellent tool and valuable exercises when performed by those who possess quality technique. If that's you, you'll know their benefits are multiple. If you don't know how to do Olympic lifts, you run a high risk of injuring yourself. You'll get far more from the numerous jumps, throws, and sprints in this program, which are far easier to learn and implement with little to no skill requirement.

What Supportive Equipment Should I Use?

Belt

Belts are to be used on main strength lifts only. Even then, be judicious with their use. Personally, I save a belt for my final one or two sets. Lifters of all experience levels will benefit from the added core engagement of beltless training. However, if you have any lower-back issues or concerns, then belt up sooner. There are no prizes for courageous but injured lifters. Be smart at all times.

Shoes

Different types of footwear are suited to different exercises/movements. To keep things simple, I have listed the different training movements and my corresponding preference of footwear:

- Warm-ups: barefoot.
- Explode (jumps/throws/sprints): good athletic shoe.
- Squat: barefoot, or flat-soled shoes such as weightlifting shoes. These are my personal preference, giving me the most secure footing and comfort. Absolutely never squat in an athletic trainer or running-type shoe. Their soles are too soft and unsuitably shaped.
- Deadlift: barefoot.
- Overhead pressing: weightlifting shoes.
- Bench pressing: good athletic shoe.
- Assistance: good athletic shoe.
- Challenge: good athletic shoe or weightlifting shoe if you prefer.
- Condition: good athletic shoe.

Neoprene Sleeves

Worn on the elbows and knees, these provide little to no support and are not a performance aid (unlike proper powerlifting wraps). I do, however, rate them highly because of their ability to keep the joint warm. A warmer joint is a safer joint, and any way in which I can care for my body whilst consistently handling challenging loads is just fine by me.

Which Exercises Can I Perform for My Main Lifts?

Below are the variations that I endorse:

Squat:
- Back squat
- Front squat

Deadlift:
- Conventional
- Trap bar

Bench:
- Floor press

Press:
- Military press
- Push press

How Should I Load the 5 × 5 and 6 × 3 Lifts?

This sample HPL program is aimed at anyone who is beginning their HPL journey. An individual with a low training age, but who knows how to perform the lifts correctly, yet has never really tested himself or herself. I recommend that they proceed with the objective of slowly building the weight lifted whilst maintaining a high quality of rep. It is far better to start too light and build slowly than to rush straight into ego territory. Long-term success is not built in such ways. Consistency is key.

Weeks one to six of the sample program use a 5 × 5 loading scheme. Each set should be heavier than the previous, with the objective being to lift the best possible weight you are capable of with good form for a maximum of five reps. Over the six weeks this amount of weight can be built upon, until in week six you'll hit your heaviest weight yet for a maximum of five reps.

Weeks eight to eleven see the set/rep scheme progress to 6 × 3, yet the principle remains the same. I want you to progressively lift heavier weights over the six sets in reps of three, working up to the best weight you can successfully lift for three reps. You have four weeks in which to build your strength and proficiency on this before setting a 1RM in week twelve... but more on that later.

I have given a short but easily understood breakdown of suggested loading for the 5 × 5 and 6 × 3.

5 × 5
1. Easy
2. Easy
3. Hard
4. Hard
5. HARD

6 × 3
1. Easy
2. Easy
3. Easy
4. Hard
5. HARD
6. HARD!

Please note that the above are work sets only. These should be preceded by a handful of warm-up sets. See the following for a detailed explanation.

How Do I Warm Up to My First Work Set?

Earlier, I mentioned the "specific" section of the warm-up. This is where you would warm up to the day's prime movement with lighter repetitions of the same movement. For example, a prime movement of squats would have light warm-up squat sets performed in advance.

The exact number of warm-up sets required will vary between individuals, depending upon their strength level. The stronger an individual, the more warm-up sets that are required to get to the first work set. Ideally this will be between two and five warm-up sets, with repetitions kept below five reps/ set in order to not wear you out before you actually work.

Below is an example of how I warm up one of my youth football athletes on the front squat. His goal on this day was to front squat 80 kg × five reps (adhering to the 5 × 5 loading parameters). I have written his warm-up sets in italics.

- *5 × bar (20 kg)*
- *5 × 30 kg*
- *3 × 35 kg*
- *5 × 40 kg*
- *5 × 50 kg*
- *5 × 60 kg*
- *5 × 70 kg*
- 5 × 80 kg

This particular athlete is both young and underexposed to strength training. He has built a solid foundation of excellent form and is now beginning to strength train with progressively heavier weights, thus he requires only a few warm-up sets.

The below example is for an international-level strongman working up to a 3RM of 280 kg in the back squat (adhering to the 6 × 3 loading parameters). Note the additional warm-up sets required for an individual with much greater strength. Warm-up sets are again noted in italics.

- *5 × 60 kg*
- *5 × 80 kg*
- *3 × 100 kg*
- *3 × 120 kg*
- *3 × 140 kg*
- *3 × 160 kg*
- *3 × 180 kg*
- *3 × 200 kg*
- *3 × 220 kg*
- *3 × 250 kg*
- 3 × 280 kg

As you can see, despite the gap in load lifted, the principle remains the same. Both athletes are strength training and both use warm-up sets in advance of their prescribed work sets.

How Do I Work Up to a 1RM?

This twelve-week program has been designed to enable you to progressively build up (weeks one to eleven) in order to test your true maximum effort or one-rep max (1RM) during week twelve. This is the heaviest single successful repetition an individual can perform. A true test of maximal strength. We do this in order to assess your current level. If you don't assess and test yourself, then how can you gauge your strength progress after a further twelve weeks? I like specifics. No gray areas, just hard facts. That way I can accurately judge progress at any given time.

When working up to a 1RM, I recommend between eight and ten sets of between five and ten reps. The exact amount of sets will be dictated by the strength level of the individual. The stronger the individual, the more sets required to hit their 1RM. Rest periods are also entirely dependent upon the individual. The sole goal at this point is to set the 1RM. If you rush through with less than optimal rest, you will still hit a final set of one rep, but it will be short of your true 1RM.

Let's continue with the previous example of my international-level strongman client. However, this time we are working to set his 1RM in the back squat:

5 × 60 kg, 5 × 80 kg, 3 × 100 kg, 3 × 140 kg, 2 × 180 kg, 2 × 220 kg, 1 × 240 kg, 1 × 260 kg, 1 × 280 kg, 1 × 290 kg, 1 × 300 kg, 1 × 305 kg = PR and a new 1RM.

A final example comes from a female client who shares your HPL mindset. She is not a competitive athlete, but is dedicated to becoming her very best. See below how her front squat 1RM testing went:

5 × 20 kg, 3 × 30 kg, 3 × 40 kg, 2 × 50 kg, 2 × 60 kg, 1 × 70 kg, 1 × 75 kg, 1 × 80 kg, 1 × 85 kg = PR and a new 1RM.

Note the difference in sets required to work up to a 1RM. Also note that both clients worked up to a successful lift. There were no missed reps or failed lifts.

How Long Should I Rest?

Rest period duration will depend upon the goal of the exercise. Using the components of my HPL training program, see below for some recommendations:

- Explode: Full recovery is required to maximize the potential of every set. Anywhere between 60 and 90 s is fine.
- Strength: As a rule, rest between 120 and 180 s between sets here. However, I much prefer you go by how you feel and rest as long as required to perform all sets in excellent form. Ensure not to rest too long and get cold.
- Build: 60–90 s between, depending upon the demands of the exercises. Generally speaking, supersets require longer rest than straight sets here.
- Challenge: I recommend between 30 and 60 seconds between such sets. Exact timings will depend on the individual.

What Is the Purpose of the Deload Week? Do I Have to Take It?

I have incorporated a deload into week seven only. Upon the completion of week twelve and your 1RM testing, I recommend you take another before moving on. The priority of the deload is to recover, not work. Hence the reduced volume on the main lifts and body-weight/band nature of the assistance exercises. A deload is not compulsory, but I advise taking one. Your body and mind will thank you.

How Do I Load the Plank Exercises in the Program?

There are various ways in which you can do this. Some are more straightforward than others:

- Wear a weighted vest.
- Have a partner place a disc(s) over your mid/upper back.
- Have a training partner place chains over your lower back. I find these easier to balance than discs.
- Attach a kettlebell to a dipping belt and hang from your waist. This is the most secure and my personal favorite, but is the most time consuming to set up.

Whatever loading methods you choose, remember to maintain perfect form throughout.

ACKNOWLEDGMENTS

This is the part where I thank you for reading my book. You now have all the tools and knowledge you need for your own High Performance Living.

You have the power to be the best that you can be. The rewards from this are continuous and evolving—and the work is daily. It's time to take action on this information and to use your discipline to make consistent choices that support your progress towards the goals you have chosen.

You must ignite the fire. Find your emotional attachment to your goals and this will provide you with the drive to push on and continually seek improvement. Play this to your advantage. Accept it, feed it, and never let go of it. This inner fire will pave your way to success. Do not change it. Do not hide it. This makes you an individual. Embrace it. Be unique and show it to the world. Be yourself.

Your inner fire can come from anywhere: a childhood challenge, a current health problem, or a future event that simply scares the crap out of you. Everybody will be different.

As a coach, my goal is to find a person's inner drive and ignite it. Only then can I apply the best strategies. This is what creates success stories, and is what will provide you with the long-term motivation to achieve your ideal body and health.

Now, it's your turn: go and ignite your inner fire.

More Thanks

I would also like to thank all of the fitness professionals who have shared their work and taught me so much about nutrition in the process. Without this I would never have been able to share the information in this book. There are really too many to name here, but you know who you are. Thank you.

Last, but not least, a HUGE thank you must go to everyone who has been part of this book creation. I didn't do it alone. If I had to list everyone, this book would be twice as long and it's inevitable that I'd still leave someone out. Nevertheless, I want to take this opportunity to specifically thank the following:

- Aleksandra—your commitment to assisting me throughout this project made this book happen.
- My family—for your love and support (especially you, Mum).
- My clients—for your commitment to me over the years.
- Aaron, Neil, Mike, and Richard—my best mates who always keep me laughing.

BIBLIOGRAPHY

Antonio J, Ciccone V. The effects of pre versus post workout supplementation of creatine monohydrate on body composition and strength. *Journal of the International Society of Sports Nutrition* 2013 August 6; 10(1):36. [Epub ahead of print].

Aragon AA, Schoenfeld BJ. Nutrient timing revisited: is there a post-exercise anabolic window? *Journal of the International Society of Sports Nutrition* 2013, 10:5.

Armstrong LE, et al. Mild dehydration affects mood in healthy young women. *Journal of Nutrition* 2012; 142(2):382–388.

Barabasi AL, Oltvai ZN. Network biology: understanding the cell's functional organization. *Nature Reviews Genetics* 2004; 5, 101–113.

Bary GA. How bad is fructose? American *Journal of Clinical Nutrition* 2007; 86(4):895–896.

Bird SP, Tarpenning KM, Marino FE. Liquid carbohydrate/essential amino acid ingestion during a short-term bout of resistance exercise suppresses myofibrillar protein degradation. *Metabolism* 2006; 55(5):570–577.

Borsheim E, Tipton KD, Wolf SE, Wolfe RR. Essential amino acids and muscle protein recovery from resistance exercise. *American Journal of Physiology: Endocrinology and Metabolism* 2002; 283(4):E648–E657.

Bosse JD, Dixon BM. Dietary protein to maximize resistance training: a review and examination of protein spread and change theories. *Journal of the International Society of Sports Nutrition* 2012; 9:42.

Brehm BJ, Seeley RJ, Daniels SR, D'Alessio DA. A randomized trial comparing a very low carbohydrate diet and a calorie-restricted low fat diet on body weight and cardiovascular risk factors in healthy women. *Journal of Clinical Endocrinology and Metabolism* 2003; 88(4):1617–1623.

Brinkworth GD, et al. Long-term effects of a very-low-carbohydrate weight loss diet compared with an isocaloric low-fat diet after 12 mo. *American Journal of Clinical Nutrition* 2009; 90(1):23–32.

British Nutrition Foundation [Online] Available at: www.nutrition.org.uk [Accessed 2014].

Buskirk ER, et al. Work performance after dehydration: effects of physical conditioning and heat acclimatization. Journal of *Applied Physiology* 1958; 12(2); 189–194.

Calder PC. n-3 Polyunsaturated fatty acids, inflammation, and inflammatory diseases. *American Journal of Clinical Nutrition* 2006; 83(6):S1505–S1519.

Chesley A, MacDougall JD, Tarnopolsky MA, Atkinson SA, Smith K. Changes in human muscle protein synthesis after resistance exercise. *Journal of Applied Physiology* 1992; 73:1383–1388.

Chromiak JA, Antonio J (2008) Skeletal Muscle Plasticity. In: Antonio J, et al. (eds) *Essentials of Sports Nutrition and Supplements*, pp 21–52. Totowa, NJ: Humana Press.

Churchward-Venne TA, Burd NA, Mitchell CJ, West DW, Philp A, Marcotte GR, Baker SK, Baar K, Phillips SM. Supplementation of a suboptimal protein dose with leucine or essential amino acids: effects on myofibrillar protein synthesis at rest and following resistance exercise in men. *Journal of Physiology* 2012; 590(11):2751–2765.

Cian C, et al. Effects of fluid ingestion on cognitive function after heat stress or exercise-induced dehydration. *International Journal of Psychophysiology* 2001; 42(3):243–251.

Dashti HM, et al. Beneficial effects of ketogenic diet in obese diabetic subjects. *Molecular and Cellular Biochemistry* 2007; 302(1–2):249–256.

Décombaz J. Nutrition and recovery of muscle energy stores after exercise. *Schweizerische Zeitschrift für Sportmedizin und Sporttraumatologie* 2003; 51(1):31–38.

De Souza RJ, et al. Effects of 4 weight-loss diets differing in fat, protein, and carbohydrate on fat mass, lean mass, visceral adipose tissue, and hepatic fat: results from the POUNDS LOST trial. *American Journal of Clinical Nutrition* 2012; 95(3):614–625.

Dreyer HC, et al. Leucine-enriched essential amino acid and carbohydrate ingestion following resistance exercise enhances mTOR signaling and protein synthesis in human muscle. *American Journal of Physiology: Endocrinology and Metabolism* 2008; 294(2):E392–E400.

Drummond MJ, Glynn EL, Fry CS, Timmerman KL, Volpi E, Rasmussen BB. An increase in essential amino acid availability upregulates amino acid transporter expression in human skeletal muscle. *American Journal of Physiology: Endocrinology and Metabolism* 2010; 298:E1011–E1018.

Eberle SG. (2008) Nutritional Needs of Endurance Athletes. In: Antonio J, et al. (eds) *Essentials of Sports Nutrition and Supplements*, pp 329–348. Totowa, NJ: Humana Press.

European Parliament, Council of the European Union. Corrigendum to Regulation (EC) No. 1924/2006 of the European Parliament and of the Council of 20 December 2006 on nutrition and health claims made on foods. *Official Journal of the European Union* 18.1.2007; L12:3.

Examine.com (2011) [Online] Available at: www.examine.com [Accessed 2014].

Familywellnesshq.com (2012) Fructose in fruits, vegetables, nuts, seeds, legumes and grains [Online] Available at: http://familywellnesshq.com [Accessed 2014].

Fink HH, Mikesky AE (2014) *Practical Applications in Sports Nutrition Fourth Edition*. Chapter 12: Endurance and Ultra-endurance Athletes. Burlington: Jones & Bartlett Learning.

Fink HH, Mikesky AE (2014) *Practical Applications in Sports Nutrition Fourth Edition*. Chapter 13: Strength/Power Athletes. Burlington: Jones & Bartlett Learning.

Fumarola C, La MS, Guidotti GG. Amino acid signaling through the mammalian target of rapamycin (mTOR) pathway: role of glutamine and of cell shrinkage. *Journal of Cell Physiology* 2005; 204:155–165.

Gopinathan PM, et al. Role of dehydration in heat stress-induced variations in mental performance. *Archives of Environmental Health* 1988; 43(1):15–17.

Gore C. (2014) The Effect of Food Sensitivities in Humans [Online] Available at: http://gorebioscience.co.uk/the-effect-of-food-sensitivities-in-humans/ [Accessed 2014].

Greenhaff PL, Karagounis LG, Peirce N, Simpson EJ, Hazell M, Layfield R, Wackerhage H, Smith K, Atherton P, Selby A, Rennie MJ. Disassociation between the effects of amino acids and insulin on signaling, ubiquitin ligases, and protein turnover in human muscle. *American Journal of Physiology: Endocrinology and Metabolism* 2008; 295(3):E595–E604. [Epub ahead of print.]

Greenwood M (2008) Aspects of Overtraining. In: Antonio J, et al. (eds) *Essentials of Sports Nutrition and Supplements*, pp 121–142. Totowa, NJ: Humana Press.

Grootveld M, et al. Health effects of oxidized heated oils. *Journal of Foodservice* 2001; 13(1):DOI 10.1111/j.1745-4506.2001.tb00028.x. [Article first published online: 30 June 2006.]

Helms ER, et al. Evidence-based recommendations for natural bodybuilding contest preparation: nutrition and supplementation. *Journal of the International Society of Sports Nutrition* 2014; 11:20.

HelpGuide.org [Online] Available at: www.helpguide.org [Accessed 2014].

Hession M, et al. Systematic review of randomized controlled trials of low-carbohydrate vs. low-fat/low-calorie diets in the management of obesity and its comorbidities. *Obesity Reviews* 2009; 10(1):36–50.

Heublein S, Kazi S, Ogmundsdottir MH, Attwood EV, Kala S, Boyd CA, et al. Proton-assisted amino-acid transporters are conserved regulators of proliferation and amino-acid-dependent mTORC1 activation. *Oncogene* 2010; 29:4068–4079.

Hite AH, et al. In the face of contradictory evidence: report of the Dietary Guidelines for Americans Committee. *Nutrition* 2010; 26(10):915–924.

Hundal HS, Taylor PM. Amino acid transceptors: gate keepers of nutrient exchange and regulators of nutrient signaling. *American Journal of Physiology: Endocrinology and Metabolism* 2009; 296:E603–E613.

Hyde R, Peyrollier K, Hundal HS. Insulin promotes the cell surface recruitment of the SAT2/ATA2 system A amino acid transporter from an endosomal compartment in skeletal muscle cells. *Journal of Biological Chemistry* 2002; 277:13628–13634.

Hyde R, Taylor PM, Hundal HS. Amino acid transporters: roles in amino acid sensing and signalling in animal cells. *Biochemical Journal* 2003; 373:1–18.

Jenkins DJA, et al. Effect on blood lipids of very high intakes of fiber in diets low in saturated fat and cholesterol. *New England Journal of Medicine* 1993; 329(1):21–26.

Johnston CS, et al. Postprandial thermogenesis is increased 100% on a high-protein, low-fat diet versus a high-carbohydrate, low-fat diet in healthy, young women. *Journal of the American College of Nutrition* 2002; 21(1):55–61.

Johnstone AM, et al. Effect of overfeeding macronutrients on day-to-day food intake in man. *European Journal of Clinical Nutrition* 1996; 50(7):418–430.

Joy JM, Lowery RP, Wilson JM, Purpura M, De Souza EO, Wilson SM, Kalman DS, Dudeck JE, Jäger R. The effects of 8 weeks of whey or rice protein supplementation on body composition and exercise performance. *Nutrition Journal* 2013; 12(1):86.

Judelson DA, et al. Hydration and muscular performance. *Sports Medicine* 2007; 37(10):907–921.

Keogh JB, et al. Effects of weight loss from a very-low-carbohydrate diet on endothelial function and markers of cardiovascular disease risk in subjects with abdominal obesity. *American Journal of Clinical Nutrition* 2008; 87(3):567–576.

Kerstetter JE, et al. Dietary protein and skeletal health: a review of recent human research. *Current Opinion in Lipidology* 2011; 22(1):16–20.

KP Body Reconstruction High Protein foods List [Online] Available at: www.kpbodyreconstruction.com/personal-diet-nutrition/high-protein-foods-list/.

Kraemer WJ, et al. (2008) The Endocrinology of Resistance Exercise and Training. In: Antonio J, et al. (eds) *Essentials of Sports Nutrition and Supplements*, pp 53–83. Totowa, NJ: Humana Press.

Krauss RM, et al. Separate effects of reduced carbohydrate intake and weight loss on atherogenic dyslipidemia. *American Journal of Clinical Nutrition* 2006; 83(5):1025–1031.

Krebs NF, et al. Efficacy and safety of a high protein, low carbohydrate diet for weight loss in severely obese adolescents. *Journal of Pediatrics* 2010; 157(2):252–258.

Kreider RB. (2008) Sports Applications of Creatine. In: Antonio J, et al. (eds) *Essentials of Sports Nutrition and Supplements*, pp 417–439. Totowa, NJ: Humana Press.

Kristo AS, et al. Effect of diets differing in glycemic index and glycemic load on cardiovascular risk factors: review of randomized controlled-feeding trials. *Nutrients* 2013; 5(4):1071–1080.

Lupton JR, et al. (2001) *Dietary Reference Intakes*, Institute of Medicine of the National Academies. Washington, DC: National Academies Press.

Manninen AH. High-protein weight loss diets and purported adverse effects: where is the evidence? *Journal of the International Society of Sports Nutrition* 2004; 1:45–51.

Maughan RJ. Impact of mild dehydration on wellness and on exercise performance. *European Journal of Clinical Nutrition* 2003; 57(2):S19–S23.

McClemon FJ, et al. The effects of a low-carbohydrate ketogenic diet and a low-fat diet on mood, hunger, and other self-reported symptoms. *Obesity* (Silver Spring) 2007; 15(1):182–187.

Mensink RP, Katan MB. Effect of dietary fatty acids on serum lipids and lipoproteins. A meta-analysis of 27 trials. *Arteriosclerosis, Thrombosis, and Vascular Biology* 1992; 12(8):911–919.

Mettler S, et al. Increased protein intake reduces lean body mass loss during weight loss in athletes. *Medicine and Science in Sports and Exercise* 2010; 42(2):326–337.

Miller SL, Tipton KD, Chinkes DL, Wolf SE, Wolfe RR. Independent and combined effects of amino acids and glucose after resistance exercise. *Medicine and Science in Sports and Exercise* 2003; 35(3):449–455.

Moore DR, Areta J, Coffey VG, Stellingwerff T, Phillips SM, Burke LM, Cléroux M, Godin JP, Hawley JA. Daytime pattern of post-exercise protein intake affects whole-body protein turnover in resistance-trained males. *Nutrition and Metabolism* (London) 2012; 9(1):91.

Moore DR, Robinson MJ, Fry JL, Tang JE, Glover EI, Wilkinson SB, Prior T, Tarnopolsky MA, Phillips SM. Ingested protein dose response of muscle and albumin protein synthesis after resistance exercise in young men. *American Journal of Clinical Nutrition* 2009; 89(1):161–168.

Morais JA, et al. Protein turnover and requirements in the healthy and frail elderly. *Journal of Nutrition, Health, and Aging* 2006; 10(4):272–283.

Muller H, et al. The serum LDL/HDL cholesterol ratio is influenced more favorably by exchanging saturated with unsaturated fat than by reducing saturated fat in the diet of women. *Journal of Nutrition* 2003; 133(1):78–83.

Nichols AB, et al. Daily nutritional intake and serum lipid levels. The Tecumseh study. *American Journal of Clinical Nutrition* 1976; 29(12):1384–1392.

Nicklin P, Bergman P, Zhang B, Triantafellow E, Wang H, Nyfeler B, et al. Bidirectional transport of amino acids regulates mTOR and autophagy. *Cell* 2009; 136:521–534.

Nikkola T. (2012) Performance Enhancement Part 2: Essentials of Repair and Recovery [Online]. Available at www.lifetime-weightloss.com/blog/2012/8/11/performance-enhancement-part-2-essentials-of-repair-and-reco.html.

Norton LE and Layman DK. Leucine regulates translation initiation of protein synthesis in skeletal muscle after exercise. *Journal of Nutrition* 2006; 136(2):533S–537S.

Norton LE, Layman DK, Garlick PJ et al. Isonitrogenous protein sources with different leucine contents differentially effect translation initiation and protein synthesis in skeletal muscle. *FASEB Journal* 2008; 22:869.5.

Nugent AP. Health properties of resistant starch. *Nutrition Bulletin* 2005; 30(1):27–54.

Parnell JA, Reimer RA. Prebiotic fiber modulation of the gut microbiota improves risk factors for obesity and the metabolic syndrome. *Gut Microbes* 2012; 3(1):29–34.

Pasiakos SM, et al. Leucine-enriched essential amino acid supplementation during moderate steady state exercise enhances postexercise muscle protein synthesis. *American Journal of Clinical Nutrition* 2011; 94(3):809–818.

Peele L. (2007) The Metabolic Repair Manual. eBook published by author.

Phillips SM, et al. Dietary protein for athletes: from requirements to optimum adaptation. *Journal of Sports Science* 2011; 29(Suppl 1):S29–S38.

Phillips SM, Tipton KD, Aarsland A, Wolf SE, Wolfe RR. Mixed muscle protein synthesis and breakdown after resistance exercise in humans. *American Journal of Physiology* 1997; 273:E99–E107.

Phillips SM. Dietary protein for athletes: from requirements to metabolic advantage. *Applied Physiology, Nutrition, and Metabolism* 2006; 31(6):647–654.

Ra SG, et al. Combined effect of branched-chain amino acids and taurine supplementation on delayed onset muscle soreness and muscle damage in high-intensity eccentric exercise. *Journal of the International Society of Sports Nutrition* 2013; 10(1):51.

Russo GL. Dietary n-6 and n-3 polyunsaturated fatty acids: from biochemistry to clinical implications in cardiovascular prevention. *Biochemical Pharmacology* 2009; 77(6):937–946.

Santos FL, et al. Systematic review and meta-analysis of clinical trials of the effects of low carbohydrate diets on cardiovascular risk factors. *Obesity Reviews* 2012; 13(11):1048–1066.

Sasaki G. Association between dietary fiber, water and magnesium intake and functional constipation among young Japanese women. *European Journal of Clinical Nutrition* 2007; 61:616–622.

Schliess F, Richter L, Vom DS, Haussinger D. Cell hydration and mTOR-dependent signalling. *Acta Physiologica* (Oxford) 2006;187:223–229.

Simopoulos AP. The importance of the ratio of omega-6/omega-3 essential fatty acids. *Biomedicine and Pharmacotherapy* 2002; 56(8):365–379.

Siri-Tarino PW, et al. Meta-analysis of prospective cohort studies evaluating the association of saturated fat with cardiovascular disease. *American Journal of Clinical Nutrition* 2010; 91(3):535–546, DOI 10.3945/ajcn.2009.27725.

Stoll B, Gerok W, Lang F, Haussinger D. Liver cell volume and protein synthesis. *Biochemical Journal* 1992; 287(1):217–222.

St-Onge M, Jones JH. Physiological effects of medium chain triglycerides: potential agents in the prevention of obesity. *Journal of Nutrition* 2002; 132(3):329–332.

Stoppani J, et al. (2008) Nutritional Needs for Strength/Power Athletes. In: Antonio J, et al. (eds) *Essentials of Sports Nutrition and Supplements*, pp 349–370. Totowa, NJ: Humana Press.

Tarnopolsky M. Protein requirements for endurance athletes. *Nutrition* 2004; 20(7–8):662–668.

Terzis G, Georgiadis G, Stratakos G, Vogiatzis I, Kavouras S, Manta P, et al. Resistance exercise-induced increase in muscle mass correlates with p70S6 kinase phosphorylation in human subjects. *European Journal of Applied Physiology* 2008; 102:145–152.

Tipton KD, Borsheim E, Wolf SE, Sanford AP, Wolfe RR. Acute response of net muscle protein balance reflects 24-h balance after exercise and amino acid ingestion. *American Journal of Physiology: Endocrinology and Metabolism* 2003; 284(1):E76–E89.

Tipton KD, Ferrando AA, Phillips SM, Doyle D, Jr, Wolfe RR. Post exercise net protein synthesis in human muscle from orally administered amino acids. *American Journal of Physiology* 1999; 276:E628–E634.

Tipton KD, Rasmussen BB, Miller SL, Wolf SE, Owens-Stovall SK, Petrini BE, Wolfe RR. Timing of amino acid-carbohydrate ingestion alters anabolic response of muscle to resistance exercise. *American Journal of Physiology: Endocrinology and Metabolism* 2001; 281(2):E197–E206.

Trexler ET, et al. Metabolic adaptation to weight loss: implications for the athlete. *Journal of the International Society of Sports Nutrition* 2014; 11:7.

Van Gammeren, D (2008) Vitamins and Minerals. In: Antonio J, et al. (eds) *Essentials of Sports Nutrition and Supplements*, pp 313–328. Totowa, NJ: Humana Press.

Veldhorst MA, et al. Presence or absence of carbohydrates and the proportion of fat in a high-protein diet affect appetite suppression but not energy expenditure in normal-weight human subjects fed in energy balance. *British Journal of Nutrition* 2010; 104(9):1395–1405.

Volek JS, et al. Body composition and hormonal responses to a carbohydrate-restricted diet. *Metabolism* 2002; 51(7):864–870.

Volek JS, et al. Comparison of energy-restricted very low-carbohydrate and low-fat diets on weight loss and body composition in overweight men and women. *Nutrition and Metabolism* 2004; 1:13.

Volek JS, et al. Carbohydrate restriction has a more favorable impact on the metabolic syndrome than a low fat diet. *Lipids* 2009; 44(4):297–309.

Walsh BP (2007) Dr. Bryan P. Walsh, Naturopathic Physician [Online] Available at: www.drbryanpwalsh.com [Accessed 2014].

Weickert MO, Pfeiffer AF. Metabolic effects of dietary fiber consumption and prevention of diabetes. *Journal of Nutrition* 2008; 138(3):439–442.

Westerterp-Plantenga MS. Protein intake and energy balance. *Regulatory Peptides* 2008; 149(1–3):67–69.

Westman EC, et al. Low-carbohydrate nutrition and metabolism. *American Journal of Clinical Nutrition* 2007; 86(2):276–284.

Wilson MG, Morley JE. Impaired cognitive function and mental performance in mild dehydration. *European Journal of Clinical Nutrition* 2003; 57(Suppl 2):S24–S29.

Zimmerman M, Snow B. (2012) *Essentials of Nutrition: A Functional Approach*, v. 1.0. Flatworld Knowledge.